RICHARD COLLINS
VINCENT PORTER

WDR and the Arbeiterfilm: Fassbinder, Ziewer and others

1981
BFI Publishing

Published by the British Film Institute
127 Charing Cross Road
London WC2H 0EA

Copyright © Richard Collins & Vincent Porter 1981

ISBN 0 85170 107 8

Printed by Tonbridge Printers Ltd, Tonbridge, Kent

Contents

Introduction — I

Chapter 1: The Political Context — 7

Chapter 2: The Growth of WDR — 16

Chapter 3: The Genesis of the *Arbeiterfilm* — 25

Chapter 4: *Rote Fahnen sieht man besser* — 39

Chapter 5: *Eight Hours Are Not a Day* — 50

Chapter 6: The Work of Christian Ziewer — 63

Chapter 7: The Demise of the *Arbeiterfilm* — 104

Appendices — 118

Glossary — 165

Bibliography — 168

Filmography — 171

Acknowledgements

Our thanks are due to Edward Buscombe and Angela Martin for patient support; to Basis Film and Westdeutscher Rundfunk for hospitality and viewing facilities; and to the Goethe Institut, London for invaluable assistance in obtaining viewing copies and making contacts. In addition, to the following individuals: Scilla Alvarado, Harald Budde, Clara Burckner, Volker Canaris, Lucy Collins, Helmut Druck, Klaus Eder, Hans-Geert Falkenberg, Merryn Grimley, Sara Haffner, Bert Hartig, Gillian Hartnoll, Friedrich Hitzer, Sheila Johnston, Winfried Kretz, Peter Märthesheimer, Helga Rulf, Andrea Siemsen, Günter Triesch, Klaus von Bismarck, Joachim von Mengershausen and Christian Ziewer.

$$* \qquad * \qquad *$$

The research for this publication was financed by the Anglo-German Foundation for the Study of Industrial Society as part of its programme of study of social and economic policy issues. Special thanks are due to the Foundation for their generosity in making it possible for us to travel to West Germany to see all the films and to meet many of the individuals associated with this period of West German broadcasting. It goes without saying that our research benefitted enormously from their support, but it must also be pointed out that our conclusions are our own and are not necessarily endorsed by the Foundation. In a world where media programming is becoming both more homogenised and more dominant, we trust that their liberal practice of research sponsorship will continue.

Introduction

Our interest in the relationship between the Cologne television station Westdeutscher Rundfunk (WDR) and the *Arbeiterfilm* (worker film) was aroused by seeing *Liebe Mutter mir geht es gut (Dear Mother, I'm OK)* in 1972 at the Berlin Film Festival and the first episode of *Acht Stunden sind kein Tag (Eight Hours Are Not a Day)** in April 1973 at the National Film Theatre in its week of German television programmes. During the German television week there was a memorable discussion between Klaus von Bismarck — then *Intendant* (Director-General) of WDR — and Huw (now Sir Huw) Wheldon, then Managing Director BBC-TV, in which it became clear that not only was the programming and organisation of WDR different from that of the BBC (or the ITV network), but that WDR stood for a different conception and practice of public service broadcasting. A further impetus for this study was established in 1975 in a weekend seminar on 'German Proletarian Cinema' which we organised at the Polytechnic of Central London. This explored the connections between the proletarian films of the Weimar Republic, in particular Piel Jutzi's *Mutter Krausens Fahrt ins Glück (Mother Krausen's Journey To Happiness)* and Bertolt Brecht and Slatan Dudow's *Kühle Wampe*, and the then contemporary work of Rainer Werner Fassbinder and Christian Ziewer at WDR. To this seminar, thanks to the Goethe Institut, London, we were able to invite Christian Ziewer to speak about and to show for the first time in England *Liebe Mutter mir geht es gut* and *Schneeglöckchen blühn im September (Snowdrops in September)*.

In this monograph we have set out to explore the relationships between the new television genre of the *Arbeiterfilm*, produced by WDR between 1968 and 1976, the concept of public service broadcasting as practised by WDR at that time and the flow of contemporary television programming into which it was inserted. It was a unique moment in public service broadcasting.

The genre of the *Arbeiterfilm* may be seen as beginning with two proto-*Arbeiterfilme* made by Erika Runge in 1968 and 1970, *Warum ist Frau B. glücklich? (Why Is Mrs. B. Happy?)* and *Ich heisse Erwin und bin 17 Jahre (My Name is Erwin and I'm 17)*, which are 'documentaries' about working-class individuals and which combine the 'objective' (i.e. exterior) tradition of the documentary with the 'subjective' (i.e. interior) thoughts and feelings of the worker who is the subject of the film. By 1971, this documentary tradition achieved feature film length and took

---

*With the exception of *Eight Hours Are Not a Day*, which is the only one to have received exhibition and discussion in Britain under its English title, we shall refer to all *Arbeiterfilme* under their original German titles.

1

on narrative form in Theo Gallehr and Rolf Schübel's *Rote Fahnen sieht man besser (Red Flags Can Be Seen Better)* (WDR/Radio Bremen/ Cinecollectif Hamburg, producer Martin Wiebel), which recounts the long and bitter story of the redundancies and layoffs at the Phrix works in Krefeld (a subsidiary of Dow Chemicals), as seen from the point of view of four of the workers made redundant. By 1972, the genre was moving into a predominantly fictional mode which rooted the characters and their actions in the lives and the experiences of the contemporary German working class, and particularly in their struggles for dignity and economic survival in the factory and at the workplace. Christian Ziewer and Klaus Wiese's *Liebe Mutter mir geht es gut* (WDR/Basis Film, producer Joachim von Mengershausen), Helma Sanders' *Der Angestellte (The White-Collar Worker)* and the five-part series directed by Rainer Werner Fassbinder, *Eight Hours Are Not a Day* (WDR, producer Peter Märthesheimer) were followed in the next few years by Ingo Kratisch and Marianne Lüdcke's *Lohn und Liebe (Wages and Love)* (WDR/Filmverlag der Autoren, producer Wolf-Dieter Brücke), Ziewer and Wiese's *Schneeglöckchen blühn im September* (WDR/Basis Film, producer Joachim von Mengershausen), Lüdcke and Kratisch's *Familienglück (Wedded Bliss)* (WDR/ Regina Ziegler Films, producer Wolf-Dieter Brücke) and finally, Christian Ziewer's masterpiece of the genre *Der aufrechte Gang (Walking Tall)* (WDR/Basis Film, producer Joachim von Mengershausen). Other films orbit like minor planets around the main stars in the constellation of the *Arbeiterfilm*. Most of them come either from the West Berlin film school, the Deutsche Film- und Fernseh-Akademie, Berlin (DFFB), such as *Die Wollands* (Lüdcke and Kratisch, 1972), *Flöz Dickebank* (Johannes Flutsch, Klaus Helle and Marlies Kallweit, 1974) and *Allein machen sie dich ein* (1973) and *Kalldorf gegen Mannesmann* (1975) (both made by Suzanne Beyeler, Rainer März and Manfred Stelzer); or alternatively from the Hamburg television station Norddeutscher Rundfunk (NDR), such as *Emden geht nach USA (Emden Goes to the USA)* (Gisela Tuchtenhagen and Klaus Wildenhahn, 1976), also titled *Im Norden das Meer*.

The term 'genre' is used loosely and we are conscious that the theoretical definition of a genre is notoriously problematic. Just as the definition of worker literature is difficult, so too is the definition of an *Arbeiterfilm*. But there are important shared characteristics in these films: their aesthetic of naturalism and/or realism, their representation of experiences and relations at the workplace as decisive, and their espousal of the point of view of the major subordinated class of the post-war social market economy of West Germany. The central place of work in these films is not simply the presence of greater footage shot at the workplace than is customary in contemporary dramas and documentaries but rather the primacy ceded to the social relations of capitalist production in determining the whole pattern of the filmic characters' experience and the perception of the social relations of production in

2

capitalism as necessarily antagonistic. The workplace is a site of conflict between capital and labour, for the interests of capital and labour are contradictory.

The expression of these contradictions is more or less extensive in different films. It is less extensive in *Erwin* than in, say, *Rote Fahnen sieht man besser* and it may, as in *Eight Hours Are Not a Day*, be presented through a romantic and anarchic optic or, as in *Der aufrechte Gang*, be seen as part of a sober and at times passionately pessimistic world-view. In all these films, life in the social market economy of the *Bundesrepublik* is seen to have a far more extensive range of problems than Britain's media merchants would have us believe.

The rich and varied qualities of the films which constitute the genre of the *Arbeiterfilm* and the different concept of public service broadcasting under which they were made offer, we feel, a new, alternative perspective on the debate about media institutions, broadcasting policy, access and accountability which continues in Great Britain in a sterile, insular and fragmented circuit. WDR clearly represented a very different resolution of the contradictions that govern the relations of television broadcasting to the state, to the public — who are mostly working-class — and to the film industry than is familiar in the United Kingdom.

Second, the aesthetic practices of the *Arbeiterfilmemacher (Arbeiterfilm-makers)* offer a perspective different from the debates about representation and ideology which have dominated film theory and criticism in Great Britain since the politicisation of Jean-Luc Godard, the changes in the editorial policy of *Cahiers du Cinéma* and the development of the strategy of counter-cinema. In West Germany, a country whose cultural and theoretical productions have not been available in the UK to nearly so great an extent as those of France or even Italy, we found a conscious, thoughtful and deliberate practice of an aesthetic of realism in the service of a critical representation of the contemporary social order and the espousal of the viewpoint of those subjugated by that order. To these two themes, the German conjuncture offered new and challenging material.

As well as contributing new material to these questions, the present publication will, we hope, begin a re-drawing of the terms of these debates. The aesthetic and ideological debate needs an institutional dimension and the concreteness that such a dimension enforces. The institutional debate in the United Kingdom needs to be unlocked from its current framework in which among all the variables of institutional form, 'product', as the messages are customarily and reductively called, remains constant. We hope too that this study will lend a comparative perspective to the study of film and television (a perspective that has been notably absent in British discussions) and that the institutional and aesthetic forms that we track will offer a fertile provocation to thinking outside the limits of the current orthodoxies in British discussions of media institutions and policies and of ideology and representation.

These are large ambitions and we are conscious that they are not fully realised within the form in which we are working and that the bounds of a short monograph have, already, been stretched beyond their customary limits by this study. Furthermore the work is not a definitive study of the genre and we are aware for instance that we have neglected the work of Marianne Lüdcke and Ingo Kratisch and in particular their films *Lohn und Liebe (Wages and Love)* (1973) and *Familienglück (Wedded Bliss)* (1975) and Helma Sanders' films *Der Angestellte (The White-Collar Worker)* (1971) and *Shirins Hochzeit (Shirin's Wedding)* (1975), which add new perspectives to the genre by extending its concerns with patriarchy.

At the time of writing, it seems as if this study may appear as an obituary. The *Arbeiterfilm* genre itself has ended with Christian Ziewer's *Der aufrechte Gang (Walking Tall)* in 1976, and the *Tendenzwende* (ideological change of direction) that closed the space in which the *Arbeiterfilm* had grown may now similarly terminate the form of public service broadcasting that has survived in West Germany since the post-war settlement. Latterly it has seemed fragile and anachronistic, embedded within the German 'strong state' and assaulted by aggressive clamour from the CDU/CSU and from capitalist interests who accuse it of being what the *Financial Times* (11 December 1979) has described as a 'system run through public sector bodies wholly responsible neither to government nor private interests'. It is, of course, precisely its system of *public* accountability that has so far protected West German broadcasting from the *Gleichschaltung* (regimentation) that these forces now wish to impose upon it.

West German broadcasting has a plausible claim to being the most successful instance of public service broadcasting in the world. It has been adequately financed. The scarcity of advertising time and the at-arms-length relation between programme origination and the sale of advertising time have ensured that in their bargain with the advertisers, the broadcasters have held the upper hand. The regionalised ARD network has ensured adequate expression of the distinct interests and traditions of the West German regions, and the modes of political control left as a legacy by the British, French and US Control Commissions have ensured that broadcasting has been accountable to the public it serves and its programming policies identified as being within the political domain. Unlike the BBC, West German broadcasting does not purvey the illusion that it is accountable to a group of Platonic 'guardians' who ensure that it appears as a neutral agent for the dissemination and transmission of the conflicts and contradictions of a separate political domain. The programming of West German broadcasting has represented the views and interests of a wider range of groups and voices in West German society than has the corresponding system in the UK, France or, until perhaps the recent collapse of RAI's hegemony, Italy.

The long and creditable history of public service broadcasting in West

4

Germany is now under threat. The broadcasting order in West Germany has, with modification but with substantial continuity, survived from 1949 and weathered the assaults of Freies Fernsehen GmbH and Deutschland Fernsehen GmbH between 1959 and 1961 under the sponsorship of the Adenauer regime (see Chapter 2). Today it is again threatened by the joint forces of state and capital, or in the words of the *Financial Times*, by 'government and private interests'.

The decision of the West German government to commission a direct broadcast satellite to transmit television programmes over the whole of West Germany doubtless owes much to the needs of the telecommunication and aerospace industries in the Federal Republic and to the propaganda need to improve reception of West German television in the German Democratic Republic, particularly around Dresden. But the technical capacity of the satellite system planned is for five colour television channels. What will be done with the two spare channels? Not Deutsches Fernsehen 1 and 2, the two channels of the German Democratic Republic, surely! More likely the long-resisted commercial channels.

In NDR (Norddeutscher Rundfunk, the Hamburg station), the cultural struggle discussed by Williams (1976, pp. 120–34) continues and may well end in the break-up of the inter-*Land* treaty by which NDR is established and the setting-up, under CDU tutelage, of commercial broadcasting in Schleswig-Holstein and Lower Saxony. (See Collins & Porter, 1980 and Druck, 1980.) NDR owes its origin to the British occupational authorities, who based their zonal broadcasting system on Hamburg. Nordwestdeutscher Rundfunk was headed by Hugh Carleton Greene until November 1948, when it was the first broadcasting organisation to be handed over to German control. In 1954, Cologne, then under CDU control, seceded from NWDR and constituted a North Rhine-Westphalian station, WDR, leaving the rump of NWDR — NDR — in Hamburg.

The CDU controlled *Länder* of the current NDR consortium are now negotiating to secede from NDR and Lower Saxony proposes to establish commercial broadcasting in order to encourage 'more broadcasting competition'. The post-war broadcasting order in West Germany seems about to end. The public service broadcasting institutions established in the post-war settlement to ensure the expression of a range of voices, accountable to the public but independent of the Federal government and of capital, stand to be forced into competition with a commercial system bound by the imperatives of profit and therefore of audience maximisation. Everywhere that broadcasting has followed this route of 'diversity' and 'competition', programming has become less diverse and opinion has congealed around the narrow middle ground, either by loss of audiences to the commercial station or by competition on the terms set by profit maximisation. Indeed, according to the testimony of one of its

5

members, 'The Annan Committee considered that the BBC and the commercial system took competition too seriously as if they were commercial enterprises whose profitability, prestige or even existence depended on maximising audiences.' (Himmelweit, 1979.)

We may anticipate then, not only a decline in 'diversity' programming such as the *Arbeiterfilme* in a chase for ratings, but, in the unregulated arcadia of the CDU, a re-insertion of the US majors as the chief providers of audio-visual programming to the West German market, a position from which they were slowly and painfully expelled in the West German film industry by the massive decline in cinema attendances, by state intervention and by the increasing importance of public service television in financing production. As Himmelweit also points out, 'the relation of size of audience to enjoyment of a programme by those who viewed it [is] low. Audience size [is] therefore an inadequate measure of the public's satisfaction.' (Himmelweit, ibid.) Since the structure of West German broadcasting has been sufficiently strong to permit the survival of its pluralism in spite of the substantial political activities of right-wing groups within the committee structures of the broadcasting institutions, the politicians of the CDU/CSU have now started to attack the system from outside, secure in the knowledge that the inelasticity of time which people devote to consuming television will ensure that any new channels will undermine existing services.

The CDU/CSU's strategy of carrying on the struggle over broadcasting outside of the regulatory boards has now been followed by the labour movement. The RFFU (Rundfunk-Fernseh-Film-Union — Radio, Television and Film Union) called a four hour strike for the evening of 19 December 1979, over the proposed destruction of NDR. This would have blacked out West German television for the first time in the country's history. The strike was forestalled by a Munich court issuing an injunction forbidding the strike, a decision which is currently under appeal in a higher court.

The remarkably successful broadcasting order, which has survived for thirty years and which offered an institutional framework within which political differences in West Germany could be expressed and negotiated, no longer seems adequate. A new institutional order remains to be contested. The prospects for the world's most important public service broadcasting system are gloomy. Whatever its faults — and the system has frequently been criticised from the left as well as from the right in West Germany — West German broadcasting to date is unlikely to be bettered by the new order of commercial competition and the dominance of the imperative of profit maximisation that will distinguish it.

CHAPTER I

The Political Context

It is impossible to comprehend the reasons why the *Arbeiterfilm* came to be produced by WDR without a full understanding of the relationship between WDR and political life in North Rhine-Westphalia and the Federal Republic. It is necessary therefore to begin with a brief survey of the Basic Law of the Federal Republic, the constitutional bedrock on which political life in the Federal Republic is built.

When the Federal Republic of Germany was established in 1949, the paramount concern of the Allied Powers was to ensure that fascism would never take root in Germany again. Accordingly two fundamental principles were built into the Basic Law, which was to form the constitutional foundation on which the new Federal Republic would be built. The first ensured that basic human rights were to be clearly and definitively specified, while the second was to establish a basic separation of powers between the authority of the eleven separate *Länder* and that of the Federal Republic. In drawing up the Basic Law, the constitutional lawyers drew upon the most liberal elements enshrined both in the constitution of the United States of America and in that of the Weimar Republic which had preceded the Third Reich. Thus in theory the purpose of the Basic Law was to ensure that it was the interests of the people that would be served and not those of the State.

The first section of the Basic Law was concerned to protect the individual citizen and asserted that human dignity was inviolable (Article 1). It then provided in Article 5 for freedom of expression:

1) Everyone shall have the right freely to express and disseminate his opinion by speech, writing and pictures and freely to inform himself from generally accessible sources. Freedom of the press and freedom of reporting by means of broadcasts and films are guaranteed. There shall be no censorship.
2) These rights are limited by the provisions of the general laws, the provisions of law for the protection of youth, and by the right to inviolability of personal honour.
3) Art and science, research and teaching, shall be free. Freedom of teaching shall not absolve from loyalty to the constitution.

Already it was clear that the commitment of the Federal Republic to the freedom of expression was not absolute. The limitations enshrined in sub-clause 2 were potentially large and the determination of 'loyalty to the constitution' provided for in sub-clause 3 was to become politically explosive some three decades later with the *Berufsverbot*, which makes it possible for public employees to be dismissed if their political beliefs are deemed to be 'against the Basic Law'. When the question of private property rights arose, however, the Basic Law was even more contradictory. Article 14 provided that:

1) Property and right of inheritance are guaranteed. Their content and limits shall be determined by the laws.
2) Property imposes duties. Its use should also serve the public weal.
3) Expropriation shall be permitted only in the public weal. It may be effected only by or pursuant to a law which shall provide for the nature and extent of the compensation. Such compensation shall be determined by establishing an equitable balance between the public interest and the interests of those affected. In case of dispute regarding the amount of compensation, recourse may be had to the ordinary courts.

When it came to industrial and natural resources, however, the Basic Law was clearer. Article 15 provided that:

Land, natural resources and means of production may for the purpose of socialisation be transferred to public ownership or other forms of publicly controlled economy by a law which shall provide for the nature and extent of compensation. In respect of such compensation the third and fourth sentences of paragraph 3 of Article 14 shall apply *mutatis mutandis*.

The rights of individual Germans to associate freely were provided for in Article 9:

1) All Germans shall have the right to form associations and societies.
2) Associations, the purposes or activities of which conflict with criminal laws or which are directed against the constitutional order or the concept of international understanding, are prohibited.
3) The right to form associations to safeguard and improve working and economic conditions is guaranteed to everyone and to all trades, occupations and professions. Agreements which restrict or seek to impair this right shall be null and void; measures directed to this end shall be illegal. Measures taken pursuant to Article 12a (conscription), to paragraphs 2 and 3 of Article 35 (dealing with natural disasters), to paragraph 4 of Article 87a (use of armed forces to avert any imminent danger to the existence of the free democratic basic order) or to Article 91 (aversion of dangers to the existence of the

8

Federation or a *Land*), may not be directed against any industrial conflicts engaged in by associations within the meaning of the first sentence of this paragraph in order to safeguard and improve working and economic conditions.

At first sight, therefore, the provisions of Article 9.3 ensure the rights of association of workers, which are firmly protected from outside interference and in particular from the use of state force whether represented by the army or by the police. Nevertheless, further restrictions on the deployment of the freedom of association in industrial conflicts were to be enacted in Federal legislation. While these did not prevent the freedom of association they were to regulate it by a series of procedures and practices in the interests of preserving industrial order and harmony.

The second and subsequent sections of the Basic Law sought to regulate the powers of the Federation and those of the constituent *Länder*. Article 28 provided that the constitutional order of each *Land* must conform with the principles of republican, democratic and social government laid down within the Basic Law, while Article 30 went on to provide that:

> The exercise of governmental powers and the discharge of governmental functions shall be incumbent on the *Länder* in so far as this Basic Law does not otherwise prescribe or permit.

This section of the Basic Law was to play an important part in the future of broadcasting in the Federal Republic, as the 1961 Decision of the Constitutional Court was to demonstrate. Among the areas over which the Federation was given power to legislate, however, were the postal and telecommunication services (Article 73.7) and industrial property rights, copyrights and publishers' rights (Article 73.9).

In addition, Article 74.12 provided for concurrent legislative powers to extend to labour law. That is, the *Länder* should only have power to legislate as long as the Federation did not exercise its right to legislate. In order to maintain economic unity throughout the Federation and in order to maintain uniform living conditions, particularly in the relations of production, the Federation enacted the Collective Agreements Act 1949 (amended 1952 and consolidated 1969) which laid down the legal conditions relating to collective bargaining; the *Montan* Industries Co-determination Act 1951 (extended 1952) which provided for co-determination in companies employing more than 1000 workers; the Labour Relations Act 1952 (revised 1972) which laid down detailed provisions for the regulation of labour relations; the Labour Courts Act of 1953 which set up a three tier system of labour courts; the Personal Representative Act 1955 (revised 1974) which provided public sector employees with consultative councils similar to those available to private sector employees; the *Montan* Industries Holding Companies Supplementary Act 1956 which extended co-determination to holding companies more than half of whose turnover came from mining, iron and steel; the Joint Stock Company Act 1966 which provided for the establishment of supervisory and managerial boards as a general principle; and finally the Co-determination Act 1976 which increased employee representation on supervisory boards in almost all companies with more than 2000 employees.

Thus Federal legislation extensively regulated the relations of production and in so doing extensively limited the rights of freedom of association of the individual workers which were enshrined in the Basic Law. (For details see Appendix 1.) The enactment of this Federal legislation was to limit not only the relations of production but the *representation* of the relations of production, as will be seen in chapter 7.

THE POLITICAL STRUCTURE OF NORTH RHINE-WESTPHALIA

The discussions about the electoral system for the Federal Republic which took place in 1948 and 1949 were centred upon the question of how to set up a system which reflected the views of the people but which also provided for governmental stability. Under the constitution of the Weimar Republic there had been a purely proportional electoral system which meant that any one political party only needed 60,000 votes in order to have a parliamentary representative. This had meant that some thirty-six parties had campaigned in one election and that as many as seventeen parties had been represented in the Weimar *Reichstag*.

For the first Federal election in 1949, the Federal Republic adopted a system which provided that 40 per cent of the candidates were elected from *Land* party lists and 60 per cent from the constituency elections. In addition, there was a limiting clause which provided that any party which did not win either three constituencies or a total of 5 per cent of the votes cast in any one *Land* lost its entitlement to any seats allocated from the party lists of the *Land*. For subsequent elections, the system was modified so that 50 per cent of the candidates came from the *Land* party lists and 50 per cent from the constituencies. Minority parties now had to win three seats or 5 per cent of the votes cast throughout the Federal Republic. The introduction of the 5 per cent provision meant that the number of political parties which were represented in the *Bundestag* fell from ten in 1949, to four in 1957 and, from 1961 onwards, three: the SPD, the FDP and the CDU/CSU alliance.

The electoral system in the *Land* of North Rhine-Westphalia, like that of the Federal Republic, combines single member constituencies with proportional representation. There are 150 constituencies and 50 seats are filled by proportional representation from party lists. In determining parliamentary representation, the total votes received by all the parties throughout North Rhine-Westphalia are added together and any minor parties which have not received 5 per cent of the votes cast or which have not won at least one constituency are eliminated. These voting totals are then used to determine how many of the 200 seats the parties are entitled to receive. If any one party has won more constituencies than it is entitled to receive, then it keeps these seats and further seats are added to the total to keep the results proportional. Table I shows party affiliations in the *Landtag* since 1947.

TABLE I: NORTH RHINE-WESTPHALIA LANDTAG

Membership by political party

Electoral Period	Total	CDU	FDP	SPD	ZENTRUM	KPD
1947–1950	216	92	12	64	20	28
1950–1954	215	93	26	68	16	12
1954–1958	200	90	25	76	9	–
1958–1962	200	104	15	81	–	–
1962–1966	200	96	14	90	–	–
1966–1970	200	86	15	99	–	–
1970–1975	200	95	11	94	–	–
1975–1980	200	95	14	91	–	–

The final outcome of the political system, and therefore its effect on broadcasting policy, depends to a large extent on which electoral system is employed. It is clear for instance, both from the results of the Federal elections and from the results of the *Land* elections in North Rhine-Westphalia, that the 5 per cent rule has progressively eliminated the minor parties such as the Zentrum party and the KPD. What is less obviously apparent is the extent to which the electoral system in North Rhine-Westphalia has favoured the CDU over the SPD. In the 1966 election, the SPD won 99 constituencies, the CDU won 51 and the FDP won none at all. However, the implementation of the proportional element in the electoral system gave the CDU a further 35 seats, and the FDP 15 seats. Thus the CDU/FDP coalition had a total of 101, a majority of 2 over the SPD. Even more political power thus accrues to the FDP, which, as can be seen from Table II, has formed coalitions both with the CDU and with the SPD and on at least two occasions has swapped political partners in the middle of an electoral period.

11

Ruling Cabinets 1947–75

Electoral Period	Minister-President	Party Coalitions	Period of Office
1947–1950	Karl Arnold	CDU/SPD/Zentrum/KPD	1947–1948
	Karl Arnold	CDU/SPD/Zentrum	1948–1950
1950–1954	Karl Arnold	CDU/Zentrum	1950–1954
1954–1958	Karl Arnold	CDU/FDP/Zentrum	1954–1956
	Fritz Steinhoff	SPD/FDP	1956–1958
1958–1962	Franz Meyers	CDU	1958–1962
1962–1966	Franz Meyers	CDU/FDP	1962–1966
1966–1970	Franz Meyers	CDU/FDP	1966 (5 mths)
	Heinz Kuhn	SPD/FDP	1966–1970
1970–1975	Heinz Kuhn	SPD/FDP	1970–1975

The FDP therefore plays a key political role in North-Rhine West-phalia, ensuring that neither the CDU nor the SPD can ever deviate far from consensus politics acceptable to the centre of the political spectrum. Nevertheless, its role has not been an entirely honourable one and according to one commentator it has come to be regarded as an opportunist party and lost a considerable proportion of its votes in 1958, 1961 and 1965 because it failed to keep pre-election promises or had broken up coalitions. (Preece, 1968, p. 65.) It is essentially an anti-socialist party. For instance, during the 1966 elections Willi Weyer, the FDP leader in North Rhine-Westphalia, declared that he would not form a coalition with the SPD even if it were to win the largest number of seats, because 'an SPD *Land* government would act party politically in the *Bundesrat* [the Federal upper house] and one cannot sever North Rhine-Westphalian politics from federal politics.' (Quoted in Preece, 1968, p. 65.)

What sort of people live under this political system? Table III shows how the people earn their living.

As can be seen from the table, the largest single grouping are those working in the factories of the *Ruhrgebiet*, who account for over one third of the working population. A further sector of approximately one-fifth of the working population are civil servants or work in the service sector of the economy. Not all of the population of the *Land* are of German origin, however. Of the over 17 million inhabitants of the *Land*, some 1.2 million are foreigners. Nearly one third of these are Turkish, while there are also large minorities of Yugoslav, Italian, Greek and Spanish origin. Nearly all of these are *Gastarbeiter* — immigrant workers brought in to carry out the menial tasks necessary to the successful functioning of the 'economic

Analysis by Occupation and Economic Sector (1971)

Occupation	Total (1000–)	Agriculture, Forestry & Fishing	Production	Business & Commerce	Other Economic Sectors
Self-Employed	528	70	154	145	158
Working in Family Business	178	76	32	33	37
Civil Servants and staff employees	3075	9	976	695	1395
Workers	2949	35	2213	320	381
Total	6279	190	3370	1193	1970

miracle' in the factories of the *Ruhrgebiet*.

By 1964, according to data collected for church tax purposes, some 8.7 million inhabitants or 53 per cent of the population of North Rhine-Westphalia were registered as Catholic, while 7 million (42 per cent) were registered as Protestant. A further 0.9 million (5 per cent) were registered as atheist or agnostic. Religion has traditionally played an important role in German politics, with strong ties between the Catholic church and the CDU. Thus in the 1965 Federal elections, the CDU/CSU obtained 72.1 per cent of the votes cast in predominantly Catholic areas (SPD 21.6 per cent) while in the predominantly Protestant areas they only obtained 42.9 per cent (SPD 40.2 per cent). In areas of mixed denomination the CDU obtained less than 40 per cent and the SPD more than 45 per cent of the vote.

Although the churches do not take any active part in political campaigning, this is not the case for some specifically religious organisations. Both the Catholic Workers Movement (Katholische Arbeiterbewegung (KAB)) and the Kolping Family Movement, an organisation headed by Catholic priests to provide hostels for apprentices while they are away from home, are permanent organisational bases for the CDU, and are actively involved in politics. Some 90 per cent of the KAB's membership is in North Rhine-Westphalia and together with the Kolping Family movement it has been the effective base for the left of centre policies which have dominated CDU politics in North Rhine-Westphalia ever since Karl Arnold's first period as Minister-President in the late 1940s. Protestant involvement in politics is much less overt, but even so there are still strong connections between the CDU and the Protestant bishops.

On the other hand, connections between the trade union movement and the SPD are not as direct as they are in the United Kingdom. Although many union leaders support the SPD, too specific a connection

13

between the SPD and the trades unions might mean defections from the German Trades' Union Federation (the Deutscher Gewerkschaftsbund) and the German Employees Union (Deutsche Angestelltengewerkschaft) to the Catholic Christian Trades Union, which actively supports the CDU.

The inner conflicts of Catholic voters who wish to vote SPD were revealed in a letter to *Die Zeit* of 22 October 1965:

> On the 19th September I went to the polls. I voted SPD. On the 2nd October as a Catholic, I fulfilled my Christian duty and went to confession. I asked the priest if I had burdened my soul with a sin as the result of having voted SPD. 'Yes,' he said, 'as a Christian you ought only to give your vote to a party based on Christian ideals.' Of course, I could have refuted the Reverend Father's point of view; the SPD is also (perhaps even more than the CDU/CSU) a party that is based on Christian ideals, that guarantees religious freedom, protects each religion, etc. But I kept quiet. I got my penance and absolution. I left the confessional contrite and disturbed, contrite and disturbed over my sinful life. (Quoted in Preece, 1968, p. 50.)

By the mid-1960s, however, the church was beginning to release its political hold on its members. Whereas in the 1965 Federal elections a Pastoral letter was read throughout the country from the pulpits more or less clearly recommending the congregations to vote CDU, by the 1966 *Land* election in North Rhine-Westphalia the Rhenish Westphalian bishops quoted the decision of their council to the effect that 'In questions of order of earthly things there can be justified differences of opinion between Christians. In such circumstances no-one has the right to claim the authority of the Church exclusively for himself and his own opinions.' (Quoted in Preece, 1968, p. 49.) Nevertheless, as can be seen from Table IV, in the North Rhine-Westphalian elections for the *Land* parliament in 1966 Catholic-affiliated working- and middle-class voters still comprised a substantial proportion of the CDU vote, and only 63 per cent of the SPD vote came from the working classes.

We can, therefore, identify two key characteristics of North Rhine-Westphalian politics. First, the split between the CDU and the SPD cannot be characterised in simple left/right terms but must also take into account religious differences. The CDU/Catholic alliance has shifted CDU policies to the left to enable them to appeal to the substantial working-class vote and the SPD has, in contrast, found it necessary to moderate its policies to capture the votes of the trade union-affiliated professional classes.

These converging tendencies, combined with the substantial proportional element in the electoral system, have given the centrist element in *Land* politics, and the FDP in particular, an especially influential role in

TABLE IV: SOCIAL/OCCUPATIONAL CLASS
AND VOTING BEHAVIOUR
(North Rhine-Westphalia, July 1966)

	Registered Electors (%)	SPD Supporters as percentage of SPD vote	CDU Supporters as percentage of SDU vote
Working Classes			
Trade union members	23	35	19
No trade union or religious affiliation	14	18	9
With expectation of advancement	7	6	10
Catholic affiliated	7	4	12
Middle Classes			
Risen from working class	6	5	6
Catholic affiliated	13	3	24
Employees	11	9	11
Independent industrial/ commercial	4	3	4
Independent farmers	1	1	2
Professional Classes			
Trade union white collar workers	10	12	7
Non-aligned			
Catholic and trade union-affiliated	4	4	5

Source: Preece (1968) p. 63, adapted from sample by *infas* (2358 cases) May-June 1966

North Rhine-Westphalian politics. This centripetal tendency in the system has had a profound influence in determining both the relationship between the *Land* parliament and the *Land* broadcasting institution, WDR, and in determining the choice of *Intendant* or Director-General of WDR. Both of these forces were to play a key role in the growth and the demise of the *Arbeiterfilm*.

15

CHAPTER 2

The Growth of WDR

After the end of the Second World War, the Allied Powers had set up separate broadcasting arrangements in their occupied zones. A pattern of decentralised broadcasting was set up in the American Zone where four institutions, Radio Frankfurt, Radio München, Radio Stuttgart and Radio Bremen, were established. In the British and French Zones on the other hand, a centralised model was adopted. Nordwestdeutscher Rundfunk (NWDR), based in Hamburg, covered the whole of the British Zone, and in Baden-Baden Südwestfunk covered the whole of the French Zone. During the early years of the Federal Republic more decentralisation followed. NWDR was split up during the early 1950s, first by relocating its Berlin service within the newly formed Berlin broadcasting organisation, Sender Freies Berlin, in 1953 and secondly by splitting the remaining organisation into Norddeutscher Rundfunk (NDR), located in Hamburg, and Westdeutscher Rundfunk (WDR), situated in Cologne. This latter split was brought about at the instigation of the *Land* government of North Rhine-Westphalia and reflected a desire for political independence by the Karl Arnold/CDU government of the largest *Land* in the Federal Republic from a broadcasting organisation which was controlled and run from Hamburg, a *Land* which was under SPD control and which was much smaller in size. As a result of the virtual secession of WDR from NWDR, the Hamburg service became NDR in 1955 and was re-established under an inter-*Land* treaty between the *Länder* of Hamburg, Schleswig-Holstein and Lower Saxony.

In the early 1950s the broadcasting stations had set up a joint organisation called the Arbeitsgemeinschaft der öffentlich-rechtlichen-Rundfunkanstalten der Bundesrepublik Deutschland or the ARD for short. This 'Joint Association of Public Corporations for Broadcasting in the Federal Republic of Germany' was very much an informal association of broadcasting institutions working together to provide the public with a service free from commercial and political pressures and which would broadcast over all the Federal Republic and West Berlin. There are no legally binding ties between any of the broadcasting institutions and the ARD. There was and is simply an established practice of working together which has grown up and developed between the constituent members. By the end of the 1950s these had reached nine in number. Six of them served areas which coincided with *Land* boundaries — Bayerischer Rundfunk (Bavaria), Hessischer Rundfunk (Hesse), Radio Bremen (Bremen), Saarländischer Rundfunk (Saar); Westdeutscher Rundfunk (North Rhine-Westphalia) and Sender Freies Berlin (West Berlin) — although strictly speaking, West Berlin is not a part of the Federal Republic. Norddeutscher Rundfunk served three *Länder* — Hamburg, Lower Saxony and Schleswig-Holstein; Südwestfunk served the Rhineland-Palatinate and part of Baden-Württemburg; and Südeutscher Rundfunk served the remainder of Baden-Württemburg. Between them they provide a public broadcasting service which covers the whole of the Federal Republic but which is funded by a licence fee fixed at a common level throughout the whole of the Federal Republic by an agreement between all of the *Land* governments. Each broadcasting organisation transmits its own programmes until 8 o'clock in the evening. After that time, the broadcasting organisations transmit a common programme throughout the whole of West Germany, starting with the main evening news bulletin. These main evening programmes are provided by individual institutions within the ARD in proportion to their wealth. WDR, which was and is the largest of the nine stations, provides 25 per cent of the networked transmissions.

THE CONSTITUTION OF WDR

The legislation setting up WDR was passed by the North Rhine-Westphalian *Landtag* on 25 May 1954 and the statutes regulating it were enacted on 6 March 1956 under the premiership of Karl Arnold. Like most of the *Land* broadcasting organisations, WDR has a three tier control structure consisting of the *Rundfunkrat* or broadcasting council, the *Verwaltungsrat* or administrative council and the *Intendant* or director-general. In addition, however, WDR has a further body, the *Programmbeirat* or programme advisory council. The law provides that the broadcasting council shall consist of 21 members and that, together with their deputies, they shall be elected by the members of the *Landtag* for a period of five years according to the principles of proportional representation. Members may be re-elected, but not more than 4 members or 4 deputies may be members of either the *Landtag* or the *Bundestag* (clauses 8.1–8.3).

The broadcasting council then elects the 7 members of the administrative council, and 19 of the 20 members of the programme advisory council (clause 9.1). The remaining member of the programme advisory council is nominated directly by the *Land* government. The 19 members of the programme advisory council are chosen from up to 3 candidates each put forward by 19 groups representing 7 social groupings. If a group does not put forward a candidate, the broadcasting council can select its own.

17

Thus the political spectrum of the *Landtag* is directly reflected in the composition of the broadcasting council, and this body in its turn selects the members of the administrative council and of the programme advisory council, acting, in the case of the advisory council, as a very selective filter, and in the case of the programme advisory council as a moderately selective filter. The broadcasting council meets four times a year to debate matters of a major political nature and to confirm the appointment of the *Intendant*. The programme advisory council, on the other hand, meets about six times per year and its role is to advise the *Intendant* on the whole programme area. The *Intendant* is required to attend its meetings and it provides him with a sounding board on the way programmes are perceived and received. The council may also give its views on the types of programmes it would like to see produced, but unless the *Intendant* wishes, which is extremely unlikely, it will not be involved in detailed programme planning.

The real power in the administrative structure lies with the *Verwaltungsrat*, the administrative council. This body, which has 7 members and which meets approximately once a month, has full responsibility for ensuring the proper management of WDR. It elects the *Intendant* and the only role reserved for the broadcasting council is to confirm its appointment. Furthermore, the *Intendant* also requires the approval of the administrative council for his appointments to the posts of programme director, the directors of the administrative sub-sections, the studio directors, the director of transmissions, the legal adviser and the technical directors (standing rules para. 28.3). This approval mechanism does not extend to a post 'with exclusively artistic duties', however (clause 21.2 (e)).

Without doubt therefore, the *Verwaltungsrat* is an extremely powerful and influential body. Its members may not be members of either the broadcasting council or the programme advisory council, nor may they be employees of WDR. Like the members of the broadcasting council, they are required in the statutes to have a knowledge and expertise of broadcasting and to be free from directives emanating from other bodies (clauses 8.5 and 12.5). Each member is elected for seven years and can be re-elected on retirement. Members retire annually in rotation. The body therefore is small, meets frequently and has a slow turnover in membership. The political balance of its membership is determined by the broadcasting council, which in its turn reflects the political orientation of the *Landtag*. Although, as Williams (1976, p. 109) has noted, it is theoretically possible for the dominant party in the *Landtag*, and thus the broadcasting council, to dominate the administrative council with its appointees, this has not happened to date. Just as the FDP holds the balance of power in the *Landtag*, so it holds the balance of power in the broadcasting council. As a result, the seven man membership of the administrative council is normally split 3:3:1 along party lines, ensuring that centrist interests are represented at administrative council level and also play a key and crucial role in the appointment of the *Intendant*.

Thus the constitution of WDR has ensured an almost direct line of political accountability between the *Intendant* and the *Landtag*, but, because of the particular politics of North Rhine-Westphalia, it has given the *Intendant* substantial independence provided that he operates within the liberal public service traditions envisaged by the British authorities when they set up NWDR at the end of the war. When, however, programming policy upsets two of the three interests on the administrative council, then the *Intendant* becomes politically accountable in a very real sense. This limitation on broadcasting independence was to play a key and important role in the history of the *Arbeiterfilm*, as we shall see in chapter 7.

THE ROLE OF THE FEDERAL GOVERNMENT

Parallel to the development of the ARD network, the 1950s also saw growing political pressure from the Federal government for a Federal broadcasting authority to be set up. The Federal Republic had been granted full sovereignty in 1955, but even before that time the battle between the *Intendanten* of the broadcasting stations and the Federal government had been shaping up. Between May 1951 and March 1953 there was preliminary political skirmishing over the Federal government's draft bill to reorganise broadcasting, which went before the *Bundestag* in March 1953. The government wanted to create a new public corporation (Der Deutsche Rundfunk) to broadcast at the same time as the other organisations. In the field of radio, it was to have its own arrangements for news and political commentaries, but other material would be supplied free of charge by the other stations. In the field of television it would supervise the Deutscher Fernseh-Rundfunk (German television broadcasting service) and the provision of long and short wave broadcasts. It would also administer the collection of licence fees and other common administrative tasks.

The *Intendanten* of the ARD stations opposed the Federal proposal. They claimed that new technical developments, including television, came within their areas of responsibility and they reaffirmed their conviction that their responsibility for broadcasting came from the sovereignty of the *Länder* in this field. They denied the contention of the Federal government that broadcasting was a part of the telecommunication services for which it had responsibility under Article 73.7 of the Basic Law, and was therefore a Federal matter. The broadcasting stations argued that they paid the Federal Post Office for its transmission services at a price freely agreed between the Federal Post Office and the broadcasters. The licence fee was administered directly by the broadcasters, and the Federal Post Office was legally contracted to transmit their programmes.

In the event, the broadcasters' case gathered wide support from other media of public opinion such as the press and the Federal government decided against forcing a vote in the Federal parliament. Accordingly the ARD went ahead and established its first television channel and in 1954, despite the lack of a proper legal identity, was accepted into the European Broadcasting Union.

The controversy between the Federal Republic and the *Länder* had only faded, however. The main lines of argument were to be deployed again in the far more intense battle over the allocation of the second television channel. In 1957, ARD announced that it was applying to the Federal Post Office for UHF frequencies to broadcast a second television channel which it planned to set up in 1960. The reply of the Federal Post Office was non-committal, saying that it was exploring various possibilities including making contracts with private capital for a second service. The following year, under pressure from the SPD opposition, the Federal CDU government referred the question to the Standing Committee for Cultural Affairs of the Federal parliament with the condition that the purpose should be to set up a second television channel 'not made by the existing broadcasting authorities'.

In December 1958, the Confederation of German Industry decided that the time had come for private control to move into the field of broadcasting. Television offered an opportunity to make large sums of money, as the commercial television companies had shown in the United Kingdom three years earlier. There was the added incentive that a network controlled by them would broadcast the type of programmes that they wanted the people to see. Accordingly, using the industrialist R. Krause to act on their behalf, they formed an alliance with a number of newspaper publishers headed by H. Merkel who were interested in extending their dominant control of media advertising. A new company, Freies Fernsehen GmbH, was founded.

In June 1959, the Minister-Presidents of the *Länder*, concerned that they should not lose their sovereignty over broadcasting, proposed the setting up of an Inter-*Land* agreement to create a federal-wide public broadcasting corporation to be called Deutsches Fernsehen. This new body would be under the control of a council which would be broadly based and would include representatives of the broadcasting authorities and the public as well as representatives of the Federal Republic and of the *Länder*.

At first, Adenauer tried to liaise with CDU colleagues in the *Länder* to combine the two proposals by using Freies Fernsehen as a vehicle for a joint company in which both the Federal Republic and the *Länder* had an interest. He even went so far as to guarantee a loan of DM 20 million to Freies Fernsehen but the links proposed between Federal Government and private capital were disturbingly close to those formed during the Third Reich between the Nazi government and big business. Adenauer, who wanted the new station to open in 1961, which was election year, changed his plans. In July 1960 he founded a joint Federal/*Länder* company called Deutschland Fernsehen GmbH. Of the basic capital, DM 12,000 was to be held by the Federal Republic, DM 11,000 was to be held by the 11 *Länder*. Adenauer himself signed the contract for the Federal Republic while the Federal Minister of Justice took it upon himself to sign on behalf of the 11 *Länder*. Forced into a choice of either having to accede to Adenauer's new proposal or of losing control of the second television channel, the *Länder* took the Federal Government to the Constitutional Court.

The historic significance of the challenge by the *Länder* to the authority of the Federal government was to stretch far beyond the decision as to who had control of the second television channel, for in its judgement of 28 February 1961 the Federal Constitutional Court laid down requirements which covered all areas of broadcasting including the activities of the first television channel, already in existence. The court found that the Federal Government's actions were unconstitutional in that broadcasting was not included in the Federal Government's constitutional responsibility for the field of posts and telecommunications. Broadcasting was a cultural activity and therefore the responsibility of the *Länder*.

More importantly, the Court went on to note that the *form* of broadcasting organisation did not debar private companies from broadcasting but, on the contrary, it was the dual guarantee that all socially relevant groups could get a hearing and that the freedom of reporting would not be infringed which was the essential requirement of a broadcasting organisation. The Court ruled that:

> The guarantee of freedom in the field of broadcasting in article 5 of the basic law does not require, of course, the form found in the *Land* broadcasting laws and assumed by the broadcasting bodies under federal law. It is above all not a requirement of the federal constitution that broadcasting can be performed only by institutions of public law. A company incorporated under civil law could also be a vehicle for this sort of undertaking provided that it offers in its formal organisation sufficient guarantees that all socially relevant groups could, as in institutions of public law, get a hearing in it and that the freedom of reporting is not infringed. (Quoted in Williams, 1976, p. 29.)

The judgment went on to be more specific about the ways in which socially relevant groupings were to be represented both in the control of the broadcasting organisation and in its programming policies:

21

Article 5 of the Basic Law does, however, require that this modern instrument for the formation of opinion should be surrendered neither to the state nor to any one group in society. The promoters of broadcasting programmes must, therefore, be so organised that all relevant forces have an influence in the organs of control and a fair hearing in the overall programme, and that binding principles apply to the content of the overall programme which guarantee a minimum balance in content, impartiality and mutual respect. This can be secured only if these organisational and material principles are made generally binding by law. (Quoted in Williams, 1976, p. 30.)

The Court went further, however. In doing so, it struck right at the heart of programming policy. It was not simply a minimum balance in content, impartiality and mutual respect which the broadcasters had to observe in relaying the views of others. Broadcasting was more than a window on the world of political debate, it was itself an active participant in the formation of public opinion and thus had a role in forming public opinion as well as in informing public attitudes. The Court ruled that:

Broadcasting is more than a 'medium' for the forming of public opinion; it is an eminent 'factor' in the formation of public opinion. Its contribution to the formation of public opinion is in no way limited to news broadcasts, political commentaries, series on past, present and future political problems; radio plays, musical presentations, the transmission of satirical and cabaret programmes, even programme settings help to form opinion. Every programme will have a certain tendency because of the selection and the form of the individual transmission, particularly when a decision is involved on what is not to be broadcast, what need not interest the audience, what can be neglected without detriment to the formation of public opinion and on how what is broadcast is to be shaped and enunciated. (Quoted in Williams, 1976, p. 31.)

Mindful, no doubt, of the total media control which the Nazis had attempted to set up under the Third Reich, the Constitutional Court had ruled quite explicitly that cultural and fictional broadcasts were also part of the field of ideological struggle for they too contributed to the formation of public opinion. No longer could the world of broadcasting be divided into news and current affairs programmes which had to observe party political balance on the one hand, and entertainment programmes which were non-political on the other. Programming policy for all programmes, whether fact or fiction, had to demonstrate a broad spread of political philosophies and to cover all aspects of human activity.

As a result of the Constitutional Court judgement, Adenauer's bid to have the second television channel run by the Deutschland Fernsehen GmbH failed ignominiously and accordingly the governments of the *Länder* set up, by means of an inter-*Land* treaty, a new public institution, Zweites Deutsches Fernsehen (ZDF), with headquarters in Mainz, to run the second television channel. The Court's judgement also had an impact on the policies of the individual institutions comprising the ARD network. Their programming policies also had to conform to the criteria laid down by the Court.

Article 4 of WDR's Constitution, which laid down the ideals of the institution's programming policy, took on a new significance. Article 4 states that:

> The WDR, Cologne is to keep its broadcasts within the bounds of constitutional order. It is to take account of various trends in ideology, science and the arts. It must respect the moral and religious beliefs of the people. The religious and ethnic divisions in the broadcasting area must be taken into account. News broadcasts must be universal, impartial and objective.

> The WDR shall foster international understanding, stand up for peace and social justice, protect democratic freedoms and pledge itself to truth at all times. It may not unilaterally serve any one political party or group, lobby, religious confession or ideology.

Following the decision of the Constitutional Court, the broadcasting authorities of WDR, and the *Intendant* in particular, had to translate these high ideals into practice, not only for news and current affairs broadcasts but also for fiction films and drama programmes. The strictures against serving any one political group, lobby, or ideology applied to entertainment programmes as well as educational ones. Similarly WDR's duty to take account of various trends in ideology and the arts were not limited to transmitting films made elsewhere and making programmes about drama productions which could be seen in the theatre. Now its duties were to ensure that all relevant social forces had a fair hearing in the overall programming of fictional programmes whether they were films or television dramas. If the dominant ideology of feature films initially developed for the international cinema market was centred in one part of the ideological spectrum, then it was the responsibility of the *Intendant* and his senior colleagues to ensure that WDR itself produced films which counterbalanced this ideological bias and to ensure that WDR's overall programming of fictional material was ideologically impartial and balanced.

This is not a requirement of public service broadcasting in the UK. Here fictional programming is dominated either by bought-in programmes such as US feature films and TV series or by homeproduced material developed for audience maximisation rather than for the achievement of an overall balance in fictional programming. The main imperatives of production are audience maximisation in the British market, overseas programme sales, particularly to the Public Broadcasting System in the USA, and the nourishing of indigenous writers. This last motive does of course mean that there are some left-wing drama productions in British television, written by authors such as Jim Allen, Trevor Griffiths or Colin Welland. But productions such as *Days of Hope, Bill Brand* or *Leeds United* are the exceptions to the general rule. Even if British television executives had the will to support the production of programmes like those on a more extensive scale, there is the battery of right-wing criticism led by the Conservative press and followed by questions in the House of Commons which has to be faced. Not surprisingly television executives are cautious when challenged on ideological grounds and retreat into a rhetoric of supporting artistic talent. Shaun Sutton, BBC Television's Head of Drama, had only this to say when William Deedes, ex-Conservative Minister and editor of the *Daily Telegraph*, attacked him for funding the production of *Days of Hope*, written by Jim Allen, directed by Kenneth Loach and produced by Tony Garnett:

> I think any large artistic group will always contain a certain number of people of left wing persuasion. This is absolutely inevitable and I think it is perfectly right. In the last two years we have produced less than ten plays of this nature before *Days of Hope* — less than 10 out of 850 original drama transmissions. That seems a very fair proportion to me. ('Jim Allen Meets His Critics', programme transcript, *The Listener*, vol. 94, no. 2427, 1975, pp. 459–60.)

CHAPTER 3

The Genesis of the *Arbeiterfilm*

1961 was a key year in the history of WDR, for in that year Klaus von Bismarck was appointed *Intendant*. The search by the WDR *Verwaltungsrat* for a new *Intendant* to propose to the *Rundfunkrat* for their confirmation had not been easy. The 3:3:1 split along party lines of the *Verwaltungsrat* meant that any candidate of either the CDU or the SPD faction also had to command the support of the FDP faction. Conversely, no FDP candidate had any chance of success unless he or she commanded the respect and the support of the CDU or the SPD factions. Furthermore, all members were looking for the ideal candidate — someone who would command universal support from all seven members.

In many ways, von Bismarck seemed to offer a unique combination of qualities for a prospective *Intendant* at the beginning of the 1960s. First, he had an impeccable pedigree since he was the great-nephew of the 'Iron Chancellor' Prince Otto von Bismarck, and he himself had given distinguished service during the Second World War as an infantry officer. After the war, he had built up a formidable reputation for his social work, closely associated with the Evangelical church, and particularly for his work with men in the mining and textile industries. In 1959, he had been awarded an honorary doctorate by the University of Munster for theoretical and practical activities in the field of religious social work. Although he was not associated with any political party, he had nevertheless played an active role in evangelical church politics, having been a member of the All German Synod of the German Evangelical Church and President of the Society for Social Progress. Thus von Bismarck embodied the aristocratic, military and religious attributes which were likely to appeal to the CDU faction, but also the progressive, social democratic and 'concerned' attributes which were likely to appeal to the SPD faction. Finally, although he was not a broadcaster by profession, he had been a member of the *Rundfunkrat* of the old NWDR from 1952 until it was split into NDR and WDR a year later. He was therefore no stranger to some of the problems of broadcasting politics and was known personally to many of those now responsible for electing a new *Intendant*.

Within the political climate of the early 1960s, the one unifying and dominant policy on which all political parties agreed was that the Federal Republic should never again fall into the terrifying grip of monolithic fascism which Germany had experienced under the Third Reich. Von Bismarck, who had already demonstrated his forthright support for individual freedom and the right of dissent, was himself firmly identified with the centre of the political spectrum. As *Intendant* he had the opportunity to put his ideas into practice, not only because they were clearly and resolutely anti-fascist in their thrust, but also because it was he, a highly respected individual, who was putting them forward. His appointment lasted for five years and was renewable, and he could be dismissed only for serious reasons by a vote of five out of seven members of the *Verwaltungsrat*. In a very real sense therefore, von Bismarck now occupied a position of enormous power in German broadcasting, where his decisions could go virtually unquestioned either by his subordinates or more importantly by the politicians on the *Verwaltungsrat*.

Given this autonomy and independence, where did von Bismarck stand in relation to the key questions which underlie the role to be played by the broadcaster in a democratic and pluralistic society? Where did he stand in that ongoing struggle between those who want society to remain the same and those who want to change it? Where, in the never-ending struggle between capital and labour, would he take his stand? How far could individual programmes challenge the existing social order? How far would he challenge the political authorities when broadcasting was at once both separate from and also part of the political structure of North Rhine-Westphalia?

Von Bismarck began to feel his way slowly, and it was not until five years later, after he had been re-elected for a second term, that he felt free to put his philosophy of programming policy into print. In a key article published in *Die Zeit* (see Appendix 2) he set out to tackle the problem of the difficult and the disruptive broadcast.

Although the article was written shortly after the decision to discontinue the satirical programme *Hallo Nachbarn! (Hello Neighbour!)* and may be read at one level as a specific comment upon that decision and the public controversy that followed, in a much more profound sense it reveals von Bismarck's more closely argued approach to a wider and more general problem which extends the conditions surrounding the genesis of the *Arbeiterfilm*. For von Bismarck, public service broadcasters should be fighting a continuous battle on behalf of the individual against the collective forces which were continuously massing in society and operating through a series of pressure groups. The most important of these pressure groups were, of course, the political parties, and one significant school of thought argued that broadcasting freedom was to be achieved by 'leasing out' broadcasting time to the various political factions. The dominance of this school of thought in WDR can be gauged from the composition of the *Verwaltungsrat* and from the more widespread operation in German broadcasting of the *Proporz* system where the political affiliations of senior broadcasting executives, and hence of their programmes, are balanced one against another both within one broadcasting company and between the output of different broadcasting companies within the ARD channel. Von Bismarck, on the other hand, from his own position in the centre of the political spectrum, and drawing on the work of the Swiss liberal and existentialist philosopher Karl Jaspers (see, *inter alia*, his *The Future of Germany*), argues for the right of the individual to put his or her point of view forward, no matter what it may be. Von Bismarck's justification for this position rested ultimately on the belief that the enduring values of a society cannot be destroyed by criticism, but that on the contrary, quoting Ulrich Sonnemann, the mind — and thus broadcasters — should be prepared to destroy until they meet qualities or ideas which are resistant to intellectual attack. Ultimately there is, he believed, a root core of values or beliefs which cannot be destroyed however hard one tries. This concept of indestructible values came very close to von Bismarck's active practice of Christian belief. Von Bismarck tempered his intellectual rigour, however, by recognising that he was putting forward an argument which may need to be at odds with broadcasting practice. Criticism is not acceptable unless these ideas are given only limited broadcasting time, not merely because of a need to balance consensus establishment views with those of dissident individuals or groups, but also because of the limited understanding by the masses of the constructive role which can be played by dialectical criticism.

Von Bismarck implied, although he never explicitly admitted it, that criticism was a suitable pastime for an intellectual and political elite, but that it was too sophisticated a diet for the simple masses, who need ideological reinforcement rather than intellectual dialectics. This pragmatic modification of his thesis related to another sub-theme, the relationship between the politicians and the broadcasters. Immediately after the Second World War, under the influence of the Allied Powers, particularly in the British Zone, there was a strong upsurge in the power and influence of intellectuals in German broadcasting, especially of course those who had distinguished themselves by their anti-fascist writings. This led to a so-called division between the broadcasters and the politicians during the early years of the Federal Republic, or between those who watched and those who did, between those who observed and commented on the political birthpangs of the new Federal German Republic and those who were actively involved. Here again, von Bismarck's personal history rendered him immune from criticism, for he had both thought and written about many social aspects of politics particularly in relation to the role of the churches and had also been an

27

active social worker in the field.

This, then, was the intellectual route by which WDR came to be known and recognised as a broadcasting institution where alternative voices were able to have their say and where voices of dissent, particularly those on the left, were able to turn their ideas into programmes exploring new philosophies and ideologies, and, on occasion, new forms. Within this general policy space there were, however, a number of other forces which led to the genesis of the *Arbeiterfilm*. Two key factors which influenced the movement within WDR were, firstly, the total failure of the German film industry to generate a policy where film-making with any artistic pretensions could flourish, and secondly, the key role played in forming the intellectual climate within WDR by the third television channel in North Rhine-Westphalia, West Deutsches Fernsehen, which only broadcasts to North Rhine-Westphalia, (unlike the first channel, ARD, and the second, ZDF, which are nationally networked).

WDR AND THE GERMAN FILM INDUSTRY

The role played by the German television networks in the development of the German film industry can only be sketched in briefly, but it is necessary to understand it for two reasons. First, it explains the economic relations that developed between the two media, and in the case of the *Arbeiterfilm* the economic relations which developed between the film-makers themselves and the broadcasting institution and which are substantially different from those which pertain in, for example, the United Kingdom. Second, it explains the feelings of creative frustration felt by aspirant film-makers during the late 50s and the 60s which almost literally forced the television institutions and particularly WDR into facing up to assessing the responsibilities and the role of a television institution as a patron of audiovisual narrative fiction.

The first involvement of the German television stations with film production and exhibition began in the late 1950s as cinema audiences declined in the face of competition from the TV network itself. Not only was television offering cheaper entertainment than the cinema, but it had also started to offer German audiences the opportunity to see films which were not available in cinemas. On 1st May 1958, the Italian film *Amici per la pelle (Friends for Life,* d. Franco Rossi, 1955) had its German première, not in the cinema, but on television, for no German distributor would distribute it. In the field of distribution and transmission, television was ready to complement the film industry in making foreign films available to the public.

At about the same time, the production side of the film industry was moving into one of its many recurring crises. At the end of the Second World War, the Americans had supported the rebuilding of the exhibition and distribution sectors of the German film industry, but only

28

reluctantly granted licences for film production. Furthermore, the various decartelisation laws should have ensured that no centralised industry could emerge from the UFA holdings. However, the new Federal Government took a different view and in 1953 in a hurried and secret move tried to prevent the Americans from selling the old UFA holdings to individual bidders by asking the Deutsche Bank to form three separate companies to develop the old UFA assets. Three years later, the three firms were openly reunited as a consortium headed by the Deutsche Bank and the Dresdner Bank. But the new monopoly was ineffective. The new organisation turned out to be an economic dinosaur and within a few years was close to collapse. At this point the television industry moved in to save the production facilities of Real Film in Hamburg and Bavaria Film in Munich by buying up over 75 per cent of their shares. This move meant that German television, and particularly WDR which had acquired a large shareholding in Bavaria Film, now had an economic interest in developing the production of television programmes which were shot on film and in film studios, in order to keep the stages of their new film studios full. At a time when much creative effort in British television was being deployed in the production of television drama programmes shot on electronic cameras, German television was developing a substantial expertise in film production.

In 1965, German television also attempted to give some financial help to German film producers when they bought the television rights of a hundred feature films in a deal agreed between the two networks (ARD and ZDF) and the German Film and Television Producers Association. For these hundred German feature films, produced between 1960 and 1964, the two networks paid 10 million DM (£893,000) or an average of 100,000 DM (£8,900) per film. Although revenue from television licences are, by law, only to be used for broadcasting purposes, it was later admitted (Hess, 1970, p. 76) that only 30,000 DM (£2,680) per film was for the television rights, and that the other 70,000 DM (£6,280) was a hidden production subsidy. Furthermore, according to one source (Berg, 1978), the films purchased in this deal were rather poor in quality.

Since 1965, German television has of course continued to purchase feature films, both from home and abroad, but it has also commissioned its own films directly from individual German film-makers, or more precisely from their private companies. In many cases, this has meant that the film-makers have been able to negotiate for themselves the theatrical and non-theatrical rights to their films, while the German television organisations have only retained the television rights, both German and foreign. (*Variety*, 10 January 1979, estimates German producers now also receive 10 per cent of their total income from foreign sales from the Goethe Institut, which promotes German culture abroad.) And so the films are not simply transmitted once on television and never seen again, as is the fate of many British television

29

productions, but frequently screened outside television and, in the case of the *Arbeiterfilm*, their non-theatrical screenings play a particularly important social role (see Chapter 6).

Table V gives the annual expenditures by the two broadcasting organisations (A R D and Z D F) both for the purchase of completed films and for the commissioning of productions by individual companies.

As can be seen from the table, during the period from 1966 until 1973 the networks followed a general policy of using higher and higher proportions of their budgets on commissioning films rather than buying them. There are of course variations from year to year, but the money spent on commissioning films rose from approximately 2½ times that spent on film purchase in 1966 to approximately 4 times in 1973. Since that time the proportion has fallen back to approximately 2½ to 1. This trend can also be seen in the figures in the last two columns, which show how the money spent on commissioning films races ahead of that spent on purchasing films when expressed as a percentage of the 1966 expenditure until 1973/74 and then starts to fall back again and by 1976 has fallen below the index for films purchased. The majority of the *Arbeiterfilme* were produced during the first period and reflect the concerns of a time when German television was relatively affluent and could afford to spend large sums developing its own film productions. The oil crisis of 1973 and the world recession meant that steadily but inevitably the networks shifted higher proportions of their expenditure on films away from commissioning them to purchasing them.

Why then, given the high cost of commissioning films as opposed to purchasing them, did German television companies spend such large sums on commissioning between the years 1966 and 1973/74? Part of the answer is to be found in their need to generate revenue from their capital investments in film studios and, in the case of W D R, from its investment in Bavaria Film studios. But a more fundamental reason is the quality of the films being produced by the German film industry during this period. These films have been succinctly described by Thomas Elsaesser as 'films about gynaecologists getting their patients pregnant, neo-imperialist "Sissi" films dreaming of Viennese pastry and Hapsburg glories, the Bavarian mountain musicals, the beer-mug and lederhosen comedies'. (Elsaesser, 1979, p.3.) While this mixture of themes and genres may have looked cosy and comfortable to the populations of Munich and Bavaria, it looked distinctly provincial from the industrial heartland of North Rhine-Westphalia and even more provincial to overseas audiences. And so German television began to think about its responsibilities as a public service in developing and building a new German film culture qualitatively different from that offered by the commercial German film industry. W D R as the major supplier of programmes to the A R D network naturally had to shoulder a large part of the responsibility.

30

TABLE V: BROADCASTING EXPENDITURE ON FILMS 1966–1976

Year	Film Purchases (million DM)	£ million at current rates	Film Purchases (as % of 1966)	Film Commissions (million DM)	£ million at current rates	Film Commissions (as % of 1966)	Film Commissions as % of films purchased
1966	44.5	4.0	100	111.3	9.9	100	2.50
1967	34.1	3.1	77	125.1	11.3	112	3.66
1968	65.5	6.8	147	142.4	14.8	128	2.17
1969	47.1	5.2	106	146.3	16.3	131	3.10
1970	46.1	5.3	104	156.7	18.0	141	3.40
1971	72.0	8.4	162	198.3	23.0	178	2.75
1972	64.3	8.0	144	202.8	25.4	182	3.15
1973	50.6	7.8	114	222.2	34.2	199	4.39
1974	60.1	10.0	135	228.1	38.0	205	3.79
1975	92.7	17.2	208	243.1	45.0	218	2.62
1976	121.4	30.4	273	289.1	72.3	260	2.38

Source: Berg (1978)

It is no easy matter to build up a culture and this applies particularly to the development of a film culture, where one film can cost several thousand Deutschmarks to produce and where the decision as to whether to produce it must be taken by one person, or at the very most, two or three, with little more to guide them than a script, a shooting schedule, a budget and a knowledge of the previous creative activities of the film's prospective director and colleagues. In the field of broadcasting, however, the British had already established a precedent after the end of the Second World War when they had to face a similar problem with literature, poetry and drama. Influenced by the Reithian tradition of the BBC, NWDR, set up in the British Zone, had set out to act as a focus for all the anti-fascist and non-fascist artists at work in post-war Germany. By putting on readings of poetry, new German prose, radio drama and programmes on other artistic events and happenings, NWDR had become not only a focus for all the young artists and intellectuals, but also a very real source of patronage for their work. And it was to this model that von Bismarck turned a decade and a half later at WDR.

The economic and technological expansion of the 1960s had made it possible for the television institutions to offer a third channel to supplement the national channel of the ARD network and the second channel run by ZDF. It was decided that this third channel would be operated by the ARD stations, but that instead of offering a national service, each *Land* broadcasting institution would only transmit its 'third' channel broadcasts to its own *Land* or *Länder*. And so, in 1965, WDR's 'third' channel started broadcasting as West Deutsches Fernsehen (WDF) to North Rhine-Westphalia. It was designed as an educational channel, and like the first channel splits the evening into two parts. Before 8 p.m. WDR provides comprehensive regional information about North Rhine-Westphalia, but later in the evening come the 'educational' broadcasts which during the week touch on all special subjects included in the secondary school syllabus, such as languages, arts, sociology, science and medicine. Within these guidelines, WDF seeks 'to be anything but an evening grammar school or a people's grammar school'. (*Public Opinion*, 1971, p. 34.) On the contrary, WDF sets out to provide education in such a way that it gives pleasure (ibid.).

The general responsibility for all cultural programmes at WDR was undertaken by Dr Hans-Geert Falkenberg, who had studied at Göttingen, Zurich and Harvard between 1945 and 1952. During his period at Göttingen he had contributed regular cultural and artistic criticism to the British occupation authorities' German radio service transmitted from Hamburg and which became the kernel of NWDR. After completing his studies Falkenberg became *Dramaturg* at the Göttingen theatre 1952-7, editor at the Fischer Verlag (book publishers) 1957-60, and editor in chief at Kindler Verlag 1960-65. In 1965 he was invited to organise the WDR third Channel, West Deutsches Fernsehen, which he did until 1970 when he assumed responsibility for all WDR cultural programmes.

In terms of his position within *Proporz* Falkenberg is firmly SPD — his association with the party dating from an early involvement with Group 47, a body of writers and intellectuals which was founded in 1947 (prior to the Godesberg programme of the SPD) and which was active within the SPD as a pressure group concerned with civil and personal liberties, intellectual freedom and cultural advance. His experience of films had been limited. In the late 1940s he had been the German correspondent for the British film magazine *Sequence,* but had found himself in the humiliating position of having no artistic developments which he could report. Like many other German intellectuals, he had read the debates in the columns of *Filmkritik* and elsewhere about the sorry state of German films both economically and artistically, but film now came fairly low down on his list of cultural priorities. In any case, the major responsibility would have to come from the drama department for the actual production of the films themselves. Even in television, film, although seen as an artistic practice, was nevertheless slightly separate from the general remit of culture. Nevertheless, Falkenberg was to play a significant role within WDR and the development of the *Arbeiterfilm.*

In line with von Bismarck's policy of attracting all new and interesting artistic talent into broadcasting, Falkenberg started to develop a liaison with the film schools in Munich, in Ulm and Zurich and later in Berlin. The Berlin film school, which had been set up with funds both from the West Berlin Senate and from the Federal Government, was officially opened in 1967, and under its director, Professor Heinz Rathsack, soon established a liberal policy which sought to have few, if any, limitations on the subject of the films made there and which stressed the general intellectual and personal development of the students. This policy was different from that practised in Munich, where the Bavarian authorities demanded a more industrially-oriented policy concerned rather with equipping students with practical skills than allowing them to express themselves or extend their cultural horizons. Falkenberg's sympathies inclined to those of the Berlin administration and over the next decade he visited the Berlin school on several occasions, frequently accompanied by staff from the WDR drama department. The purpose of these visits was to establish a two-way exchange of views with the students. While, no doubt, the students saw the exchange as an opportunity to try and gain employment in WDR, Falkenberg was looking for ideas, talent and the seeds of a new film culture.

The nature of this exchange between a film school and a television station says much about the role that a film school can play in the genesis of a national film culture. In the CSU-dominated Bavaria, the role of the film school was seen as being primarily industrial, and the syllabus was

33

biased towards producing students with craft skills, who could work either in the big Munich film studios or within Bayerischer Rundfunk. The premium was not on producing students with ideas but on students who would move up through the industry to the higher and supposedly more creative grades only when they had already demonstrated their professional skills. Berlin, on the other hand, with its liberal approach, had a much more ambitious aim. This was to equip young people with the basic skills of expressing themselves on film and then to concentrate on the artistic problems of translating ideas into filmic form. The German film industry, however, most of which was located in Munich, was not very sympathetic to this approach, and therefore the Berlin film school was crucially dependent on the television stations to allow its students to put their work into professional practice after they left the film school.

For Falkenberg, the visits to the film school were not a way of seeking professionally produced student films which could be brought and screened on television, since these films were usually pale imitations of conventional forms or genres. What interested him and his colleagues from the drama department were the themes which concerned both the students and the staff of the film school, and which were frequently different from those which interested the programme editors. He was also interested in tracking down individual film students who seemed creatively gifted and who might have the potential to become future programme makers — not because they aped professional styles and tricks but because they had a genuinely original form of visual expression.

In this crucial but too often ignored area therefore, Falkenberg played a key role in creating inside WDR, both within his own department and within the drama department, a path by which student film culture might mature and make a positive contribution to television film culture. Unlike many television institutions in Western Europe, WDR was prepared to explore and develop the talents coming from its national film schools.

The students of the Berlin film school played a formative role in the development of the *Arbeiterfilm*. Christian Ziewer, director of *Liebe Mutter mir geht es gut, Schneeglöckchen blühn im September, Der aufrechte Gang* and *Aus der Ferne sehe ich dieses Land,* was a student there, as were Ingo Kratisch and Marianne Lüdcke, who assisted him and Klaus Wiese on *Liebe Mutter* and went on to make *Die Wollands, Lohn und Liebe* and *Familienglück. Flöz Dickebank* by Johannes Flutsch, Klaus Helle and Marlis Kallweit was made at the film school and later transmitted by WDR. Many of the student ideas were also developed outside WDR, such as the productions of *Allein machen sie dich ein* and *Kalldorf gegen Mannesmann* by Suzanne Beyeler, Rainer März and Manfred Stelzer, who were also at the film school.

34

The other executive at WDR who played a significant role in the genesis of the *Arbeiterfilm* was Dr Günter Rohrbach. Rohrbach had been on the staff of WDR since 1961 and had therefore joined the institution in the same year as von Bismarck. For two years he worked as an editor in television management and then moved on to being leader of the planning group for the third programme. When WDR started, however, he moved on to being head of television drama, where he soon demonstrated his flair for producing plays which tackled the current problems of society and where he acquired a reputation for heading one of the most liberal and imaginative drama departments in the ARD network, to which he attracted a very talented group of young *Redakteuren* (editors).

Volker Canaris, one of the *Redakteuren* of the WDR Drama Department during this period and now at the Cologne theatre, has written that 'The West German theatre of today is a directors' theatre' (see Canaris, 1975) and that 'The two other chief participants in a theatrical occasion — author and actor — [have] generally become subordinated to the director's stylistic whim.' Canaris' emphasis on the director in theatrical production in West Germany is also appropriate to West German television, which was and is marked by a very different constitution of the relations between director and producer, author and institution, from what is customary in British television. Anthony Smith outlines the German situation in the research paper on West German broadcasting commissioned and published by the Annan Committee in its Report (Appendix I, section IV) and emphasises there the high proportion of commissioned work transmitted by West German television and the consequential status of permanent employees of the TV companies as editors not authors. A different configuration of institutional space therefore exists in West German television from that in UK television, where programme policy tends to be directed from the centre and permanent or (fewer than in Germany) freelance workers are commissioned to produce to order. In West Germany the *Redakteur* fosters his or her 'authors' and rather than commissioning a writer to produce, say, 13 scripts of 25 minutes all to be shot on film starring x and y in a given format, he or she will respond to the author's ideas and aspirations. Thus the formation of a *policy* in the WDR Drama department to develop a programme genre was highly unusual in German TV.

The institutional space opened up in West German television by von Bismarck and others did not of course lead only to the *Arbeiterfilm* genre, which was more particularly the result of the interaction of that space with the wishes, aspirations and aesthetic explorations of students at the Berlin Film School in the late 1960s and with the creative support of liberal executives at WDR. Other conjunctures have produced different genres. Some few years later in 1974-75 for instance, WDR's drama inputs into the ARD and to its own third channel network, WDF, featured

35

six plays concerned with sexual politics under the general title *Frauen 74*. These were *Anna* by Uschi Reich, *Marianne findet ihr Glück (Marianne Finds Happiness)* by Hannelore Klar, *Mira* by Jens Heilmeyer and Francisco Alcala-Taca, *Kampf um ein Kind (Fight Over A Child)* by Ingemo Engström, *Zwei Schwestern (Two Sisters)* by Haroun Farocki and *Monolog eines Stars (Monologue of a Star)* by Rosa von Praunheim.

Also at about this time, the ARD stations and ZDF signed a film co-financing agreement with the Filmförderungsanstalt (FFA) which arose out of the debates in the *Bundestag* and the *Bundesrat* on the second Film Aid Law. The agreement was designed primarily to finance films suitable for both cinema exhibition and television transmission. Naturally this agreement encouraged film-makers to prepare scripts on subjects which would be acceptable both to cinema owners and to television viewers and so new genres began to emerge. (For some further discussion see Collins and Porter, 1980.)

Since the Oberhausen Manifesto in 1962, the West German film industry, like the television industry, has been dominated by the director — the *Autor* (see Johnston, 1979). Eligibility for state subsidy whether as script premium or as tax relief on exhibition is characteristically dependent on the 'artistic value' of a film (assessed on the basis of the detectability of the expression of the authorial personality in the film text). Thus in the West German film/TV industry a massive space exists for a plurality of different and antagonistic voices to express themselves. Balance (*Ausgewogenheit*) does not in West German television inhere in the elimination of partisanship (or its reduction to the invisible and 'neutral' ideology of the dominant order) but rather in a balanced representation of the spectrum of partisanship.

However, this structure, whilst offering a certain potentiality for programming like *Arbeiterfilme*, is in other respects inimical to it, for realist films that offer themselves as a representation of general truths about the world are clearly less readily justified in terms of their properties as authorised texts than films that are concerned to represent no more than a personal view. Syberberg or Schroeter rather than Ziewer or Lüdcke/Kratisch are favoured. Rohrbach's paper at the Mainzer Tage der Fernsehkritik 1978 may be seen as a response to this skew in the financial system and as a defensive accommodation to it. Rohrbach's 'Case for more fantasy in television drama' (Rohrbach, 1979) is an argument for a distinctive fictional route to cognition and knowledge of reality. He imagines a criticism of crime series on the grounds of the statistically unrepresentative, unreal number of major crimes shown and consequent under-representation of minor crimes and argues, appropriately enough, that such social scientific criteria are inappropriate to the assessment of fictional forms and their mode of representation. However, the thrust of Rohrbach's argument is for the emancipation of television drama from naturalistic representation; TV

36

drama must emancipate itself from its reality fetishism and become free again for fantasy. It is substantially a retreat from the work done in the *Arbeiterfilme*, into line with the ethos of the *Autor* system and for a substantial depoliticisation of the concerns of TV drama. Rohrbach's deployment of Schiller in his argument is one of the most piquant of his *trahisons*, invoking the author of one of the major theorisations of the relations of aesthetics and politics ('On the Aesthetic Education of Man') in order to legitimise his politics of retreat to fantasy.

In 1972, von Bismarck reorganised the administration of WDR television programme production. Programme units were no longer to be responsible for programmes for either the third channel or the first channel, but were to produce programmes of a given type for both channels. Werner Höfer became Director of Television for both the first and the third channels, Günter Rohrbach became Head of Television Drama and Entertainment and Hans-Geert Falkenberg became Head of Cultural Programmes. This reorganisation was to impose itself on the development of the *Arbeiterfilm*. The early examples of the *Arbeiterfilm* may be associated with the educative ideals of the third television channel and are frequently more documentary than fictional in content and in tone. The later films move progressively away from the documentary elements to become more full-bloodedly fictional and, in the case of the Lüdcke/Kratisch films, almost romantic in their tone.

Early beginnings of the genre can be traced back to Erika Runge's personalised documentaries *Warum ist Frau B. glücklich? (Why is Mrs B. Happy?)* (1968) and *Ich heisse Erwin und bin 17 Jahre (My Name is Erwin and I'm 17)* (1970), which look at the personal lives and attitudes of a miner's widow (Frau B.) and a young apprentice (Erwin) and their personal struggles in a capitalist world. Theo Gallehr and Rolf Schübel's *Rote Fahnen sieht man besser (Red Flags Can Be Seen Better)* (1971) adds narrative to the genre as it follows the progress of the struggles against enforced redundancy at the Phrix factory in Krefeld by a group of workers. Klaus Wiese and Christian Ziewer's *Liebe Mutter mir geht es gut (Dear Mother I'm OK)* (1971) lies poised interestingly between the two periods. It is a fictional film about fictional characters, but it has a very real dependence on documentary verisimilitude and is an interesting interpretation of WDF's ambition of providing education with pleasure. Significantly, *Liebe Mutter* was shown first on the third channel and then rebroadcast on the first channel some months later, and it is from *Liebe Mutter* that the inception of the *Arbeiterfilm* genre is usually dated.

Within the second period, the development of the *Arbeiterfilm* shifts from the third channel to the first channel and while continuing to be realistic in tone, the shift from documentary to fiction is complete. With Ziewer's next films, *Schneeglöckchen blühn im September (Snowdrops Bloom in September)* (1974) and *Der aufrechte Gang (Walking Tall)* (1976) the break with the documentary becomes complete and the same goes for Helma

Sanders' *Der Angestellte (The White-Collar Worker)* (1972) and *Shirins Hochzeit (Shirin's Wedding)* (1976). With *Lohn und Liebe (Wages and Love)* (1974) and *Familienglück (Wedded Bliss)* (1975), the struggle as seen by Marianne Lüdcke and Ingo Kratisch becomes more elegiac. Finally with Fassbinder's *Acht Stunden sind kein Tag (Eight Hours Are Not a Day)* (1972/3) there was a marriage of the family series and the *Arbeiterfilm*.

It is clear therefore that the major flowering of the genre which occurred during the second period took place in Günter Rohrbach's drama department. The genesis of the ideas contained in the films, however, had taken place a few years earlier in the cultural department of W D F and those ideas, in their turn, had developed from ideas which had emerged among students at the Berlin film school. In a very real sense, von Bismarck's policy of supporting and patronising emergent talent and Falkenberg's association with the Berlin film school had come to fruition with the flowering of the *Arbeiterfilm* under Günter Rohrbach. Whether the authorities liked the results of their policies was to be another question entirely.

38

CHAPTER 4

Rote Fahnen sieht man besser

Rote Fahnen sieht man besser (Red Flags Can Be Seen Better) was one of the programmes in the celebrated 'Red Week' ('Rote Woche') of the WDR third channel in September 1971, and in a lecture at the Polytechnic of Central London, 2 November 1975, was picked out by Christian Ziewer as a milestone in the development of the *Arbeiterfilm* and a decisive moment in the reconstitution of the broken trajectory of proletarian cinema in Germany. That trajectory (through *Mutter Krause, Kuhle Wampe, Brüder* and others) was broken by the Nazi seizure of power in 1933 and began to be reformed in the mid to late 60s, a period in West Germany that, for the first time since the foundation of the BRD, the Federal German Republic, was marked by a serious internal economic crisis, unemployment peaking in the official statistics (*Bundesanstalt für Arbeit*) in 1967 and 1968 with 674,000 and 673,000, figures unprecedented since 1960 (684,000) and not repeated until 1974 (946,000). The period was marked also by less readily quantifiable challenges to the political and ideological hegemony of capitalism in the BRD, notably a number of oppositional strands in the *Reideologisierung* of society in Germany and the formation of the student movement. (The attempted assassination of Rudi Dutschke took place in Berlin in 1968, and between 1960 and 1968 the number of students in West Germany trebled.) In 1971 working days lost through strikes in the BRD peaked at 4.483 million, a figure unprecedented since 1951 and not exceeded by 1976.

The 'Rote Woche' was characterised thus in the *Fernseh-und Rundfunkspiegel des Deutschen Industrieinstituts:*

> On five days during the week of the 3rd September the red flag was unfurled by the WDR. Commentaries, reports, documentaries, films and discussions were broadcast with the aim of making the 'wage slave' of 'capitalist society' conscious of his 'situation'. Dr Hans-Geert Falkenberg, Head of the Department of Culture and Entertainment, claimed responsibility for this crash course in Marxist politics and for this 'Red Week' on WDR. Artists and workers, troupes of actors and cabarets, trade union officials and film-makers were mobilised, not merely to demonstrate the shortcomings of our social order but in the last analysis to condemn the entire system of the social market economy. (See Appendix 3.)

The critique ended with the hope that WDR would in future operate with higher standards of journalistic objectivity and artistic quality.

Rote Fahnen was later to become the site for an extended conflict over such questions as journalistic objectivity and artistic quality. This conflict was fought out in the regulatory boards of WDR, in the pages of the daily press — notably the *Frankfurter Allgemeine Zeitung* — and in a variety of specialist journals, in Radio Bremen (the co-producer with WDR) and in question time in the *Bundestag*.

This 'rotes Lehrstück', ('red didactic play'), as *Fernseh-und Rundfunkspiegel* referred to it (23 September 1971), was made by Theo Gallehr and Rolf Schübel in a five month collaboration in 1971 with a number of workers at the Phrix chemical works in Krefeld. The film adopts the point of view of the workers in narrating the closure of the works: 'Eine Betriebsstillung aus der Sicht der Entlassenen' ('The closure of a works from the point of view of those made redundant'). The openness of its commitment ('Schon das ist parteilich und dazu wollen wir uns auch bekennen'; 'Certainly it is partisan and we're happy to admit it' — Gallehr and Schübel, 1971, p. 20) occasioned opposition to the film and to WDR — 'Rotfunk' as it came to be called — and set the film-makers a number of interesting, ultimately unresolved, aesthetic problems in reconciling the documentary conventions within which *Rote Fahnen* is cast with its contentious espousal of an anti-capitalist position: 'from the point of view of those made redundant'.

The film proceeds by juxtaposing and integrating a series of fragments — the experiences and observations of a range of people concerned with the Phrix closure. Each element is allowed its integrity and the film-makers establish a series of motivated connections and relations between the discrete elements. But the complex relations of the time scheme of the film bring it into conflict with the usual canons of documentary film-making practice. The film's present time, in fact, shifts in its relation to the chronology of the actions it presents. In the first prologue sequence the present of the image is the present of the narration. 'August 1970. Arbeiter des Krefelder Werkes Phrix A.G. hissen schwarze Fahnen' ('August 1970. Workers at the Phrix works, Krefeld, hoist black flags') is spoken over shots of workers on a factory roof raising a flag. The second sequence, a short interview with Heinz Steinke, a DGB official in Krefeld, has Steinke commenting on *past* events:

'Herr Steinke, als die Stillegung bekannt wurde, hissten Arbeiter schwarze Fahnen auf den Phrix Gebäuden. Sie vertraten in einem Presse-Interview die Aussicht, rote Fahnen wären besser gewesen. Warum?'

Steinke: 'Rote Fahnen sind besser zu sehen. Rote Fahnen sieht man bis zum Rathaus, sie sieht man bis zur Landesregierung nach Düsseldorf, sie sieht man sogar bis zur Bundesregierung nach Bonn.'

40

('Herr Steinke, when the closure was known about, workers put up black flags on the Phrix buildings. You said in a press interview that red flags would have been better. Why?'

Steinke: 'Red flags can be seen better. Red flags can be seen from the town hall, from the *Land* Parliament in Düsseldorf and even from as far away as the Federal Government in Bonn.')

The third sequence immediately following the title, *Rote Fahnen sieht man besser*, remains, as did the first two, in a documentary mode. The film reports a factory meeting, at which Phrix workers and trade union officials speak; their statements locate the action that the camera witnesses and represents in the past, at a moment when the outcome of the Phrix events is not clear and a moment from which the retrospective and political judgements of Steinke's speech and the film's title are absent. Thus in the first sequences the film-makers establish both a contemporaneity, an immediacy, a present with its uncertainty and repleteness of possibilities, a here-and-nowness that has the characteristics of an authentic record, *and* a historical perspective from which the described and documented events are placed, comprehended, ordered and judged. We see a black flag raised — events of the Phrix closure documented — and hear in Steinke's statement and in the sentence lifted from his talk that was to become the film's title ('Rote Fahnen sieht man besser') an interpretative framework for those events, a notion of how they might have been and should have been otherwise. We learn that the experience of the Phrix workers as victims (the experience that *Rote Fahnen* actually documents) should have been reconstituted in political struggle, that the black flag of mourning is one which does not force itself into view throughout the political levels of the BRD — the *Rathaus*, the *Landesregierung*, the *Bundesregierung* — and that, indeed, Red Flags *Can* Be Seen Better. The film presents not just what was, the phenomena, but also what might have been, the concrete potentiality of the situation. *Rote Fahnen* thus forces into view some of the absences in the Phrix campaign and some of the lacunae in the point of view which it both espouses and transcends, that of 'der Sicht der Entlassenen'.

The contentious political aspect of the film lies, therefore, in its refusal to be bound by the canons of the conventional documentary practice within which it seems, at first sight, to be operating. Its transgression of the 'rules' of passive reportage, of balance, impartiality and objectivity, comes not through the exclusion of 'the other side', of management and its rationale — as we shall see, they are present. Rather, it is a matter not of leaving out one side of the argument but of putting into an account of the Phrix events what was potential in them even if 'untrue' because unrealised.

Nevertheless, it is striking how far the customary rhetoric of television documentary film-making is retained in *Rote Fahnen*. The events and locations shown are those which one would expect in a documentary on a factory closure and the subsequent unemployment: the factory itself, scenes of different kinds of work in the factory, the labour exchange, the homes of the workers and a director of the company, the factory pay and pensions office, a farewell party, workers outside the factory and a demonstration at the company's head office. Similarly, the people who appear are just those one might expect in a 'balanced' documentary: a range of workers in their 20s, 30s, 40s, 50s; a woman worker, disabled, unskilled, skilled and white collar workers, officials of the trades unions (IG Chemie and the DGB) and the *Betriebsrat*, a representative of the local employers' association, the manager of another firm, members of the company management.

The statements of these individuals, either direct to camera or in social interaction observed by the camera, are unified by their common theme: reflection and speculation on the Phrix factory closure, its causes and entailments. A series of common questions are raised and discussed by workers and by the owners and management of Phrix, notably that of the relation of labour and capital in the economy. The debate is of course orchestrated so that only one conclusion is possible: that the power of capital is greater than that of labour and that the experience of the workers as victims of forces outside their control is to be mourned. In some senses *Rote Fahnen* never breaks definitively with the problematic and view of events and their relations which are symbolised by the 'schwarze Fahnen', the black flags.

The main part of the film is occupied with the presentation of four Phrix workers: Fritz Thomas, a 57 year-old handicapped cleaner who has worked for Phrix for 31 years, Elly Scholz, 44, at Phrix for 9 years; Dieter Süllwold, 26, 8 years at Phrix as a fitter; Heinrich Göbel, 39, 8 years at Phrix first as a chemical process worker then as a white collar worker. Clearly the choice of these four is one that enables the film-makers to represent intensively, through the choice of 'typical characters in typical circumstances', the totality of the situation of the Phrix workers. Each character, too, is presented in his or her totality. They are seen outside work in their homes and recreations, with their families and friends, reflecting on and recounting their lives, their history at the Phrix factory and anticipating their problematic future after the closure.

The representatives of capital, Dr Morawski, Dr Bischof of the Phrix management *(Vorstand)* and Erich Selbach of the board of directors *(Aufsichtsrat)* are, although allowed to speak in the same ways as the four principals, not presented in their totality. We do not see them (as we also do not see Steinke and Hasslach) in other than a single role as reified spokesmen for the forces that oppress and victimise the four central people. What, though, differentiates Steinke and Hasslach (member of

the Phrix *Betriebsrat*) from Morawski, Selbach and Bischof is that the
union figures articulate in a more or less theorised form the experiences,
uncertainties and incomprehensions of the four workers. The discourses
of Steinke *et al.* are caught in a reciprocal relation of legitimation and
support with those of Elly Scholz, Dieter Süllwold, Heinrich Göbel and
Fritz Thomas. The statements of the representatives of capital, of course,
are not. And when Selbach is seen in his home — a place of considerable
luxury — that location serves only to fix him firmly as an unjust and
insensitive exploiter of the workers. To see the Scholz family or Fritz
Thomas and his wife at home (a sequence of Thomas and wife is intercut
with the major presentation of Selbach) is to see them not as an
abstraction but concretely, not as a particular functionary in a factory,
and a part of a collective category 'labour', but as a total human entity
(or at least as closer to that than a simple presentation of either their
work or their home life alone would show). To see Selbach at home is to
see a man who does no work and whose utterances display no knowledge
or understanding of those who do. In the same way we hear Dr
Morawski use the word 'Freisetzung' — setting free — as a synonym for
the dismissal of the 2000 workers in the Phrix works after having seen
Fritz Thomas in his garden in the immediately preceeding scene
responding, not as Morawski's vocabulary implies, like a prisoner in the
ninth scene of *Fidelio* but concerned rather with his likely inability to get
another job and the difference between his position ('dann lebe ich lieber
von der Landesversicherung oder von der Stempelkarte'; 'I'd rather live
on social security or the dole') and that of those who 'sitzen Nachts in den
Hotels wo Sekt und kalte Ente gesoffen wird' ('sit at night in hotels
boozing champagne and cocktails').

Morawski's statement is followed by a report from the *Arbeitsamt* in
which workers, including Elly Scholz, are either unable to find work or
find it on worse terms than they were able to command at Phrix. To see
Morawski's statement juxtaposed with the subjective perceptions of
Fritz Thomas that contradict his account and the objective report from
the *Arbeitsamt* is to experience a contradiction, a paradigm clash. Schübel
and Gallehr have in presenting the workers in their totality decisively
inflected the audience's choice of whom to believe, towards labour and
away from capital.

Towards the end of the film the pattern of the preceeding sections
changes. The relatively concrete and urgent questions of the closure of
the works, its effect on different individuals and the groups whom those
individuals represent and exemplify give way to talk around more
abstract questions announced by headings in the script: 'Uber das
Risiko' ('On Risk'), 'Kapital und Internationalismus' ('Capital and
Internationalism'), 'Solidarität' ('Solidarity'), 'Mitbestimmung' ('Co-
determination'). The structures and forms of organisation of the
narrative of the earlier parts of the film are retained — juxtaposition of

43

statements either elicited in interview, given straight to camera or 'observed' by the camera, by different people: Steinke, Bischof, Göbel, Süllwold, etc. These sessions of reflection and argument (though the argument is, of course, constructed by Schübel and Gallehr *post hoc* rather than actually experienced in interaction between the participants) are then interwoven with the more concrete, personal and integrated sections showing the experiences and way of life of some of the four main figures. The principal sections of this kind are those of the last days at work of Elly Scholz and of Fritz Thomas and the *Sylvesternacht* party at the Scholz home. The whole of *Rote Fahnen* is punctuated by a repeated shot of the black flag on the factory roof. The flag becomes successively more tattered until in the final shot it hardly exists. The diminution of the flag and a date given over the flag shots mark the passage of time during which the events the film reports occurred, beginning with August 1970 and ending after January 1971.

The organisation of the film's fifth (of six) sections, December 1970-January 1971, is representative. It begins with a shot of the black flag — tattered and almost finished — with a voice over the flag and date saying, 'Die letzten Arbeiter werden entlassen. Die meisten Angestellten sind inzwischen freigestellt.' ('The last workers have been dismissed and most white-collar workers have also left.')

Heinz Göbel tells of the situation of those left at the works, attending each day with nothing to do. A major section follows: Fritz Thomas' last day at work. Fritz Thomas converses with Hans Hasslach and an older worker. They talk of their age and the time they've spent at Phrix and of the 260-300 marks per month they will receive. The conversation ends with this interchange:

—Wir kriegen mit Kind, Mann und Frau 260 Mark im Monat, mehr nicht, lass es 280 sein.
—Nein, etwas mehr, über 300 im Monat.
—Dann ist es erledigt.
—Was, Wohlfahrt.
—300. Mark, stell' dir vor, 300 Mark. 150 Mark Miete und dann sind noch 170 Mark und dann darfst du nicht mehr rauchen und so weiter und so fort.
—Licht, Strom, Gas und das alles.

(—We get for a child, man and wife, 260 marks a month, no more, let's say 280.
—No a bit more: over 300 a month.
—Then we're washed up.
—What, Social Security.
—300 marks — imagine that, 300 marks. 150 marks for rent and then

44

you've got 170 marks left and that won't allow you to smoke and so on.
—Lighting, electricity, gas and everything else.)

This is followed by a statement from Dr Thomarek of the Krefeld employers' association that the disadvantages of the system have to be accepted and that no-one proposes an end to traffic in the streets although each year 16,000 people are killed in road accidents in West Germany. Four speakers, Hans Hasslach, Heinz Göbel, Heinz Steinke and Dr Bischof, are then juxtaposed in a 'discussion' under the head of 'Capital and Internationalism'. The workers' conclusions are that multi-national corporations can switch resources and production rapidly to maximise profit and that this flexibility and the concentration of capital into increasingly fewer and larger units gives capital increasing advantages in the wage bargain. Steinke concludes that absolute solidarity is necessary amongst the labour movement, particularly in the EEC, in order to fight. These conclusions are privileged by being articulated at greater length and by a larger number of voices than are the conclusions and ideology of the apologists for the system, and by their being articulated by individuals who — unlike Thomarek and Bischof— are represented in *Rote Fahnen* as human beings in a variety of activities, reflecting on themselves, not as puppets with a repertoire limited to sitting behind a desk and obfuscating. The abstractions of Steinke are rooted in the experiences narrated by Elly Scholz at her Sylvester celebration:

Und ich muss jetzt zum Jahreswechsel sagen, also wir müssen uns sehr einschränken. Es ist bei uns so, weil dadurch, dass Ingrid Kurzarbeit macht und sehr wenig bekommt, dass ich viel weniger verdiene wie vorher, nicht, und ja an sich alles teurer ist und noch teurer wird. Also muss ich sagen das Jahr war gar nicht so gut.

(I must say at this New Year that we are really having to cut back. The reason is that Ingrid is on short time and earns very little. I earn much less than before, don't I, and everything has got, and will continue to get much dearer. So this last year hasn't been so good.)

The final section of the film opens with a vestigial flag fluttering over the factory and the dateline of January 1971, and represents the final closure of the factory. Shots of the dismantling of the Phrix works, the destruction of the old machinery and other debris are framed by elements that come from outside the world of the Phrix workers that the film has previously delineated. Hasslach, Süllwold, Göbel, discuss a demonstration at the head office of Phrix in Hamburg, reported in the film through the inclusion of footage from an amateur home movie shot

45

during the demonstration. Their discussion turns on the questions of whether a demonstration in Hamburg is the most effective way of resisting a factory closure in Krefeld and on the related question of the colour of the flags they raised over the factory. The demonstration is the only form of action the film presents and offers an example of resistance to the factory closure and to the exploitation that the film documents through its victims' own testimony.

The final section of the film contains a song by Dieter Süverkrüp about the Phrix closure. It is sung over shots of the empty factory halls and the final image of the flag, existing in this last shot only as tatters.

The Süverkrüp song had been sung in an earlier section of the film (the beginning of the November 1970 section) and, in spite of going no further than other parts of the film in its critique of the Phrix management and owners and the relations of labour and capital exemplified by the Phrix sackings, it was the Süverkrüp song that became a major target for hostile criticism of the film. The song was deleted from the film by Radio Bremen, the co-producers with WDR, when it was repeated on 14 December 1971 under a Radio Bremen, not WDR, station identification.

The first occurrence of the song in *Rote Fahnen* comes half way through, where Süverkrüp is shown singing outside the Phrix works as workers leave at the end of a shift. The Süverkrüp song was thought to be an inadmissible inclusion in the film and the film-makers were accused of introducing an element that was not part of the Phrix situation, and of compromising reception of the documentary by adopting, for polemical reasons, procedures more appropriate to fiction and feature film-making. Schübel and Gallehr replied that the appearance of Süverkrüp in their documentary presentation of the Phrix closure was quite legitimate because he had not been invited to sing at the factory gate, but had appeared there spontaneously in order to publicise his local concert. Whether or not Süverkrüp did appear spontaneously or whether he was invited is not really relevant. What is important is the effect that that appearance has in *Rote Fahnen* as a whole and the principles on which the film-makers made the inclusion.

The Süverkrüp song thus exemplifies the general problem of the documentary mode in which *Rote Fahnen* is cast: that of the representativeness of its material. Documentary implicitly legitimises its presentation of the world by asserting the authenticity of the events it represents. The here-and-nowness, the unacted, unfictionalised nature of the events shown in *Rote Fahnen* are testified to by its use of footage marked by camera noise, the grainy and ill-focused material of the Hamburg demonstration, the incredible brutality of the statements of the Phrix directors and management, and by the evidently unscripted, heavily accented raw colloquial reflections of the workers. In this scheme of aesthetic — or as the film-makers would probably say, journalistic or documentary — values, the filmed presentation of events is to be judged and legitimised by the closeness of those representations to historical events, rather than by their relation to other elements in the film text, to their place in its dramaturgy. To say that Süverkrüp really was outside the Phrix works, that Erich Selbach really does live in a luxurious house, is accordingly a sufficient vindication of the presence of those elements in the film. And Gallehr/Schübel reply to the criticism of the tendentiousness and absence of objectivity in *Rote Fahnen* in just these terms, that what is shown actually happened. They deny that the payments to the four principal workers influenced the statements made by Göbel, Scholz *et al.* and adduce the sworn testimonies of the workers that they did not collaborate in *Rote Fahnen* for the money and that the opinions they uttered in the film were their own. Schübel and Gallehr use the terms 'Dokumentation' and 'Geschichte' about *Rote Fahnen*. They refer to the enormous footage (31,000 metres) of film exposed and the length of time spent on production and research. And they quote Heinrich Göbel writing after the award of the Grimme-Preis to *Rote Fahnen*: 'Ich freue mich, dass *unser* Film einen so grossen Erfolg hat.' ('I'm very pleased that *our* film is so successful.') — all evidence of their attempt to find an identity between the events of the Phrix closure and their representation in *Rote Fahnen*.

Göbel's letter and characterisation of the film as 'unser Film' is quoted by Gallehr/Schübel as evidence of their accomplishment of their partisan project. They rationalise the contradiction between contentiousness and documentary in terms of the relativism of truth:

Bei einer Betriebsstillegung zum Beispiel gibt es nicht die Wirklichkeit. Wie man sehen kann, ist das für ein Aufsichtsratsmitglied etwas Anderes, als für einen Arbeitnehmer und für einen dreissigjährigen Arbeiter etwas Anderes als für einen sechzigjährigen. Wenn es die Wirklichkeit absolut also nicht gibt, kann es auch kein Abbild dieser Wirklichkeit geben. Wir konnten unsere Arbeit also nur verstehen als Montage von Fragmenten dieser verschiedenen Wirklichkeiten.

(There's no one truth about, for example, a factory closure. As you can see, for a director the truth is different from that for a worker, and that for a 30 year old worker, it is different from that for a 60 year old worker. When there is no absolute truth then there can be no representation of this absolute truth . We can then only understand our work as a montage of fragments of these various truths.) (Gallehr and Schübel, 1971.)

The contradiction in which *Rote Fahnen* is locked is the classic contradiction of naturalism: between a representational practice that depends for its legitimacy on the closeness of the approximation of its mimesis to reality — its lack of mediation, structuring and organisation

47

— and the necessary choices of point of view, editing, subject, narrative order that inevitably and evidently structure the representation.

The retreat to relativism, to the modest self-deprecatory rhetoric of 'Wir konnten unsere Arbeit also nur verstehen als Montage von Fragmenten dieser verschiedenen Wirklichkeiten' is a retreat into an indefensible position. If the film is only one truth among many what grounds of objection remain to the revision of *Rote Fahnen* by Radio Bremen? What grounds exist for demanding assent to the view of the Phrix factory presented in *Rote Fahnen*? Why rote Fahnen and not schwarze Fahnen?

We have suggested in our exposition of the film that Gallehr/Schübel adopt a number of artistic devices in order to command evidence for their version of events, for 'rote Fahnen': the choice of a representative range of workers, showing the workers in and outside their workplaces, reflecting on and puzzling over their whole lives, having a theorised articulation of the relation of the worker to the employer and labour to capital linked to a display of the concrete manifestation of those relations in the closure of Phrix-Krefeld. These procedures are ones that structure, orientate, and weight the reading or *Rote Fahnen*. Schübel/Gallehr's statement that 'Schon das ist parteilich und dazu wollen wir uns auch bekennen' is a far more satisfactory articulation of the import of *Rote Fahnen* than their agnostic 'Wenn es die Wirklichkeit absolut also nicht gibt, kann es auch kein Abbild dieser Wirklichkeit geben'.

Finally, *Rote Fahnen* remains hung on the unresolved contraction of naturalist aesthetics, torn between its impulses on the one hand to document truth and on the other to assert the compelling primacy of the experience and understanding of Elly Scholz, Heinrich Göbel and Heinz Steinke over that of Erich Selbach *et al*. But the documentary mode, if it is to retain the legitimacy that espousal of 'here-and-nowness' is generally supposed to lend it, must necessarily refuse evident structuring and *parti pris*. Yet no film can be an unmediated witness and testimony to truth; rather it is only those films that remain within the bounds of the dominant ideology that will generally appear to be balanced, impartial and truthful documentary. Further, the here-and-nowness embraced by Schübel and Gallehr cannot readily offer general statements. The very authenticity that documentary seemingly offers by confining itself to specific incidents, to what actually happened, necessarily precludes generalisation and the articulation of extensive and typical representations.

The film had a massively important place in the development of the *Arbeiterfilm* in the 'window' of critical programming opened up by the beginning of WDR 3 and closed in the mid-seventies by shifts to the right in the *Reideologisierung* of West Germany society. But the aesthetic practised by Schübel/Gallehr, and by Erika Runge in, for example, *Ich heisse Erwin* and their epigones in *Kalldorf gegen Mannesmann, Flöz*

Dickebank and *Wir waren vorbereitet* is seriously flawed both in its epistemology and its suitability for the attraction, retention and education of mass audiences. It was to these problems that the WDR drama department, the Programmbereich Spiel und Unterhaltung, addressed itself after *Rote Fahnen* (itself a product of the Programmbereich Kultur). The same problems were to be confronted by Christian Ziewer and Rainer Werner Fassbinder through the fictional modes of representing working-class experience adopted in the *Arbeiterfilme* they made with WDR.

Rote Fahnen sieht man besser

CHAPTER 5

Eight Hours Are Not a Day

Following the 'pilot' productions of *Rote Fahnen* and Erika Runge's *Ich heisse Erwin und bin 17 Jahre (My name is Erwin and I'm 17)*, a naturalistic documentary of much more conventional and simple form than *Rote Fahnen* concerned with the experience at work, at home and with his contemporaries of an apprentice, transmitted 19 May 1970, the Drama Department of W D R addressed themselves, as a collective project, to the question of making working-class entertainment.

These major categories — 'Drama Department of W D R', 'collective project' and 'working-class entertainment' — require further exegesis. The Drama Department (Programmgruppe Fernsehspiel) consisted of Dr Günter Rohrbach, Head, and a number of *Redakteuren* ('editors') and supporting staff. The editors, W. D. Brücker, V. Canaris, P. Märthesheimer, J. von Mengershausen, G. Witte, operated rather like the editors of a traditional publishing house, each responsible for contact with his own 'authors'. In the case of the *Arbeiterfilme*, Peter Märthesheimer collaborated with Fassbinder, Joachim von Mengershausen with Ziewer, and Martin Wiebel — formerly a member of the Bereich Kultur, then headed by Dr Hans-Geert Falkenberg — with Gallehr/Schübel. However, in spite of a system which allowed for greater individual autonomy on the part of the editors than would be usual for their equivalents ('producers') in British television, and a model of production which was based on fostering and developing the aspirations and initiatives of the film-makers rather than commissioning film-makers to produce for a programme concept developed in the television company, a shared commitment developed in the *Fernsehspielgruppe* to develop working-class entertainment. The flagship production of this policy was *Eight Hours Are Not a Day*.

The examples of *Rote Fahnen* and *Erwin* were considered inadequate models for programme development, since they were not attractive to mass audiences (*Erwin* achieved a viewing figure of 19 per cent), nor did they display workers positively (*Rote Fahnen* is subtitled 'Aus der Sicht der Betroffenen', ('from the point of view of the victims') as well as 'Aus der Sicht der Entlassenen' ('from the point of view of those sacked')). Rather, they maintained the practice dominant in capitalist ideology of representing the working class as irremediably subordinate. Other programmes which were concerned with the fictional representation of working-class experience and an account of contemporary life in Western Germany from a working-class perspective had been transmitted by WDR and offered further positive and negative experience for the *Fernsehspielgruppe* to draw upon. Some of these programmes (e.g. *Der Angestellte* and *Liebe Mutter, mir geht es gut*) had been originated by WDR. Others were drawn from foreign sources (e.g. *Coup pour coup*, director Marin Karmitz, production MK2 Paris; and Colin Welland's three plays, *Bangelstein's Boys*, director J. Mackenzie, LWT, *Slattery's Mounted Foot*, director M. Apted, LWT, *Roll on Four O'Clock*, director R. Battersby, Granada).

Eight Hours Are Not a Day represented WDR's attempt to appropriate the positive and attractive elements of an established programme type — the family series — and invest them with progressive content. The title of Märthesheimer's essay, 'The Occupation of a Bourgeois Genre', explains the aims of the project (see Appendix 15).

The series is set in contemporary Cologne and centres around the families of the male and female protagonists Jochen and Marion. Jochen is a skilled factory worker, a toolmaker and the son of a factory worker, Wolf; Marion works in the advertising department of the *Kölner Stadt-Anzeiger*.

Fassbinder, interviewed in *Konkret* ('Kommt die Proletwelle?') stated of *Eight Hours Are Not a Day*:

Was wir versuchen, bewirkt wahrscheinlich immer noch sehr viel mehr als reine Dokumentationsfilme wie Schübel-Gallehrs *Rote Fahnen sieht man besser*. Da hört's halt auf, da ziehen die Arbeiter nicht mehr mit. Drum wollten wir in der Serie auch ohne politische Parteien auskommen und ohne Gewerkschaften. Damit das Ganze nicht gleich in den Geruch kommt, was Linkes zu sein. Denn wir wissen doch, dass das auch viele Arbeiter verschreckt.

(What we're attempting probably achieves much more than pure documentary films like Schübel/Gallehr's *Rote Fahnen*. The workers don't go along with it and because of that we wanted to make the series without political parties and without trades unions. So that the whole thing doesn't get the reputation of being Leftist. Because we know that that frightens off a lot of workers.) Röhl, 1973.)

He went on to say:

Man kann jedes Genre benutzen, um damit etwas Eigenes zu treiben. Ob man nun eine andere Sensibilität an den Mann bringen will oder einen politischen Inhalt. Familienserien sind gerade das, was Deuts-

51

che gerne sehen. Dadurch schafft man erst mal eine Zuschauerpotenz. Danach gibt's die Schwierigkeit, über die erste halbe Stunde zu kommen. Wenn die Leute dann noch nicht abgeschaltet haben, ist man übern Berg. Dann kommt so eine Familie den Leuten regelmässig ins Haus, und sie können nachvollziehen, was die einzelnen Figuren machen. Von diesem Moment an kann man versuchen, politische Inhalte unterzubringen. So dass die Zuschauer möglicherweise auch bereit sind, mit den Figuren in die DKP einzutreten, um es mal ganz primitiv auszudrücken.

(One can use any genre to put over a message, whether you want to introduce a new sensitivity or political content. Family series are what Germans like watching. That way you create a potential audience, then you have the problem of retaining the audience for the first half hour. You're over the hill then if people haven't turned off. Then such and such a family comes to people regularly in their homes and they can do what the characters do. From then on one can attempt to introduce political content so that viewers are possibly prepared to join the DKP (German Communist Party) along with the characters, to put it very crudely.)

There is, then, a clear intention in the makers of *Eight Hours Are Not a Day* to use a familiar 'compromised' genre as a vehicle for the raising of the political consciousness of the German working-class TV audience, through that audience's identification with the characters and action of an 'occupied' family series.

Equally evident in the series, however, is Fassbinder's idiosyncratic *mise en scène*, the elements of distantiation in his film-making. In *Eight Hours Are Not a Day* there is much of a characteristic motif of Fassbinder's film-making: the blocking of the camera's uninterrupted view of the subject by the interposition of flowers, chair-frames, glasses, etc. There are moments in the five episodes where these obtrusions into the composition of the frame are motivated and signify in relation to the other cinematic codes at work. For example, in Episode Five when Jochen and his workmates present to the firm's boss, Dr Betram, their nine-point programme for the improvement and, most important, their control of their working conditions in the new Westhofen factory, Betram is shown with the head of an open-mouthed, fanged leopard in the foreground. Völkmar Gross, the Manager of the tool room, is frequently shot with the bars of his office's venetian blinds interposed between him and the camera. Both the blind and the leopard are used by Fassbinder in the classic manner of Hollywood *mise en scène*, functioning as an objective correlative to signify the nature of the person with whom they are juxtaposed. But elsewhere in the episodes there are plentiful instances of the more characteristic manner of Fassbinder's own *mise en scène*: the deployment of the elements of a shot in a superfluous or mannered form. The recurrent foregrounding of flowers or the bars of a chair-back carry not the motivated correlative meanings of the bars of the venetian blind or of the leopard's fangs and spots (the spots that never change), but an excessive, superfluous and gratuitous intervention into the bundle of motivated signifying relations in the shot. In Episode Two, when the manipulative effect of television is being discussed by the characters, the camera zooms into a close-up of one of the participants in the conversation, Peter Märthesheimer, the producer of *Eight Hours*.

Thomas Elsaesser (1979) argues persuasively that there are two aspects to the evident stylisation or mannerism in Fassbinder's *mise en scène*. First that the blocking of the audience's access to the actions depicted in a scene and to the characters who enact them is an assault in the classic Brechtian manner on Aristotelian aesthetics and the uninterrupted relation of audience to spectacle; that Fassbinder is practising a *Verfremdungseffekt*. Clearly the blocking of the audience's customary relation to the cinematic spectacle, identification with characters and rapt involvement with the unfolding narrative is a strong element in Fassbinder's work — a practice whose lineage can be traced through the continuity in German theatre from Brecht and Piscator to Fassbinder and the *anti-teater* and, perhaps no less directly, through the cinema of Douglas Sirk. The reader who is *au courant* with the course of contemporary theory on how to make political films will need no reminding of the importance that is now ceded to the *Verfremdungseffekt*. But Brecht and Piscator's deployment of alienation effects was always to position and orientate the spectator to the text in a quite specific way that would 'usher them [the audience] into their own real world with attentive faculties' (Brecht, 1961). In Fassbinder and in *Eight Hours Are Not a Day*, the alienation devices are not orchestrated to perform a specific attentive orientation of the spectator but rather to disorientate, to create an unresolvable uneasiness in the relation of the spectator to the characters and action of the spectacle.

Elsaesser argues that, as he puts it, the 'unsettling dephasing element' in Fassbinder's *mise en scène* stems from Fassbinder's own present self's uneasy relation to his past: 'it seems equally possible that the particular form of distanciation and stylisation in the early films points towards the unresolved dilemma hinted at above — the troubled relationship of the would-be commercial film-maker to his one-time addiction as spectator-consumer.' (Elsaesser, 1979, p. 29.)

There is in *Eight Hours Are Not a Day* also the possibility of the unresolved dilemma of a director (whose films had hitherto been centred around his own autobiography and emotional economy) making a series that extends over a milieu, experience and consciousness — that of the German working class — of which he has little knowledge.

53

In Wolfgang Röhl's interview with Fassbinder on *Eight Hours Are Not a Day* (Röhl, 1973) Fassbinder is questioned on this point:

Röhl: 'Herr Fassbinder, Sie sind ein Sohn des Burgertüms, Schüler der Rudolf-Steiner-Schule und mittlerweile ein gemachter Mann. Jetzt drehen Sie Filme über den Alltag des bundesdeutschen Arbeiters. Woher wollen Sie eigentlich wissen, wie der aussieht?' Fassbinder: 'Ja mei — Ich weiss natürlich auch nicht, wie der aussieht. Ich hab' nur so Ahnungen. Und ich habe Freunde, die Arbeiter sind. Wenn ich meine Ahnungen zusammengeschrieben habe, gebe ich ihnen den Text, dass sie's lesen und mir was dazu sagen. Und dann ändere ich noch mal, bis sie irgendwann einmal sagen; ja, so ungefähr ist es.'

(Röhl: 'Herr Fassbinder, you're a son of the bourgeoisie, and ex-pupil of the Rudolf Steiner School and you've made it in the world. Now you're making films on the daily life of West German workers. How do you actually know what it's like?' Fassbinder: 'Ah yes. Of course I don't really know what it's like. I just have an idea of it. And I have worker friends and when I have written up my ideas I give them the text so that they can read it and discuss it with me. Then I alter the text until they finally say — yea, it's like that near enough.')

Konkret do not press Fassbinder very much further — unfortunately, perhaps, since little is established except that both parties to the discussion assent to the anachronistic and long-transcended notion of the social equivalent of art. Each tests the authenticity and value of the representation of *Eight Hours Are Not a Day* in terms of its suspicious origins in the mind of a middle-class director educated in a tradition of irrationalism and the assent given to it by workers friendly with the director. The origins and associations of a film-maker are no guarantee of anything; rather the criteria for assessing the adequacy of the representation offered in *Eight Hours Are Not a Day, Rote Fahnen sieht man besser* or *Schneeglöckchen blühn im September* are aesthetic and political, not simply questions of 'social equivalence'. And Fassbinder's invocation of the legitimacy ceded to *Eight Hours* by its scripting being performed in collaboration with workers is surprising and perhaps misleading. What is most evident about the dialogue in *Eight Hours* is how *unlike* it is to that recorded live in *Rote Fahnen, Flöz Dickebank*, or *Erwin*. The syntax and vocabulary of the workers in *Eight Hours* is much less varied and complex than that of the direct speech of the workers in the documentary films.

The difference between the shortness of the utterances of the *Eight Hours* characters, the simplicity and brevity of their sentences and their restricted vocabulary, and the lengthy, well-articulated complexity of

54

structure and range of vocabulary of the Krefeld workers in *Rote Fahnen* is striking. These absences in *Eight Hours* are similar to the absence in the five episodes of any of the institutions of the working class — their political parties, trades unions, co-operatives or cultural and sporting organisations.

The representation of the working class in *Eight Hours Are Not a Day* is, then, one that does not meet the criterion of a simple appeal to reality and it is surprising that Fassbinder should choose to fight for the legitimacy of his work on those grounds. It is, rather, the impulse implied in the title of Märthesheimer's article, 'The Occupation of a Bourgeois Genre', which is most apparent in the programme — an attempt to re-order the combinations and relations of the familiar elements of the family series — the soap opera — to show and promote an anti-authoritarian and self-determining practice in the working-class family on whom the narrative centres and in whom the German working-class television audience is invited to see its own positive image. Certainly the construction of this representation entails the introduction of novel elements into the family series, notably the experience of the work place, and this impulse can genuinely be called a movement towards realism; towards a more extensive depiction of the experience of wage workers — the mass of the German people — and the introduction into the 'world' of the television series of the central determining feature of the way people live and themselves experience the capital/labour contradiction. But the rhetoric of *Eight Hours* is emphatically within the conventions of a 'bourgeois genre'. It remains, as Christian Ziewer put it, a *Märchen*, a fairy tale. But a fairy tale that introduces novel elements into the customary repertoire of a staple genre of family viewing and which attempts to rework the usual combination of familiar elements of the family series and thus to re-articulate its meanings in a progressive way, to present workers positively struggling for and achieving their own liberation.

There is, one could argue, a conspicuous unease in the programmes — an uncertain and ambivalent relation of three elements that it is useful to distinguish analytically. First, the endeavour to engage with, to represent extensively the experience of German workers plotted around the two geographical co-ordinates of the workplace and the home in which the social relations that govern the workers' experience are reproduced. Second, the choice of an established programme genre and its defining rhetoric — that of the family series — as a carrier of this representation. And thirdly, the choice of Fassbinder as the series director, a choice that carried numerous positive entailments — the director's inventiveness, his ability to bring in a project on time and within budget and to offer the formidable package of a company of actors used to working with him and each other, a brilliant art director and other members of the production team familiar with each other, his celebrity/notoriety in Germany and the attendant likelihood of audience and network interest in the programmes. But it was a choice which carried — perhaps inevitably — a certain gratuitousness of *mise en scène* and — notably in Episode Two, 'Oma und Gregor' ('Grandma and Gregor') — an unbalancing of the series' concern with the unfolding of a representation of working-class experience (the relations of work and family in contemporary Germany), towards the privileging of a hermetic internal dynamic in the playing out of variations of character and role in the series' extensive project of the representation of working-class experience and that class's struggle to transform its life.

The privileging of the playful elaboration of the established 'star' personae of Luise Ullrich and Werner Finck is a path that the relative absence of institutions and practices other than those of work and the family in the series lays wide open. *Eight Hours Are Not a Day* has none of the institutions that the working class created for itself in opposition to the dominant culture of capitalism (using the term 'culture' here in the sense ascribed to it by Raymond Williams in his conclusion to *Culture and Society*): no trades unions, no co-ops, no political parties, none of the survivals of the magnificent range of cultural, sporting and leisure groups that the German working class organised for itself around its political parties, the SPD and the KPD-DKP. Nor, in Fassbinder's *Märchen*, is there any extensive presentation of the complex hierarchy of strata and roles that the negotiation and living out of the labour bargain in capitalism generate. No *Betriebsrat*, no shareholders, no supervisory board, no changes in the economy, no rupture of the prosperous arcadia of the Federal Republic of the 1970s. No more politics, no more history, no more presentation of the working class as the object of history than in, say, the untroubled reaping of the reward for his ambition, energy and hard work that the James Stewart character experiences in the *The Glenn Miller Story*.

The establishment of the *Kindergarten* in Episode Two, 'Oma und Gregor', is an account of the creation of just such an institution — outside the family, indeed acting as an agent in the transcendence of the roles prescribed for mother and child in the nuclear family. A conflict between the traditional pattern of child care — mother at home — with its attendant subordination of mother and children to the wage-earning father, and the new order of wage-earning mother liberated from her economic dependence and subordination to the pater familias by the *Kindergarten* is concretely enacted by Jochen's sister and brother-in-law, Monika and Harald. But this 'citizens' initiative' — the establishment of the *Kindergarten* — is magicked into existence with almost as mysterious a sleight of hand as Oma's materialisation of a playing space for children in Episode One. (There she puts on an authoritative manner, flashes her pensioner's card, pretending it is an official Town Councillor's accreditation, and vanquishes bumbledum in the shape of the park-keeper.)

56

Though the *Kindergarten* certainly permits the re-drawing of the relations within the marriage of Monika and Harald (and by extension, of course, offers a means of realising some of the potential for the emancipation of women in other marriages) and a better time for the kids, it remains an institution conjured into existence by Oma's personality. And by choosing to represent the general potentiality of *Kindergarten* for women and children concretely through its productivity for Monica and her daughter, Fassbinder in fact invokes the extensive family as redress for the problems of the nuclear family: Gran re-assumes the role of caring for children while the mother is freed for productive labour.

Of course, the specific developments enacted in 'Oma und Gregor' carry very happy entailments for all concerned; Oma and Gregor find roles that please them, enable them to be useful to others and that fortuitously provide them with a flat. Monika begins her emancipation from Harald, the children are saved from the loneliness or danger from traffic that has attended their collective play before the foundation of the *Kindergarten*. But the *Kindergarten* cannot be seen as the expression of collective will and action (to be sure a gang of mothers and children descend on the Town Hall and fill its corridors with noisy and messy play to force official assent to it but that collectivity and its co-ordinated action has no life beyond that which Oma gives it). It is her doing, not the realisation of a self-conscious collective will. Rather it is a practical re-articulation of the maximum collective unit of the ideology of individualism — the family.

The choice of limiting the ambit of the series to that of the consciousness of its heroes precludes expression of the real relations that govern their lives and are unrecognised by their false consciousness, except through the direct praxis of the characters. In many ways, this choice carries positive consequences. The audience may follow Jochen, Marion *et al.* through a process of discovery and their development of an understanding of reality in the classic manner of the *Bildungsroman*. And through this process the audience may appropriate the discoveries, understanding and consciousness of its heroes as its own. But the exclusion of the institutions that are the expression and thus the carriers of the maximum realised potential class consciousness of the proletariat means that in, for instance, the absence of their political parties, the memory of the class is absent from *Eight Hours Are Not a Day*. The institutions that are present in its articulation of the life of the contemporary German working class are those of the dominant class and its culture — institutions so deeply naturalised as to be invisible: the social relations of capitalist production (and in particular the wage bargain), and patriarchy and its central embodiment of male dominance — the nuclear family. To be sure, the project of *Eight Hours Are Not a Day* is to crack the glass through which we see and experience reality, and in cracking its transparency demonstrate the presence of a screen that

57

constrains, directs and determines the actions of its characters and the real lives their performances represent; and in their actions thus to contest the legitimacy and necessity of the social relations that flow from wage labour in a capitalist society and from family life. But the framework of that, often admirable, contestation is emphatically that of the consciousness and culture that *Eight Hours Are Not a Day* has, in Märthesheimer's felicitous pun, occupied.

Unfortunately, whether the director and the trajectory assumed by the series in the five extant episodes could have accommodated the projected shift in the proposed Episodes 6, 7, 8, is unresolvable. It was proposed to extend the action to the milieu of the institutions and contestations that are absent or unquestioned in the extant episodes; Manfred and Jochen were, for example, to become active in their company's *Betriebsrat*, hitherto complicit in the operations of capital, and the competence of the central unifying institution of the family series — the family itself— was to be assaulted in Jochen and Marion's divorce.

The project embodied in these three unshot episodes would have fundamentally challenged the ideological framework overarching the first five and the central integrating device of the narrative which is a major axis of the ideological system of each episode. For the narrative is organised around the lives of two families who are related by the connection of Jochen, the representative of one, and Marion, the representative of the other — a connection that is sealed and institutionalised in their marriage. The connection between these two families, systems of relationships, is the agency whereby the variety of the other characters encountered in the two principal milieux — home and work — are brought and held together.

The figures of Jochen and Marion, then, are the foci around which the other characters cohere. The major net of relationships plotted from the centres of Jochen and Marion are those of family — in the case of Jochen, four generations and in that of Marion, two (or effectively three, due to the closeness in age of Manni and Sybille) — and of friendship, all their respective friends being colleagues. And the friends themselves enter parallel relationships that 'echo' that of Jochen and Marion (Irmgard and Rolf, Manfred and Monika).

But the two major axes are the vertical ones of the families and the horizontal ones of friendship/love. Both axes are attenuated in the case of Marion, and her experience is presented much less extensively than that of Jochen; it is she who is integrated into Jochen's world and the active role she is given there is qualified by her world being abbreviated. However perceptive and active an agent there, she remains a woman in a man's world. The choice of the family as the agency whereby the narrative maintains and reproduces the relations between the characters carries less 'critical' potentiality than does that of, say, The Street in the most evident British equivalent to *Eight Hours Are Not a Day*, *Coronation*

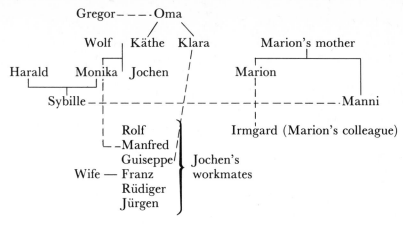

Street. For, should the institutional form of inter-personal relationships in *Eight Hours* be broken, as in the divorce of Jochen and Marion, then it is hard to see how the fictional world can be maintained. The 'accidental' nature of the relationships between neighbours in *Coronation Street* permits a much wider repertoire of events, personalities and transformations than does that of a narrative organisation that demands the maintenance of a particular form of human society, 'family life', for its continued existence, and permits the playing out and interrogation of a variety of roles and relations between men and women. Whilst *Eight Hours Are Not a Day* offers a model of how the family series might be inflected towards a critical representation of capitalism and the social relations it produces and that reproduce it, the potentiality of the family series for performing a similar representation of patriarchy and how it may be transformed is less evident.

Fassbinder certainly treats the most fundamental aspect of women's relation to capital — that of wage labour — but it's apparent that whilst Marion and Irmgard are wage workers, their potential struggles as wage workers are never expressed. Marion may play an exemplary role in gingering up the men to struggle at the point of production and voice the analysis of their experience that Jochen, Manfred and the others are groping towards, but the world of the advertising department of the *Stadt-Anzeiger* is never shown as other than the petty bourgeois arcadia that Irmgard's not rose- but black-tinted ideological spectacles see it as. We have a positive heroine, whose economic subordination no more enters the fictional world than does her woman's subordination within patriarchy. And in the workplace which patriarchal ideology constitutes for women — the home — we see (in contrast to the excellent treatment of the factory workplace) little actual work going on. Käthe, Jochen's mother, occupies that territory, but her place in it never enters the action as a major concern. It is only Monika who experiences any real nastiness at the hands of patriarchy; hers is served to her by her rather contemptible *Spiessburger* husband, Harald. Happily for her though, she readily emancipates herself from him and is manoeuvred into the ready arms of the friendly and sensitive proletarian Manfred by Oma, the benevolent and powerful matriarch.

In this respect then, *Eight Hours* is a tendentious *Märchen* with only one heart in its breast — and that on the left side — but no breasts to go with the heart.

Sheila Johnston, in an exploration of Fassbinder's status and role as an *auteur*, has commented on the absence of fathers in Fassbinder's films. A paradoxical absence, since his films are suffused with a central concern with the playing out of patriarchal values. We see this pattern at work in *Eight Hours*; of the two families that animate the series Marion's has no father and Jochen's has the most amiable of domestic tyrants — Wolf, who plays at the role of pater familias, but exorcises the power of the father through his happy inability to command the obedience of those whom patriarchy constitutes as subordinate to him. For representations of the articulation of social relations under capitalism and patriarchy and the concrete living out of those contradictions, we have to look elsewhere in the *Arbeiterfilm*, to the work of Ingo Kratisch/Marianne Lüdcke, Helma Sanders and to Christian Ziewer, particularly to his third *Arbeiterfilm, Der aufrechte Gang*.

Fassbinder's *Arbeiterfilm* nevertheless remains a most important landmark in the institutional history of the *Arbeiterfilm* genre. For in *Eight Hours Are Not a Day* the Drama Department of WDR committed large resources in an attempt to develop a popular form for the representation of working-class experience. The series expresses in a way no other *Arbeiterfilme* do, whether the documentaries of Runge and Schübel/ Gallehr or the fiction features of Lüdcke/Kratisch or Ziewer, an institutional policy of initiation and active development of a new form of programming that proved popular with audiences. But it seems to us that in the aesthetic history of the *Arbeiterfilm Eight Hours Are Not a Day* is less remarkable. The series is flawed by its conception of working-class life, by the absences of trades unions, politics and the institutions of the working class, by the adoption of the family as the integrating unity of the narratives and by the excesses of Fassbinder's *mise en scène*.

60

Eight Hours Are Not a Day

Eight Hours Are Not a Day

Eight Hours Are Not a Day

62

CHAPTER 6

The Work of Christian Ziewer

DEUTSCHER ALLTAG: ZWISCHEN ANPASSUNG UND WIDERSTAND (GERMAN EVERYDAY LIFE: BETWEEN ACCEPTANCE AND RESISTANCE)

> The return of the boundless dreams, the boundless explosion of the history of heresy, the ecstasy of self-respect ('aufrechten Gangs'), of the impatient, rebellious and serious desire for paradise. (Ernst Bloch, *Thomas Munzer: Als Theologe der Revolution*, Frankfurt 1960, p. 63.)

Christian Ziewer's work has an exemplary status in the *Arbeiterfilm* genre; and in a certain sense the trajectory in his work from *Liebe Mutter*, his first feature of 1971, through *Schneeglöckchen blühn im September* in 1974 to *Der aufrechte Gang* (1976) marks both the passage of the whole genre from documentary to fiction and a movement from the unproblematical primacy ceded to the capital and labour contradiction in the presentation of 'Deutscher Alltag' to situating that — still central — contradiction in an ensemble of contradictions; the relations of men and women in patriarchy, city and country, different modes of production caught in the same system of exchange, and so on. The focus shifts over the period marked at one end by *Rote Fahnen* and *Liebe Mutter* and at the other by *Der aufrechte Gang*, *Familienglück* and *Eight Hours Are Not a Day*, from a straightforward concern with class confrontation at the point of production to operations in the spheres of social reproduction, from the base to the superstructure or, better, from a conception of straightforward primacy of the master contradiction rooted in the economic to a concern with the complex articulation of a plurality of contradictions in the totality.

THE INSTITUTIONAL CONTEXT

Ziewer's film making is conceived as an instrument of struggle and a major focus of his activity as a political film-maker has been not only the production of film texts but also the creation of Basis Film, an institution in which the relatively profitable activity of production subsidises the unprofitable activities of distribution and exhibition. All Ziewer's features have been made as co-productions between WDR and Basis Film GmbH Berlin. The main activity of Basis is film distribution and Basis Film Verleih was established, like the Filmverlag der Autoren, as an attempt to escape the domination of film distribution by the American majors. Though the Filmverlag was conceived as an agency for facilitating the dissemination and continued production of *Autorenfilme* — the self-expression of film-maker artists — Basis acts as an agency for the distribution, and development of circuits of exhibition, of progressive films. It has enjoyed some success in this: an expanding catalogue, outright purchase of some titles by unions such as I. G. Metall, and the slow cultivation of non-commercial and often non-theatrical exhibition. But these activities are conditional on continued subsidy from the production section of this mini vertically-integrated media co-operative of seven full-time workers. Ziewer and Wiese (the principal collaborator on *Liebe Mutter* and *Schneeglöckchen*) have, for instance, waived their authors' rights in *Schneeglöckchen* in favour of Basis in order to sustain the enterprise. Control of film distribution by foreign capital has long been a weakness of the West German film industry and it is control of distribution and exhibition in television by non-commercial public service institutions that (with the large sums available for expenditure on programming, since television revenues are not bled off to finance corporate diversification or shareholders' dividends as they are in the UK) goes a long way to account for the importance of the television sector in the West German film industry. The sole major distributor of the post-war era that was not owned by US capital, Constantin, recently went bankrupt and the Filmverlag der Autoren itself now survives only through a take-over by Rudolf Augstein, the publisher of *Der Spiegel*.

The condition of Basis Film Verleih's existence as a channel through which critical films may circulate is continued activity in production by Ziewer and to a lesser extent (because of their more 'at arm's length', 'commercial' relation to Basis) by other film-makers such as Max Willutzki and Helke Sander. The revenues from production *can* be formidable. The case of *Liebe Mutter*, the film that made Basis possible, is instructive. It cost 350,000 DM. From WDR came 150,000 DM, while from the Kuratorium 200,000 DM. Thus any receipts from theatrical or non-theatrical exhibition, prizes and so on are pure 'profit'. Yet a necessary condition of attracting subsidies from the Kuratorium, the Filmförderungsanstalt, the Bundesministerium des Innern (e.g. the script premium received for *Der aufrechte Gang*), or for tax relief from the Filmbewertungsstelle is artistic excellence — i.e., continued approval by film critics, regular appearance of films at film festivals and clever manipulation of the *Gremienpolitik*. Thomas Elsaesser (1979) argues: 'Fassbinder seems condemned to over-produce in order to produce at all, and in this sense he is the only independent film-maker in Germany whose working methods reflect the objective conditions of a capitalist mode of production.'

Ziewer and Basis are caught in the same dynamic. Over-production of course is a relative term and Ziewer's output is nowhere near that of Fassbinder's, but produce he must, once every two years, a film that is not only profitable in terms of marks and pfennigs but one which also maintains its director's par value on the cultural exchanges, a sphere where the denomination of the paper is constantly changing under the pressures of public taste and political contestation. (It's salutary for the British intelligentsia, enjoying its arcadia where cultural politics is the undisputed territory of the left, to recognise that in Western Germany that field is very actively contested by a well-organised, well-financed and capable right.)

Some further location of Ziewer is perhaps worth making before discussing his three *Arbeiterfilme*. Like a number of other makers of *Arbeiterfilme* (notably Lüdcke and Kratisch), Ziewer came from the Berlin film school of the late 1960s. The Berlin school had, and continues to have, an orientation towards documentary film-making and thus towards engagement with the course of social life. Ziewer's films before his entry into feature production exemplified this current. For example, *Einsamkeit in der Grosstadt* (1968, with Klaus Wiese) was described by Ziewer (1975) as a film

> on the loneliness of life in big cities; it dealt with the sociological as well as psychological aspects of living conditions in cities. We described in this film how this was reflected in the individual. We were working on this film with West German workers who were working and living in West Berlin and we realised how terribly isolated they were. We interviewed them and realised that it would be easy and interesting to write and make a feature film on this subject. But we realised we could not deal with only one aspect of the matter in the feature film, that is what they were doing in their leisure time; this could only be described by including their working life.

Exemplifying his conception of cinematic reflection of reality as an instrument of struggle were Ziewer's *Kinogramm 1* and *Kinogramm 2* (1970, with Max Willutzki). These films were made during Ziewer's (and Willutzki's) residence in one of West Berlin's post-war architectural showpieces and residents' nightmare, the Märkische Viertel, during which he was active in community politics, such as initiatives to secure *Kindergarten* and playgrounds, rent strikes, etc.

> During the period 1968–70 an initiative developed among the people living on the Märkische Viertel who got together in order to try and solve problems jointly. We, the film-makers, lived there ourselves for

two years and participated in many of their group initiatives. For instance, parents got together with students in order to deal with the lack of *Kindergarten*, with the problem of constantly rising rents, with problems that occurred in the flats and tower blocks, school problems, etc. We made our films with these ' people. They were mostly documentary films but eventually what could be called education films developed, in which demands were expressed to the political authority [i.e. the Berlin *Land* government was the landlord] and this was done by showing the state of affairs that existed; albeit in a somewhat exaggerated form, we tried to express the conflict that existed between the people and the state. These *Kinogramme* were used for short spots in political campaigns and actions for demonstrations, etc., and the active citizens who were working in these initiatives tried to inform others in this way and tried to get their co-operation and participation. Our participation and active work in all this led, of course, to a very close relationship with the people concerned, who were producing their own papers, *Bilderzeitungen*, and they collaborated with us in these films. (Ziewer, 1975.)

THE AESTHETIC CONTEXT

Film production, of course, whilst necessarily located and determined by the political and economic structures of the society in which it takes place, necessitates aesthetic choices. Ziewer has referred to three distinct lineages which have informed his film-making: Italian Neo-realism, British realism of the late 1950s and lastly, the proletarian cinema of the Weimar Republic, those films that came out of the rich militant and class-conscious cultural and political practice of the German working class up to its brutal suppression in 1933 and half-suffocated revival after 1945. To retrieve that broken tradition is for the contemporary German film-maker a somewhat abstract project, though those films are for Ziewer the most important of the lineages on which he draws.

Perhaps the lost continuity between culture and politics in the German working-class movement, first generated during the ninteenth century period of anti-socialist laws, is irretrievable. But the strength that continuity represented and which found expression in the cultural institutions and practices created by and for the working class — its theatres, sports and music clubs, its press, radio stations and film productions — may still offer the present, very different situation a principle of hope and an enlivening example of concrete possibilities.

As Ziewer says:

We can try as outsiders, as middle-class artists, to make films which give an outline of the working class and which will, as we hope, help the working class to present their own arguments.

66

Now what I just said shows, I think, that we have no link with the tradition of the proletarian film. During the time of the Weimar Republic, during the 30s, these films came from the Socialist and Communist movements and were used by these organisations. This is something that does not apply to us because there has, in the meantime, been a break within the tradition of the workers' movement in Germany itself. And therefore I feel that we cannot use old traditions. There is no connection to something that did exist at the time and that still continues to develop. What we have done is to start new work in this particular field and I do realise that in doing so we run the risk of losing contact with the history of the workers' movement, but on the other hand I think we have an advantage because it does enable us to rethink matters, to get rid of old ideas which we feel especially apply to the work done during the period of the Weimar Republic. (Ziewer, 1975.)

For Ziewer the most positive inheritance from the past has been the body of reflection and theory in Marxist aesthetics on the relation of artistic representation to cognition and to social transformation, especially the work of Brecht, Ernst Bloch and Georg Lukács.

For Lukács mimetic representations required categorisation under two heads: realism and naturalism. Naturalism was simply ideological (and open to the critiques mounted by the anti-realists in British film culture). However, realism was a mode of cognition and representation that could enlighten, liberate and 'adequate the real'. For Lukács naturalism, whatever its actual historical productivity (which in the case of Zola or Strindberg could be argued to have been progressive), was based on a false epistemology and thus offered no adequate basis for cognition, no way of satisfactorily knowing the world. Naturalism is distinguished by scrupulous fidelity to the here and now; to the immediate and the apparent. It is an aesthetic that seeks to minimise the mediation through consciousness of the real in perception and representation. In film theory the classic site of a naturalist aesthetic is in Bazin. In his 'Ontology of the Photographic Image' Bazin states:

The aesthetic qualities of photography are to be sought in its power to lay bare the realities. It is not for me to separate off, in the complex fabric of the objective world, here a reflection on a damp sidewalk, there the gesture of a child. Only the impassive lens, stripping the object of all those ways of seeing it, those piled up pre-conceptions, that spiritual dust and grime with which my eyes have covered it, is able to present it in all its virginal purity to my attention and consequently to my love. (Bazin, 1967.)

This strict naturalism is often contradicted in Bazin's critical writings, which approach at times a conception of representation closer to Lukácsian realism than the strict naturalism of his explicitly theoretical essays as exemplified above. Lukács, though, argues that scrupulous fidelity to the here and now, the immediate and the apparent, is an inadequate mode of knowing. Events, objects, phenomena are chimerical, caught in a process of change and a network of causal relations that require representation if the real is to be fully adequated and understood. Therefore some analytical and constructive activity of human consciousness is necessary for the real to be produced for representation.

> The artistic correctness of a detail thus has nothing to do with whether the detail corresponds to any similar detail in reality. The detail in a work of art is an accurate reflection of life when it is a necessary aspect of the accurate reflection of the total process of objective reality, no matter whether it was observed by the artist in life or created through imagination out of direct or indirect experience. (Lukács, 1970.)

Whether a particular mimesis is realist or naturalist cannot be determined by the presence or absence of particular formal qualities; rather the criterion is the degree to which the major determining forces in the social totality which fix and produce particular phenomena are represented.

> The work of art must therefore reflect correctly and in proper proportion all important factors objectively determining the area of life it represents. It must so reflect these that this area of life becomes comprehensible from within and from without, re-experienceable, that it appears as a totality of life. This does not mean that every work of art must strive to reflect the objective, extensive totality of life. On the contrary, the extensive totality of reality necessarily is beyond the possible scope of any artistic creation; the totality of reality can only be reproduced intellectually in ever-increasing approximation through the infinite process of science. The totality of the work of art is rather intensive: the circumscribed and self-contained ordering of those factors which objectively are of decisive significance for the portion of life depicted, which determine its existence and motion, its specific quality and its place in the total life process. In this sense the briefest song is as much an intensive totality as the mightiest epic. The objective character of the area of life represented determines the quantity, quality, proportion, etc., of the factors that emerge in interaction with the specific laws of the literary form appropriate for the representation of this portion of life. (Lukács, ibid.)

For Lukács the extensive totality of the material world required ordering in the intensive totality of the artistic representation, and the major agency whereby this process of transformation and representation was to be performed was that of 'typicality':

> The typical is not to be confused with the *average* (though there are cases where this holds true), nor with the *eccentric* (though the typical does as a rule go beyond the normal). A character is typical, in this technical sense, when his innermost being is determined by objective forces at work in society. Vautrin or Julien Sorel, superficially eccentric, are *typical* in their behaviour: the determining factors of a particular historical phase are found in them in concentrated form. Yet, though typical, they are never crudely 'illustrative'. (Lukács, 1967.)

Both realism and naturalism are mimetic systems or practices of representation but are based on different epistemologies and this distinction between realism and naturalism within the category of mimesis is of great use in exploring the competence of documentary and fictional modes of mimesis in the *Arbeiterfilm* (though there is no perfect fit between documentary and naturalism, realism and fiction). The *Arbeiterfilme* themselves offer a more productive site in contemporary aesthetic production from which the strictures of the anti-realists may be rebutted than do the British instances (e.g. Loach/Garnett, Trevor Griffith) that have been pressed into service to defend the citadels of realism.

In Brecht's essays 'Against George Lukács' (Brecht, 1977) the critique of Lukács is principally of Lukács's formalism, of Lukács's lack of recognition of realism in literature other than in the big bourgeois novels of Balzac, Tolstoy or Thomas Mann. Brecht's critique is not of realism as such nor of the central tenets of Lukács's theory; indeed he shares its major axioms that art is a mode of cognition, that enlightenment follows the rupture of the surface of the phenomenal world and the apprehension of its organising principles and their relations, the necessity for 'legibility' in artistic representation and so on. He even adopts the central 'integrationist' category of Lukács — that of totality — when he criticises the Lukácsian practice of anathematising Joyce in favour of Tolstoy:

> In Joyce's great satirical novel, *Ulysses*, there is — besides the use of various styles of writing and other unusual features — the so called interior monologue. . . . Astonishingly, some Marxists associated themselves with this nonsense [i.e. criticism of the Molly Bloom monologue], adding in their revulsion the epithet of petty bourgeois. As a technical method the interior monologue was equally rejected; it

was said to be formalistic. I have never understood the reason. The fact that Tolstoy would have done it differently is no reason to reject Joyce's method. The criticisms were so superficially formulated that one gained the impression that if Joyce had only set his monologue in a session with a psycho-analyst, everything would have been all right. Now the interior monologue is a method which is very difficult to use, and it is very useful to stress this fact. Without very precise measures (again of a technical sort) the interior monologue by no means reproduces reality, that is to say the totality of thought and association as it superficially appears to do. (Brecht, 1977, p. 73.)

The lineage of aesthetic and representational theory behind the *Arbeiterfilme* (and particularly those of Ziewer) is not exhausted by George Lukács and Bert Brecht. It is worth considering too the influence of Ernst Bloch (1885–1977), whose category 'Der aufrechte Gang' was appropriated by Ziewer as the title for his third film and by Märthesheimer in his essay 'What can the hero do?' Bloch's work is much less well known in Britain than that of Brecht or even Lukács.

For the *Arbeiterfilm* the elements of his thinking that seem to have been principally important are those concerned with contradiction and Utopia. For Bloch human existence is teleological, its project directed towards the free expression and realisation of human potentiality, unconstrained by necessity. The liquidation of necessity and creation of a realm of freedom entails struggle in the here and now. But what animates, makes sense of and legitimises that struggle is the aspiration to the realisation of freedom as a general human state. The general human aspiration to and struggle for freedom surfaces in irrational philosophies and beliefs, in religion, in the praxis of reactionary classes, as well as in the beliefs and praxis of those with the most advanced, truest, intellectual and political positions. Habermas (1969), the inheritor of Horkheimer's mantle as the centre of the Frankfurt School, says: 'What Bloch wants to preserve for socialism, which subsists on scorning tradition, is the tradition of the scorned'. Thus there is a positive potentiality that needs to be recognised, valued and fostered in much that confident Marxists have identified as fit only for the rubbish heap of the present.

Bloch insists that for S to become P, for the Subject to become Predicate, for 'nature' to become 'home', for humanity to realise its potentiality for freedom and fulfilment, the general aspiration for Utopia needs to be recognised and integrated into a strategy for social change. To follow the current of Marx and Engels' anathematisations of Utopianism (see *inter alia* Section III, 3 of the *Manifesto of the Communist Party*) is to yield a potent force for human liberation, the aspiration to Utopia, to the enemies of liberation. Bloch's emphasis on the productivity of the dream implies attention and respect for the attempts of individuals to realise partially the promise of human freedom contained in 'lawfulness without law', for example in private pleasure and in an accommodation to the dominant order that a sterner Leninist tradition regards as simple backsliding and objectively reactionary. In his theory of representation Bloch admits an aesthetic dimension; the architecture of his thought precludes the Lukácsian reduction of aesthetic problems to ones of epistemology, of art to philosophy, and finds in that aesthetic dimension, in its characteristic 'purposiveness without purpose', a principle of hope; a testimony to the possibility of Utopia, to S becoming P. In terms of cognition Bloch demands of art different cognitive principles and systems of explanation from those of the dominant Marxist tradition of Marx, Engels, Lenin and Lukács. His celebrated rejoinder to Lukács's theory of the totality does not repudiate a cognitive dimension to art or rule out the pertinence of epistemological criteria in the judgment of artistic representation, but argues rather for a different model of the totality and the principles of cognition through which the totality may be known:

> But what if Lukács's reality — a coherent infinitely mediated totality — is not so objective after all? What if his conception of reality has failed to liberate itself completely from classical systems? What if authentic reality is also discontinuity? Since Lukács operates with a closed objectivistic conception of reality, when he comes to examine Expressionism he resolutely rejects any attempt on the part of artists to shatter any image of the world, even that of capitalism. Any art which strives to exploit the *real* fissures in crevices appears in his eyes as a wilful act of destruction. (Bloch, 1977.)

Bloch argues for a reality of contradiction, the contradiction between, for instance, an individual's own economic interest in the maintenance of capitalism and his or her ethical commitment to a praxis of revolution; or between non-synchronous but contemporaneous modes of production, the dominant, residual and emergent as formulated by Raymond Williams in *Marxism and Literature*, and for a hermeneutic system that attends to the dialectical aspect of these contradictions.

Bloch stands, then, in the construction of the *Arbeiterfilm* as a sign of the importance of the representation of imaginary as well as real relations, of the 'personal' as well as the 'political', of the domestic as well as the productive economy, and for the importance of ethical as well as material aspirations in the living out of people's lives. If for Lukács the real can only be known through its process of becoming, through knowledge of the past and a survey of causal relations and their temporal extension into the present, then for Bloch that real can only be adequately known and represented if the temporal extension is directed *forwards* in a kind of prospective mimesis that embraces the moment of S

71

becoming P, nature becoming home, and Utopia being realised. The sign of this hope is the aesthetic dimension of representation, the disinterested pleasure that attends the spectacle of, for example, Ziewer's *mise en scène*, and itself signifies the possibility of a state of freedom, of 'lawfulness without law'.

It is beyond the scope of this monograph to perform a full exegesis of the ways in which Lukács, Bloch and Brecht (who in spite of his affectation of vulgar thinking could be as Kantian as the next, for example in his argument for pleasure and entertainment as vital principles) have attempted to invent the aesthetic absent in classical Marxism by re-working the formidable and contradictory inheritance of Kant, Hegel and Idealist philosophy. Rather, we wish to indicate the different versions of Marxist aesthetics that have been drawn on, consciously or unconsciously, to a greater or less extent, in the making of the *Arbeiterfilme* from that which has achieved a common currency in British and French film studies and which is, we judge, likely to form the reader's frame of reference.

It's worth pointing out that Ziewer's relationship to Brecht also has a biographical dimension. At the DFFB, Ziewer's tutor in direction was Egon Monk (whose production for NDR of Fallada's *Bauern, Bonzen and Bomben* was shown in 1979 by the BBC). Monk had collaborated with Brecht as a member of the Berliner Ensemble in a number of productions during the early 1950s. Canaris (1975) remarks that: 'As a director too Brecht has had his disciples; four of them are amongst the most important directors of the German-speaking theatre and of television: Peter Palizsch and Egon Monk in the Federal Republic; Bruno Besson and Manfred Wekwerth in the GDR.' In 1950 Monk had been assistant director of *The Tutor*, Brecht's adaptation of Lenz's work, and assistant on *Mother Courage* at the Kammerspiele in Munich. In 1951, he directed Brecht's adaptation of Hauptmann's *Beaver Coat* and *Red Cock*, and Brecht's *Herrnberg Report*. In 1952 he was the director of Brecht's Goethe adaptation, *Urfaust*, and of Brecht's *The Rifles of Señora Carrar*.

Monk's productions were some of the most controversial mounted by the Berliner Ensemble in their first season of plays (*Mother Courage, Puntila, Vasya Shelesnova* (Gorki), *The Tutor, The Mother, Beaver Coat* and *Red Cock*). *The Herrnberg Report*, although published by the Central Committee of Free German Youth (FDJ), had been omitted from Brecht's *Stücke*; though eventually awarded the National Prize First Class, it was only reprieved from early cancellation on the instructions of the SED (Socialist Unity Party) after a private performance which Pieck, Grotewohl and other members of the DDR government attended. And *Neues Deutschland* attacked Monk's *Urfaust*:

Monk copied models we have already encountered in *The Tutor* and *The Broken Jug* (Kleist). They too were fatalistic and pessimistic pictures of static conditions; they had only one hero: *Deutsche Misère* ('German miserableness'). This expresses an attitude — an attitude in fact directed against Germany's cultural heritage, against Germany's national culture. . . . We feel we must say that the young members of the Berliner Ensemble, many of whom are very talented, are being led into a wrong direction by the methods and principles applied in the adaptation of the classics by Bertolt Brecht, the artistic director of the Ensemble. ('Weitere Bemerkungen Zum Faust-Problem', *Neues Deutschland*, 27 December 1953. Translated by M. Esslin, *Brecht: a choice of evils*, Eyre & Spottiswoode, London, 1959.)

Willett and Mannheim print Monk's notes for the Lenz project in their edition of *The Tutor* (Brecht, *Collected Plays*, vol. 9, ed. J. Willett and R. Mannheim, Vintage Books, New York 1973), and also reproduce the Ensemble's defence of their project:

The Tutor has been criticised in some quarters for being a 'negative' or unconstructive play. In the opinion of the Berliner Ensemble this play, containing as it does three portraits of schoolmasters (privy council-lor, Wenzeslaus, and Läuffer) and three of students who intend to become schoolmasters (von Berg, Pätus, Bollwerk), and being set in the period when the German bourgeoisie was evolving its educational system, offers a stimulating satirical view of this aspect of the German *Misère*. The production was a perfectly valid contribution to the great process of educational reform which is currently being undertaken in our republic. As can be seen from such works as *Tartuffe, Don Quixote, Candide*, and *The Inspector General*, satire is not normally concerned to set up exemplary characters as a contrast to those which it mocks; in the concave mirrors which it uses to exaggerate and emphasise its targets the 'positive' character would not escape distortion. The positive element in *The Tutor* is its bitter anger against inhuman conditions of unjustified privilege and twisted thinking. (Willett and Mannheim, op.cit., p. 362.)

In spite of the plurality of lineages against which Ziewer defines his film-making it is only the lineage of theory that achieves more than brief echoes in his films. In each of his *Arbeiterfilme* there are few moments which bear more than a very general relation to Neo-realism (in, as Ziewer says, the use of amateurs or, perhaps, location shooting), to Godard (some breaks — particularly in *Liebe Mutter* — in the unity of the main diegesis), or to the English realists (wage labour, an alienated relationship to the world, a sense of impotence). But the films do represent an attempt to discover and practise an aesthetic of realism that will provoke in audiences a recognition of the pertinence to their own lives and projects of the issues that animate the fictional characters, that

73

will 'develop models of the social life of human beings in order to help the spectator to understand his social surroundings and to help him control them rationally and emotionally' (Brecht, 1961, p. 9), and that will provide a catalyst whereby the cognitive advances the films offer the audience will be translated into organisation and action by and for the audience themselves. The films' project extends beyond the naturalism implied in the cinematic lineage of *Bicycle Thieves*, *A Kind of Loving* or even *Vivre sa vie*, towards ushering the audience into 'its own real world with conscious faculties' — and offering a principle or promise of hope for the audience to change their own real world; in short to realise the inheritance from Brecht and Bloch.

LIEBE MUTTER, MIR GEHT ES GUT (DEAR MOTHER, I'M OK)

Ziewer's first feature film, *Liebe Mutter, mir geht es gut (Dear Mother, I'm OK)*, was made by Basis Film in co-production with WDR. The financing of the film and the consequences of securing the Adolf Grimme Prize (the principal documentary prize of German television) make *Liebe Mutter* a graphic case study in the possibilities and potentialities of television finance and distribution, financial contributions from the state sector, and critical legitimation for a young film director and producer. Ziewer was not only able to make a film of considerable interest concerned with an exposition of class confrontation at the workplace but acquired sufficient legitimacy to continue his career as a film-maker, to secure finance, distribution and critical attention for further productions and to establish Basis Film.

This, the first film of the Berlin school of *Arbeiterfilme*, is a 'documentary feature film', located at the same point of contradiction in cinematic conventions as *Rote Fahnen* and demanding the same kind of critical exegesis of the aesthetic solutions chosen to surmount the antagonisms of naturalism (with its attendant specificity that guarantees the authenticity, and limits the pertinence, of the information it presents) and fiction (offering the potentiality of a general referent but unguaranteed by the actual enactment in reality of the events it documents).

We called it a documentary feature film because it consisted of two elements; on one hand, research, that is documentary scientific examination, and on the other artistic imagination, and the two elements were led together and were based on interviews, on visits to the factories, etc. We discussed the manuscript with the workers in the early stages as well as its treatment and added their and our ideas and imagination. Therefore it is not purely documentary but shows stories that serve as a kind of model. (Ziewer, 1975.)

74

The kinds of research that Ziewer outlines (scrupulous field work; participant observation, drawing on his own and Wiese's experience as factory workers; integrating the suggestions of the workers who were drawn into the project as non-professional actors; checking the draft against the comments of the subjects) are familiar to any anthropologist or social scientist and to many documentary film-makers. What is perhaps not so familiar is the recognition that after the research stage in the preparation of the film there remains a problem of representation; of finding an aesthetic that simultaneously makes possible the transmission of the reality defined in the research stage and which realises both the specific (the unique) and the general (generalisable) elements of the film's material for an audience who are to be offered entrances to it so that they can make it their own.

The mediations that the material undergoes in its transformation into a filmic spectacle are foregrounded through evident devices of narration like the separation of the film into prologue, epilogue and main action. Each section is separated from the others by intertitles and the main action is broken by intertitles, by voice-over exegetical narration and commentary, by the use of expository flashback and by representative characters — a director, a worker, a *Betriebsrat* — voicing to camera their understanding of the events that the film's action presents.

Liebe Mutter begins with a title scene showing male hands putting a floppy vinyl promotional record on to a record player; the titles give the name of the film and the date 1967. The record plays the opening of the march 'Berliner Luft', which is followed by the voice of Willy Brandt (the former Mayor of West Berlin) inviting West German workers to the city: 'Deine Chance ist Berlin!' ('Your Opportunity is in Berlin'). In a device of juxtaposition echoed several times in the film the rhetoric of the official version of events is set against a specific experience of the reality to which the dominant ideological rhetoric refers; here, the daily routine of male West German workers in a hostel, getting up, making sandwiches, negotiating their enforced communality. In the first two sequences, then, a very specific experience has been initiated by the actors, captured by the camera and offered to the audience as a veritable account of living conditions in a workers' hostel. And this experience has been set in critical juxtaposition with the bombastic music and promotional rhetoric that specify 'West Berlin 1967' as the site of the film's action and which, if they are to be believed, must manage and encompass the documentation of West Berlin 1967 that *Liebe Mutter* offers its audience. The prologue ends with a series of stills that offers a *prospect* of the film to come, and over these stills an account of the prospect is narrated:

Ein Arbeiter, der seine Arbeit nicht tut, Schlägerei anzettelt, Kollegen beschimpft, gegen Vorgesetzte hetzt, ein solcher Arbeiter bekommt seinen Lohn, kriegt das Maul gestopft, fällt auf die Schnauze, wird

75

erledigt. Dieser Film zeigt, wie solches geschieht, und warum es uns alltäglich erscheint. Arbeiter die gegen erhöhte Mieten Kämpfen und unterliegen und daraus lernen, die sich gegen den Verlust des Arbeitplatzes empören und erfolglos bleiben und daraus Schlüsse ziehen, die schliesslich den Streik organisieren und ihre Kraft erkennen und ihre Lage zu ändern beginnen, solche Arbeiter zeigt dieser Film, und er stellt die Frage, warum sie uns nicht alltäglich erscheinen.

(A worker who doesn't do his work, who fights, swears at his workmates, agitates against his superiors, gets what's coming to him, gets a punch in the nose, falls flat on his face and is finished off. This film shows how all this happens and why we consider it normal. Workers fighting against increased rents, learning from their defeats or fruitlessly fighting layoffs and drawing their own conclusions, finally striking and discovering their strength, beginning to change their lot: this film shows us these workers and poses the question why we don't regard them as normal.)

It would perhaps be too much to claim that the prospect for the film laid out in this prologue is one in which all surprise at the course of events that follow is eliminated. But the attention that the audience invests in the action that follows is closer to a Hitchcockian suspense (or Brechtian sceptical and curious attention) than to simple curiosity as to the course of the diegesis, for the audience knows the course of the diegesis that is to follow; they are 'made perfectly aware of all the facts involved' (Truffaut, 1967, p. 88). The audience's attention is caught not in an expectation of surprise but in an engagement with the argument that the film's course is there to demonstrate.

This argument is essentially one of showing that the dominant order is not the only possible one and that the customary system of categorisation that places 'Streik organisieren und ihre Kraft erkennen' as 'nicht alltäglich' and 'fällt auf die Schnauze' as 'alltäglich' is by no means a necessary system. And that the material and ideological system that leads the figures in and the audiences for *Liebe Mutter* to find 'fällt auf die Schnauze' more normal than 'ihre Kraft erkennen' may be challenged.

The film's manner of address is defined from the beginning as being conceived to contest and re-order the modes of cognition, the *alltäglich* customary or commonsense category system — the imputed dominant ideology — which the audience brings to its perception of workers' lives.

The principal worker's life to be shown is that of Alfred Schefczyk, whom we see at his workplace, in the hostel and at leisure, in a series of vignettes (given coherence by the unity of their common protagonist, chronological temporal sequence and common location: West Berlin 1967). These establish the terms of his existence. His work is shown to be

76

the badgering of other workers into making do with an inadequate supply of crates for transporting components from one part of the factory to another. Put like that it sounds as though he is a manager — he isn't. He's an unskilled worker who shifts components from work station to work station. That he is a displaced skilled worker is evinced by his unofficial design and manufacture of steel garage gates for a workmate. He lives in a hostel where, as at work, the autonomy he enjoys in his life comes from his creative negotiation of the authoritarian structures that govern the situation. He and fellow West German *Gastarbeiter* may be resented by Berliners, for example. These nuggets of naturalism — the documentation of the parameters of Alfred's *Alltag* — are explicated by the narrator's voice (e.g. confrontation with the foreman is explained as ending Alfred's chances of securing skilled work) and broken up by intertitles (e.g. 'Rent rise in the hostel'), and are separated from each other by sequences in which Alfred does not appear but which lay out the extensive network of relations which structure his experience and in which it is embedded. Thus the first and second sequences of Alfred's life ('Alfred works from 6 to 2.45' and 'Rent rise in the hostel') are divided by a succession of short statements observed by the camera, uttered as if to an annual general meeting of a company, by the hierarchy of people who together coalesce as the boss: the foreman, the works manager, the director, the majority and minority shareholders. They agree substantially in their statements on the need to squeeze the workers; that item of policy concluded the meeting moves to consider distribution of profits. A scene in a Berlin bar in which Alfred and his class-conscious friend from the hostel are ejected after an argument with a chauvinistic Berliner (a personification of 'Berliner Luft'?) is separated from a scene in which Alfred returns to the hostel drunk by the exposition of the management decision to close W14, a workshop at the engineering factory where Alfred works, and transfer its production and machinery to the Federal Republic.

The closure of the W14 sequence shows the hierarchy of power inside the company, the objective situation of the workers and their own reasoning out and accounting to themselves of their place in the world. There are four moments to the sequence. One, the workers chat about work and football pools inside the factory. Two, the *Betriebsräte* complain at the meeting of the company board that they have been the catspaws of the management, have been kept in ignorance of company policy and in particular of the shift of W14 from Berlin to Hanover, and that the politics of *Mitbestimmung* are such as to render them impotent to resist even so fundamental a change in the conditions of work. Three, after the board vote in favour of closure (*Betriebsräte* voting against) the directors toast their achievement in *Sekt* (this scene was cut on the instructions of the Head of the WDR Drama Department when *Liebe Mutter* was first shown on the ARD network). Four, a number of the workers affected by the decision drink at a pavement bar in Wedding and one 50 year old worker articulates, informally, his history and sense of place in the world: the total destruction of Berlin in 1945, the exploitation of Germany by the USA, USSR and France (Wedding is in the French Zone of Occupation of Berlin), the introduction of the new coinage (i.e. the establishment of the Federal Republic of Germany and West Berlin as distinct state entities in Germany and the beginning of the cold war), and the ideology of all Germans working together: the period of perceived social solidarity, working together, national reconstruction, the *Wirtschaftswunder* and now. . . . Thus the situation of Alfred, which has been intensively and specifically defined to the audience, is placed in a context of the collective historical experience of his class from 'Year Zero' and in the relations of power that govern and determine his place in the world. The directors toast the closure in *Sekt*, the workers conduct their wake in beer.

Alfred returns to the hostel drunk and maudlin, attacks the impotent verbiage of his militant and active friend and rejects the qualified optimism and sense of possibility in struggle of the friend for his own perception that 'Life stays as it always was'.

There is, then, a feeling in the film explicitly articulated by Alfred, internalised and lived by other workers, that their lives are impotent, subordinate, immutable. There is a clear congruity between this ideology and the presentation of their experiences in the naturalistic vignettes of working class *Alltagsleben*. Each lacks a perspective of other-ness, a relation to what Alfred's sober interlocutor in the hostel terms the 'total picture'.

We have indicated above some of the devices of narration that are employed in *Liebe Mutter* to contextualise the fragments of experience lived by the workers and to place those elements in the network of relations that constitute the social totality. The final sections of the film are animated by integrative impulses — formally in the way the narrative unfolds — and in the integration of the workers' experience and consciousness through their struggle with the 'whole picture'. They enact a movement in their 'actual consciousness' towards their 'maximum potential consciousness'.

The strike sequences are preceded by three 'voices'. One, that of a director of the firm, who speaks whilst escorting a party of visitors around the factory, is the voice of the German model 'social market' economy as articulated by its progenitor Ludwig Erhard. It speaks of solidarity, effectivity and mutual benefit for the 'social partners', capital and labour. A second, a *Betriebsrat*, states that there is no unity of interest between workers and bosses, that the workers do not have the strength to resist the imperatives of the bosses and that the employment laws offer no effective protection to workers. He voices this analysis to a group of angry workers after their dismissal: 'Stuff the laws up your arse and you'll find who's Master here.' The third, a worker, like the director and the *Betriebsrat*, begins his statement to camera and continues as a voice over shots of the workplace; his idea is that whilst he has no illusions about his own subordination his job is safe if the company continues to make profits. These three ideologies are challenged by the strike.

The workers strike piecemeal and spontaneously after a reduction in piece work rates; the solidarity of all sections of the factory labour force is in doubt and, consequentially, so is the success of the strike. The strike leaders are seen by the bosses individually and are inhibited from further action by the management rationale (that changes in the investment situation necessitate changes in piece rates and other measures.) The strike collapses. It is clear, though, that the workers' action, and their inability to defend their leadership from victimisation, fails only because they are insufficiently united. The unofficial leadership and the *Betriebs-räte* do not unite; consequently the *Betriebsräte* have no effective leverage on the management and the strike leaders lack the specific information about the firm's policy which would enable them to contradict the management's arguments. The different sections of the work force do not recognise their common interest *vis-à-vis* the employers and do not take action together. The agency whereby the shared interest of the workers and potential solidarity might be made active and actual is informed, conscious, human action. The anger and energy of Alfred that earlier in the film has been articulated destructively (the fight with the Berliner in the bar, the arguments in the hostel) is directed towards informing and activating his fellow workers. Alfred sees more of the 'whole picture' than does any other shop floor worker and his informed activity points the way forward. And his work in transporting components around the factory makes possible his activities of passing information, covertly agitating and acting as an integrative agent. After resumption of work, the dismissal of the militants and Alfred's ineffectual attempt to gain signatories to a petition for re-instatement (cf the similar scene in *Eight Hours Are Not a Day*), he narrates an epilogue.

The epilogue is spoken half to camera, half to an 'invisible' inter-locutor. Alfred concludes that the strike marks a beginning, and that the potentiality for the workers to understand the world and their place in it and to act to control their own lives rationally and consciously is on the way to realisation. This clear, rational optimism, vindicated by certain aspects of the current of events that the film has outlined, is juxtaposed with Alfred writing on a postcard: 'Liebe Mutter mir geht es gut . . . Dear Mother I'm OK. The machine work is better, I'm earning more and will move out of the hostel soon.' A series of delusions? At least an absence of the understanding evinced previously of his real situation and the lessons he's learned. The consciousness of the protagonist and his struggle to comprehend and take command of his life remain in doubt. The banal rhetoric of the postcard encompasses and suffocates the vitality of experience and enlightenment that the film has presented to the audience.

The film ends with an image of the postcard and the voice of the narrator over it, explaining that the first post-war recession is over, that investment is being raised and that the newspapers say that recovery is well under way.

The device of juxtaposing real relations and their ideological rationalisation and management that the first sequences in the film initiated closes *Liebe Mutter*. It is clear how ideology is lived, realised and reproduced. It is no less clear how it is to be transcended and the real relations it mystifies transformed: through the united praxis of conscious, active humans.

Der aufrechte Gang

Liebe Mutter, mir geht es gut

Liebe Mutter, mir geht es gut

81

Liebe Mutter, mir geht es gut

SCHNEEGLÖCKCHEN BLÜHN IM SEPTEMBER

Ziewer's second feature, though still evidently engaged in the contemporary world of the working class, represents that world substantially differently from *Liebe Mutter*. The world of *Schneeglöckchen* is more extensive, embracing the struggles and 'politics' of the domestic as well as productive economies, and is organised around a plurality of characters rather than being integrated only through Alfred as was *Liebe Mutter*. A more evident, and perhaps decisive, break is in the *mise en scène* of the two films. That of *Liebe Mutter* is very spare, with minimal signification coming from framing and camera movement. That of *Schneeglöckchen* is much richer, drawing on a wealth of cinematic conventions and adding to the variety of uses of the speaking voice the music of a political-rock group, Lokomotive Kreuzberg.

Ziewer, in 'More about the Uses of Film' (see Appendix 18), speaks of a shift in intention by the film-makers from *Liebe Mutter* to *Schneeglöckchen*, a shift from presentation of material, a kind of transmission by film-makers to a, hopefully receptive, audience, towards the engagement of the audience in the action of the film and through that engagement the development of an informed and transforming consciousness and praxis in the audience.

Much of Ziewer's argument and the construction of the film (its five sections, intertitles, chorus-like dialogue, interruption of dramatic and emotionally charged scenes) is, as his rejection of positive heroes, Aristotelian unity of action and character dramaturgy, and the invocation of Schiller suggest, an espousal of the form of the epic and the aesthetic of alienation. Yet against this there is a strong contradictory impulse in the aesthetic theory Ziewer enunciates (and practises in *Schneeglöckchen*), an impulse that combines with the element of alienation to offer the audience just that dialectic between involvement and reflection, emotion and reason which Ziewer perceives in the history and praxis of the labour movement. That impulse is located in the pleasure taken by the audience in their vicarious experience through identification with the struggles and activity of the film's characters. This identification, dispersed among a group of characters and thus with a collective problematic, is orchestrated by the songs, which refer not to the *peripeteia* of an individual but to the collective experience — 'Mehr Arbeit für weniger Lohn' ('More work for less pay'), 'So ein Tag so wunderschön wie heute' ('A day as wonderful as to-day'), by the *mise en scène*, and by the *activity* of the characters whether in a wage struggle or car rallying.

The first of the five sections of *Schneeglöckchen* is introduced by the title:

Ein Mann soll eingespart werden
Die Kolonne bestimmt ihren Preis.
(Reduced by one man,
The crew set their price.)

A chorus-like discussion of the demands the workers will make is laid over shots of their work and workplace and followed by a scene of three of the workers led by their *Vertrauensmann* (shop steward) Hannes striding through the factory yard accompanied on the sound track by Lokomotive Kreuzberg belting out 'Mehr Arbeit fur wenige Lohn'. These early scenes exemplify the movement in the unfolding of the film between distanced and involved moments of audience relation to the film text; distanced by the contradiction between the naturalistic location photography and the titles and formal diction of the speakers (unfamiliar cinematic conventions) and involved through the invitation offered by the insistent rhythm of Lokomotive Kreuzberg, the echoing of the forward movement of the three men through the factory yard by the camera into the rhetoric of the western (familiar cinematic conventions).

We do not propose to discuss *Schneeglöckchen in extenso* but to comment on the parts of the film which seem to us to distinguish it from *Liebe Mutter*. First of all, there is a more extensive representation of the levels and mediations in the relations lived by the characters. This appears chiefly in the treatment of the relation of the shop floor workers and their initiatives to their *Vertrauensmann* and *Betriebsräte* (the two levels of representation legitimised for plant bargaining in the BRD) and in the

83

relation of homelives to worklives.

Hannes, the group *Vertrauensmann*, is the central figure in the first part of the film. And it is predominantly his analysis and practice in the workplace struggles that is vindicated. The early scene of the three delegates crossing the yard is followed by a contestation in an office with an antagonistic besuited man. Shooting from over the shoulder of the man, the camera presents the situation as one of mutual hostility, and it is open to the audience to interpret the scene as confrontation between workers and management. It is only when the camera pans and reveals a shirt-sleeved colleague in the office and union posters on the wall that we know the suited man to be a *Betriebsrat*.* Later in the film the firm's *Vertrauensmänner* meet the management on whose side of the table the *Betriebsräte* sit. And at this meeting (the final scene in the second part of *Schneeglöckchen* — 'Der Betrieb wird an einen Konzern verkauft. Grosse Veränderungen kündigen sich an.' ('The firm is sold to a big combine. Big changes in prospect.')) Hannes in raising the question of the possible closure of the factory challenges the practice of the company and its owners who effectively, he argues, buy and sell workers. The chairman of the *Betriebsrat* closes the discussion by saying that Hannes' argument is political and outwith the remit of the meeting. The *Betriebsrat* is constituted principally as an agent of management in its negotiation of the demands and discontents of the workforce. (Though the expertise of the *Betriebsräte* is instrumental in achieving the qualified success through negotiation of the first struggle for 20 pfennigs.) However, the plurality of characters in *Schneeglöckchen* permits the presentation of another *Betriebsrat*, one on the side of the workers and it is he (the Diemal Ziewer refers to in Appendix 18) who tips off Hannes about the future developments in the company and mobilises the excavator shop. But it remains Hannes who is most consistently, centrally and successfully active for the workers and it is he who is shown extensively in his domestic economy and relations as well as at work.

In the first section Hannes and his wife are intending to go out for an evening at the *Volksbühne*; in the event she goes alone and he and another militant spend the evening typing and distributing a counter-statement to that day's letter from the management sent to all the workers (like petition signing, the management letter is a motif that recurs in *Arbeiterfilme*). The scene hints both at the range of German working-class culture and institutions and the strength which that extensive alternative culture offers the labour movement; and at the customary subordination of women to men and their imperatives, and at the frustration of the desires of the working class by the imperatives and agenda set by capital. The most striking instance in which the central thematic concern of *Schneeglöckchen* and its dominant aesthetic motif are realised,

---

*Betriebsrat can mean either 'works council' or 'works councillor'.

84

where the place of the male worker is posed relative to family and to social struggle and the formal dialectic between alienation and involvement is articulated, is the magnificent scene between Hannes and his daughter Katja. After an interview with Katja's teacher in which he learns that she has not been attending classes he seeks out Katja at a camp site where the family spend holidays. The argument between them takes place in the family tent and is constantly interrupted by friends' greetings and enquiries. Thus the charged dramatic scene between father and daughter constantly has its emotional intensification arrested, and so the audience may better reflect on the relations of the two antagonists and on the arguments that they offer each other. The points at issue between Hannes and Katja are of considerable interest but it's worth observing that this particular management of the dramaturgy permits both the maintenance of a reality principle for the scene through the motivated unidiegetic nature of the interruptions and also the channelling of audience attention towards reflection on the scene and interrogation of the issues it raises, rather than swamping sceptical interest through emotional intensity and direction of identification to either father or daughter to the exclusion of the other.

Hannes' argument is that Katja should accept the values of the *Gymnasium* and the implicit upward social mobility that the institution offers, and that the family as a whole is going short for her education. Katja rationalises her rejection of the *Gymnasium* by truanting in terms of the non-pertinence of its teaching to the class struggle. Hannes closes the argument by telling her that the class struggle should be left to those who know about it and further attempts resolution of the clash by wielding the threat of patriarchal authority over Katja — by locking her up (in a tent!). She continues to defy him. The framework of the argument is lost and resolved into a naked clash between authority and its refusal. The interest of the scene resides in the clash between on the one hand Hannes' attempt to subordinate at home (in the name of the values of the dominant culture) just the values that he, subordinated at work by the class that wields them, lives out in his resistance at work; and on the other Katja's adolescent ultra-leftism, preaching to her father the values by which he lives without the understanding by 'those who know about it' of the mediations through which class struggle, in whose name she argues, is expressed and fought. She does not, for instance, recognise the need for education as a means of survival and of augmenting the value of a wage worker's labour power in capitalist society. The conflict between Katja and Hannes is re-articulated in a coda where Hannes reproaches his wife for the absence of domestic harmony — his dream of an arcadia without conflict and contradiction if not to be achieved in macrocosm is to be enforced in microcosm — and she replies that he is always absent!

The other major character who is portrayed extensively, at work and at leisure, is Ed, a worker in the same shop as Hannes whose individualism and self interest is expressed in his hobby of car rallying, his refusal to accommodate or to recognise as legitimate the demands of his fiancée Erika, and his willingness to break solidarity with fellow workers in struggle to serve his own interests, and later, as the *Bildungsfilm* structured around him develops, to strive for solidarity among his workmates so that their leverage in the wage bargain may be increased. Ed also figures in what is for someone soaked in Fassbinder's *mise en scène* one of the most delightful scenes in *Schneeglöckchen*. He and Erika sit down at a café table divided by a bowl of flowers. Instead of the flowers obtruding between the lovers and between them and the camera throughout the scene, Ed simply picks them up and removes them — they never bother us again!

Ed represents a seemingly more rational and pleasurable principle of living than does Hannes. Instead of spending his evenings in the crucifyingly boring activity of addressing envelopes and the other small change of active trade unionism Ed goes drinking and hots up his car. During the day at work, rather than acting on the abstract principle of solidarity with other, unseen, workers he earns himself a bonus. The development of the narrative can be characterised as the unfolding of a convergence between Ed and Hannes; part of the unity in practice that Hannes and Diemal so carefully construct and that finds its expression in the successful strike for better compensation, the '40 pfennig mehr' and the triumphant mass singing of 'So ein Tag, so wunderschön wie heute' in the factory yard. It is in the construction of that solidarity that Hannes demonstrates the necessary condition for the realisation of the plurality of individual aspirations held by the workers (of whom Hannes and Ed are the most extensively represented): united action.

Schneeglöckchen, like *Liebe Mutter*, has a coda, its *Nachspiel* in which the contradiction between individualism and class solidarity seemingly transcended in the synthesis of the strike re-articulates itself. The unity that the workers have constructed, which the leadership, the conscious directed activity of Hannes and Diemal, has been instrumental in achieving, is threatened by Ed's affirmation of that unity in his scapegoating denunciation of a workmate, Udo, who hadn't joined their action. Hannes retorts that Ed and the others too could have been like Udo; that their unity is precarious and that just as their solidarity represented a real potentiality for Udo, a potentiality that it is, to a certain extent, just to rebuke him for not realising, so too Udo's scabbing is a real potentiality for all of them. The film ends with a tableau of a solemn, silent group of men sitting around a table covered with the wreckage of their celebrations.

Schneeglöckchen blühn im September

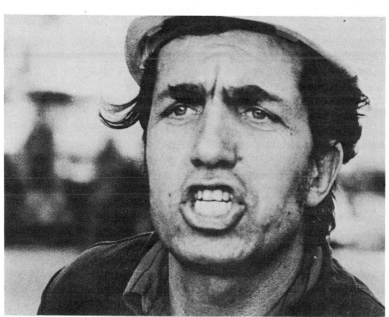

Schneeglöckchen blühn im September

Not all people exist in the same Now. They do so only externally, by virtue of the fact that they may all be seen today. But that does not mean that they are living at the same time with others.

Rather, they carry earlier things with them, things which are intricately involved. One has one's times according to where one stands corporeally, above all in terms of classes. Times older than the present continue to affect older strata; here it is easy to return or dream one's way back to older times. Certainly, a person who is simply awkward and who for that reason is not up to the demands of his position, is only personally unable to keep up. But what if there are other reasons why he does not fit into a very modern organisation, such as the after-effects of peasant descent, what if he is an earlier type? In general, different years resound in the one that has just been recorded and prevails. Moreover, they do not emerge in a hidden way as previously but rather, they contradict the Now in a very peculiar way, awry, from the rear. The strength of this untimely course has become evident; it promised nothing less than new life, despite its looking to the old. Even the masses flock to it since the unbearable Now at least seems different with Hitler, who paints good old things for everyone. There is nothing more unexpected, nothing more dangerous than this power of being at once fiery and puny, contradicting and nonsynchronous. The workers are no longer alone with themselves and the bosses. Many earlier forces, from quite a different Below, are beginning to slip between. (Bloch, 1977.)

In *Der aufrechte Gang* the shift towards a more extensive representation and intensification of the dialectic of distanciation and involvement evident in the passage from *Liebe Mutter* to *Schneeglöckchen* is continued. *Der aufrechte Gang* poses more general problems than do the earlier films, although still located within the milieu and experience of wage workers. Instead of implicitly asking how exploitation is manifested and fought at the place of work in the wage bargain, *Der aufrechte Gang* asks how exploitation is experienced by men and women. How must they struggle in order to achieve an 'aufrechter Gang'? This category ('self respect') Ziewer draws from Ernst Bloch, who articulated it in relation to Thomas Münzer, a leading communist ideologist and organiser of the 16th century Peasant's War — the location of Ziewer's current, as yet unrealised film project. How do the relations that flow from the primary capital-labour contradiction in capitalism manifest themselves in other contradictions; between men and women, Germans and Turks, youth and age, city and country, craft and mass production; between direct experience and the representation of those experiences in ideology, in the consciousness of those who live the experiences and in the discourses of mass communication?

Ziewer takes one of the *Montan* industries, steel production, as the site for the dispute around which a major theme of *Der aufrechte Gang* is articulated. This is an industry in which co-determination is weighted more favourably towards labour than elsewhere, and which is thus the most favourable site for a positive treatment of the 'social partnership' between capital and labour. Thus the inability of a *Montan* industry to satisfy the aspirations of its workers makes more thorough any critique of the 'social market economy' in general. Another difference between the construction of the fictional world of *Der aufrechte Gang* and those of Ziewer's other *Arbeiterfilme* is achieved by showing the worker as a consumer as well as a producer. To be sure the moment of consumption is part of *Schneeglöckchen*; Ed requires more money to enable him to compete effectively in car rallying and part of his tranformation in *Schneeglöckchen* comes as he learns that the 'obvious' response to a desire for more consumption, more production, is not applicable in the labour market of capitalism. His electrical maintenance work produces him a bonus, but the higher production the flexible disposal of his labour power incurs does not offer him any enduring benefit. In capitalism, he learns, wage workers paradoxically can only raise their wages, and hence their consumption, through temporary curtailment of production in a strike. But in *Der aufrechte Gang* Dieter's aspiration to a car and the wah-wah that his son Andy regards him as responsible for providing could be paid for in a number of ways — through successful militant action at the steelworks, through his wife Hannah taking the job she desires as a manageress, or through the adoption of the craft production and small capitalist route of Dieter's father and brother. The resolution of the economic lack in *Der aufrechte Gang* can therefore follow a number of routes.

This uncertainty makes the narrative itself more interesting. It seems to us no accident that Ziewer returns in his writings ('More about the Uses of Film' is a good example) to quite formal, classical problems of narration; the place of suspense, for example, and the ideological problematic of a film more complex and extensive than that of *Schneeglöckchen, Liebe Mutter* or other *Arbeiterfilme*. The integrating centres of the narrative are the institutions of family, work place and, perhaps, the hero — though centring the film on Dieter strikes us as a weakness. Hannah's emancipation and directing role in the action come, perhaps, over-late. But compare Ziewer's treatment of *Der aufrechte Gang* and the hero with Fassbinder's (see Märthesheimer's attribution of Bloch's category to Jochen, the hero of *Eight Hours Are Not a Day* in 'What can the hero do?', Appendix 14). For Ziewer the hero and his aspiration towards self-confidence and self-respect are problematic; in Fassbinder's film, Jochen's moral stature and his status as a positive directing hero are never in question. He, as Märthesheimer says, can change the world whereas the Ziewer hero has to change himself before he can change the world.

These centres, hero, family and work place, are placed in relation to a set of like institutions; variations and oppositions in the form and practice of the institutions are played in the film. Thus work is shown in the form of craft, small-scale independent capitalist production, in the wrought-iron business run by Dieter's father and brother Werner; in the form of the distribution and service sector, in the *Konditorei* where Hannah works and which she aspires to manage; and in the form of large-scale basic industry, in the skilled work of Dieter. The family is present, centrally, as a two generation German working-class family, but that nuclear family is placed in relation to the extended family of the grandparents, the brother and uncle, and in relation to the enigmatic but clearly very different life of the Turks.

The practice of extension through pairing and variation is also manifested in a temporal plane, though in an attenuated form. The film takes place in a tightly compressed 'present' of a week or so. Temporal extension is achieved by showing Dieter's retention of a press photograph and report of the successful 1969 strike in the steelworks and by similar witnesses to history such as Franz Wittkowski's certificate of craft skill (issued during the Third Reich). These objects testify to different historical possibilities from those realised in the present and give a kind of materiality to the non-synchronous contradiction that is pre-eminently played out *within* Dieter but also between him (and the other workers) and the steel employers, and him and his family.

Throughout *Der aufrechte Gang* Dieter is thrown out of the solid and familiar structures of his 'lived ideology'. The circumstances that attend his participation in the steelworkers' strike force him into a new, more conscious, relation to his roles of worker, father, son and husband, and towards recognising the contradictions within those roles and between them and his 'project' of self-respect. Dieter's place as hero is situated in the narrow margin between tragedy, in which the hero is subordinated by the world, and *Bildung*, in which the hero learns to comprehend and thus possess himself and the world. Dieter neither experiences the enlightenment and confidence that customarily accrue to the fortunate positive hero of a *Bildungsroman* nor does the world and its order subjugate him as is customary in tragedy. Rather, he comes to know more surely but with greater personal uncertainty the project of the positive hero: changing the world.

The first section of the film shows Dieter displaced from his customary patterns of existence by his participation in the strike. Far from dominating his world either as father or worker, he is thrown into an enforced leisure that is difficult to fill. He becomes an instrument in the directed lives of his children (they casually allocate him the task of getting the record player mended) just as he, soon, directs Hannah to economise on their household expenses so he may buy a v w Passat, and refuses her desire to become manageress of the *Konditorei,* an action that would raise their disposable income. Following the film's first 'punctuation' by a shot panning with a bus travelling through a lush rural landscape to discover the steelworks (this shot is repeated later in the film as the third punctuation mark; the second shows a train moving through a rural scene with a distant skyline of cooling towers), extensive sequences show Dieter and Hannah at their separate workplaces. Hannah is at the *Konditorei,* where she is in command of her world and troubled only by her husband's refusal to permit her to become manageress of a new branch shop.

Dieter is shown joining other strikers outside the gate of the steelworks; the workers converse and offer a variety of attitudes to their action, the strikers are photographed by management, the full-time official of IG Metall goes in to the works to negotiate and a *Betriebsrat* reports to the strikers that another plant in the combine, at Osnabrück, has struck.

The antagonisms within the family are further articulated in a scene between Dieter and his son Andy. Both are musicians, but their music *divides* them. Dieter stops Andy playing his guitar, just as he covers the canary to stop it singing, so he may play his accordion undisturbed. Dieter and Gaby discuss her homework, Hannah returns from work and is greeted by a friendly patriarchal slap on the bum. The nuclear family undergoes a fissile reaction to Dieter's bad temper when hearing the news on the radio and is dispersed to their separate territories; the children, Andy and Gaby to their bedrooms, Hannah to the kitchen, Dieter to the living room. The news states that some strikers are returning to work. The family fuses into a silent group around the radio, only to be dispersed again by Dieter's projection of his anxiety at the course of the strike into antagonism directed at his family. This scene and most others in *Der aufrechte Gang* are presented in 'real time', with few ellipses and very little cutting to speed up the narrative. Generally fictional time and the real time taken for actions *within* a scene are the same.

The family quarrel provokes Dieter to go to the factory gate and complain to the *Vertrauensmann,* Georg, that his domestic peace is being disturbed by the strike. What's 30 pfennig compared to that? It may be a lot for a Turk but not for a German worker. The enigmatic Turkish *Gastarbeiter* at the steelworks are presented from the outside but appear models of solidarity, experiencing no contradiction between their struggle as workers, their place as individuals or as members of families. The film briefly presents them as inhabiting an autonomous sub-culture insulated from the mass media and the imperatives of the dominant order and its ideology that assail Dieter. The unity of the Turks is juxtaposed with scenes portraying the isolation and alienation of the

91

film's two central figures, Dieter and Hannah. Before the film's second punctuation (the shot of a train travelling through the countryside) we see Dieter travelling at night on a bus; fade to Hannah standing alone outside a *Konditorei* that is being renovated. Finally Dieter watches the news on television in a bar and learns that the Osnabrück night shift has returned to work. A drunken worker expresses his satisfaction that the strikers are suffering; why should they do better than us?

The first section of the film tracks the fragmentation of the integument — not of the body politic under pressure from the workers' actions but of Dieter's life. He is not changing the world, rather the world is changing him, and the familiar roles and relations he has lived are thrown into question. Participation in the strike has not led him to experience greater control of his life, rather it has isolated him in a destructive asociality.

The central section of the film explores the possibility of solidarity offered to Dieter by his father and brother; the appeal to a proletarian of petty bourgeois life and ideology based on small-scale artisanal production. The presentation of the mass media is a major theme of the film, and this requires exposition before discussion of the film's movement towards re-integration of Dieter into sociality, passing through the false unity offered by his parents and their mode of life, to the possibility of a more *aufrechte* comradeship.

Broadcasting, the television at home and in the bar and the radio at home have all been presented in *Der aufrechte Gang* as performing their customary task of reporting on industrial disputes, emphasising the factors that tend towards the resumption of work, the unreasonableness of the workers' demands and the impropriety of their action. The relation of Dieter and his family to the news broadcasts is on the one hand one of dependence on it for information of vital concern. On the other hand, there is a paradigm clash between the dominant ideology that has socialised them and which is expressed by mass communications, and their own experience, here most importantly of the strike, which cannot be reconciled with this dominant ideology. This clash between experience and the dominant ideology when experience lacks an interpretative paradigm — a counter-hegemonic ideology — within which it can make sense produces scepticism, confusion, isolation and violent, petulant discontent.

The most extensive treatment of mass communications in the film is concerned with the press. During Dieter's spell in the steelworks on emergency duty he is interviewed by a journalist, Dohm, who is being conducted around the works by a foreman, Axmann. Prior to the encounter with the journalist the foreman has removed from display at Dieter's work bench a newspaper photograph of Dieter with accordion, in a group of striking workers during the successful 1969 steelworks strike. Dieter refuses to assent to the journalist's definitions of the strike, which Dohm attempts to get him to make his own and quote back to him, but finally allows Axmann to speak for him. He refuses to adopt the views offered by the journalist but does not actively contest them. The interview ends with a question on the relations between Germans and *Gastarbeiter*. Dieter again refuses the journalist's definition of a gap between German and Turkish workers and states that a *cultural* gap exists but that this does not affect their working together nor the common desire for a speedy end to the dispute. The final shot of Dohm photographing Dieter pretending to work is a mid-shot with a dark foreground and the frame bisected by diagonal steel struts and is accompanied by discordant downbeat music. The implication of trouble to come is realised, on the train journey to his parents' home. Dieter reads the newspaper account of his views on the strike in which he is represented as a racist blackleg.

The central section of the film takes place principally in the home and workshop of Dieter's father. Dieter's brother Werner greets the Rheine Wittkowskis (Dieter and his family) at the railway station (built in archaic rural half-timbered style) with the news that the conformity of his family, notably the Mother's diligent churchgoing, has been rewarded by an order for their metalworking business. The sociality represented by the parental family is one of conformity and involves the subordination of individuals; as such it is perceived to be inadequate by Dieter. He refuses assent to his father's and brother's congratulations on his position as represented in the newspaper, but this time, instead of his refusal being articulated passively as in the interview with Dohm, he actively contests his father's view. The rejection of the viewpoint of the father, i.e. the ideology of conformity to the dominant order, takes place in the workshop of the small family metalworking business run by Werner and his father.

Dieter and his father enter the workshop talking of the family business and the deal with a local entrepreneur, Berghof, who will resell the production of wrought iron candlesticks to department stores. As Dieter enters, the camera pans with him and the first shot of the workshop scene ends with Dieter at right of frame looking at the candlesticks, his father to left of frame looking across to Dieter, the two men separated by a pillar in the centre. We cut to a two-shot, Dieter and father occupying the left half of the frame facing each other and discussing the iron church screen the firm has made (the order secured by the mother's obsequious piety); the father expresses his approval of Dieter's statements in the newspaper. There is then a sequence of shot/counter-shot between Dieter and his father as his father reads aloud the anti-Turkish views the newspaper attributes to Dieter. Dieter protests that he has been misquoted and that he has never stabbed anyone in the back. His father generalises this into a kind of petty bourgeois *misère*; it is often the innocents who get beaten in life. Dieter turns this platitude back to a specific instance and refers to a childhood beating by his father for, supposedly, breaking the windows of

93

the editor of a Communist newspaper when his father knew that he was not responsible. He argues that the beating was administered to protect the children of a local capitalist who, in return, granted the family business a soft loan through the *Genossenschaft* (an association for mutual assistance of craftsmen and small businessmen). Dieter's argument for the primacy of the principle of justice is countered by his father with the pragmatic argument that in comparison to the prosperity of the family an unjust beating administered to a child was, and is, of trivial importance. During the increasingly heated argument Dieter moves across to his father and the shot/counter-shot *mise en scène* returns to a two-shot. There is then a cut to the oxygen bottles and welding gear in the workshop, behind which Hannah is revealed. The camera tracks to reveal her and the sound track continues with the sound of the men's argument. Then we track to a medium close-up of Hannah's face and cut to a close-up two-shot of Dieter and his father at the point of the clearest and most intense articulation of the conflict between the principles of pragmatism and justice they are arguing — ethics that are rooted in the places in the sphere of production that both men occupy. To survive as a small capitalist and producer Dieter's father had and has to conform to the norms of the dominant order. Within the terms set by his own experience his son Dieter's imperatives are Utopian. Dieter lives in a world in which he has no stake in the maintenance of the *status quo* (at least in the social relations of production, though arguably he has an interest in the maintenance of female subordination to male dominance). Rather, in order to realise his own interests and what he perceives as justice he has to refuse the dominant order, hence his reluctant and predominantly passive participation in the strike. Following the culmination of the argument between the two men, there is a cut to a close-up of Hannah's face and a return to a mid-two-shot of the two men at opposite sides of the frame facing each other. Then there is a cut to Hannah silently leaving the workshop. The camera remains on the door and witnesses her re-entry as she tells the men to return to the house. Next we cut to a two-shot of the men. Hannah enters the shot and the father leaves, with Hannah and Dieter remaining in two-shot. Dieter leaves without addressing Hannah. This workshop scene exemplifies the characteristic operation of Ziewer's *mise en scène* in disposing the audience's attention and involvement amongst a plurality of characters and viewpoints. *Mise en scène* is used as a signifying code to intensify and underscore elements in the action, and to orientate and re-orientate the audience to different elements in the drama.

Dieter's refusal of the role offered him by his parents and their values is confirmed by Werner's appropriation of Dieter's opportunity to propose a toast at the family dinner table and by Werner taunting him with his inability to provide a car or a wah wah for Andy, to achieve as an economically potent male, and is echoed by the father who lectures

Dieter on the irresponsibility of the steel strike and the necessity for men to act consistently with a responsibility to provide for their family. Thus family relationships present themselves to Dieter as an integument of oppression in which there is no place for his half-articulated, half-understood strivings. He refuses that construction of sociality and leaves the family party alone. Dieter's re-integration into sociality begins only after his return home, when Hannah forces him to attend to her and recognise her decision to take the job at the *Konditorei*, and after his refusal of the threat contained in a letter from the steelworks management that dismissal will follow continuation of strike action and the role in which the newspaper report has cast him. He and Hannah exchange looks after each has affirmed their challenge to the forces that subordinate and exploit them: for Hannah, Dieter and patriarchy; for Dieter, the boss, the newspaper and capitalism. They go to the steelworks picket together.

The management succeed in reopening the plant and dispersing the pickets. Dieter is restrained by Georg from a quixotic gesture of defiance that would lose him his job and the film ends with Dieter, Hannah and Georg together in a cafeteria. Dieter, despondent at the failure of the strike and the emptiness of the rhetoric of solidarity, writes 'Scheisse' on the strike leaflets, and claims that no one can be trusted, that everyone cringes before they are hit. Georg answers that the defeat of the strike was simply a question of incorrect tactics, but his answer is not adequate to the intensity of the despair and isolation experienced by Dieter. Hannah reflects that Dieter's pessimism is unjustified, that there were people who acted honourably: Dieter himself, who would strike again, the Turks, the lorry driver who refused to cross the picket line, the worker Bahlke who defied the management, the police who were guilty at their role as strike breakers. All these, she argues, represent a certain principle of hope, but, she goes on, it's not enough. The film ends with a shot of the steelworks in production and a title giving the shop stewards' resolution on the return to work: 'Our justified demands still stand'.

The contradictions presented in *Der aufrechte Gang* remain unresolved. The course that the film has followed is one that, through the microcosm of a family, tracks the project of emancipation and achievement of an 'aufrechter Gang' in contemporary life. For Hannah some definite progress has been made. For Dieter the possibility has come to exist. He has been presented with experiences of conflict that challenge the ideological paradigms by which he lives, but whether he is able to consciously integrate these experiences into principles for future struggle remains uncertain.

Ziewer describes *Der aufrechte Gang* (in *Film in der Bundesrepublik Deutschland*, March 1976):

Liebe Mutter and *Schneeglöckchen* were particularly concerned with the

95

situation at work. In *Der aufrechte Gang* the centre is now the microcosm of a family. A man is confronted with the question of the moral content of his existence; his wife tries to emancipate herself by querying her own position in the marriage. The film's content is how the two people arrange their lives, how they try to find themselves and each other . . . Most people are united in their longing to emancipate themselves from dependences and unnecessary adaptation to strange circumstances. I think they want to have a value of their own. How this is to be brought about, that is the question confronting every individual person in his own specific circumstances. *Der aufrechte Gang* I hope encourages this. For it shows people who want to make their dream come true without escaping everyday life in the course of it.

WDR's drama department received in Ziewer's exemplary *Der aufrechte Gang* fulfilment of their project of fostering the development of an aesthetic adequate to the representation of the articulation and weight of the social contradictions that structure the experience of the contemporary German working class. The critical realism that grew out of a long heritage, but specifically the experiments of *Erwin, Rote Fahnen, Eight Hours* and *Liebe Mutter*, peaks in *Der aufrechte Gang*, which seems in retrospect the swansong of the genre. Ziewer's latest feature, *Aus der Ferne sehe ich dieses Land (I See This Country From Afar)* is concerned with isolation. Using Chilean refugees living in West Berlin, and particularly 16 year old Lucho, who is marooned between two cultures, an uncertain future and a closed past, it signifies a general alienated relation between people and their contemporary world and 'alienates' (*verfremdet*) the presentation of daily life in West Berlin by showing it from the point of view of the Chileans. Of the films made after *Der aufrechte Gang*, the most powerful candidate for recognition as an *Arbeiterfilm* is Gisela Tuchtenhagen and Klaus Wildenhahn's documentary *Emden geht nach USA* (1977). Made for Norddeutscher Rundfunk in co-production with WDR's third channel, West Deutsches Fernsehen (WDF), it's a film about the closure of VW Emden. But its account of the history of Friesland and its workers is too specific, too little fictionalised to be really considered as addressing the same kind of problems of representation as *Lohn und Liebe, Eight Hours* or *Schneeglöckchen*. It is a matter for regret that the *Arbeiterfilm*'s engagement with the *Alltag* of the German working class and its insertion into the public sphere of network TV programming is at an end. Particularly so because a number of the aesthetic problems that the WDR drama department set themselves in initiating the experiments from the late sixties to the mid seventies had been solved in *Der aufrechte Gang*.

96

The aesthetic category within which we have discussed Ziewer's work and other *Arbeiterfilme* is that of realism, an aesthetic system and practice that has been almost unassailably constituted as archaic and conservative by contemporary British film theory and criticism. Since the first of *Cahiers du Cinéma's* new courses and the founding of *Cinéthique* (1969), the backwash of the post-1968 French current in film analysis has dominated British film culture. *Afterimage*, founded in 1970, printed Godard's political film manifesto 'What is to be done?' in its first issue and *Screen*, flushed with a shot of French imported iodine, metamorphosed from a sleepy axolotl into an aggressive salamander following the trajectory implied by the reprinting of the *Cahiers* article 'Cinema/Ideology/Criticism' by Comolli and Narboni in 1971. The polemical acts of *Screen* and *Afterimage* in appropriating the lessons of the French and mediating them in Britain successfully constituted film analysis as a political activity. The central thesis of Comolli and Narboni was that:

> In France the majority of films, like the majority of books and magazines, are produced and distributed by the capitalist economic system and within the dominant ideology . . . What the camera in fact registers is the vague, unformulated, untheorized, unthought-out world of the dominant ideology . . . the film-maker's first task is to show up the cinema's so called 'depiction of reality'. If he [*sic*] can do so there is a chance that we will be able to disrupt or possibly even sever the connection between the cinema and its ideological function. . . We would stress that only action on both fronts, 'signified' and 'signifiers', has any hope of operating against the prevailing ideology. Economic/political and formal action have to be indissolubly welded. (Comolli and Narboni *Screen* vol. 12, no. 1.)

In Britain, though, it is principally on the front of the signifiers that battle has been joined; the second front, apart from sporadic raids, remains to be opened. And the Althusserian problematic that informed the work of Comolli and Narboni and which retained a notion of determination, albeit one that like the shattering of the illusion that attends the transformation of Cinderella's coach (ideology) into a pumpkin (economy) occurs only at a very late moment, has been displaced by a post-Althusser epistemology of 'no necessary correspondence' between the major instances of the political, the ideological and the economic. This tendency has constituted film-making (and theory) as a 'struggle in ideology' in which disruption of the customary procedures, codes, of the dominant ideology is the appropriate activity for progressive film-makers. This emancipation of the subordinated polysemic potentiality of the sign from the repressive metalanguage of the dominant ideology has been seen as necessary and sufficient and, of course, entails a comprehensive hostility to the aesthetic supposed to be the instrument through which the ruling class continue to rule: realism.

Latterly, a major source that is drawn on to legitimise this anti-realism is the theory of Bertolt Brecht. It is interesting to examine the different appropriation of Brecht by Ziewer and other *Arbeiterfilm* makers in their film-making — and their rationale for their film-making — and their emphasis on a realism in Brechtian theory and practice. The classic sites at which a post-Brechtian anti-realism is articulated are Colin Mac-Cabe's articles in *Screen* (MacCabe, 1974 and 1976), the latter written in response to Colin McArthur's (1975) engagement with some of Mac-Cabe's theses in his article '*Days of Hope*'.

MacCabe (1976) summarises the argument of his first, substantial, article:

> While traditional debates about realism have centred on content and the ability to reflect reality, classic realism should be considered as centrally defined by a certain formal organisation of discourses whereby the narrative discourse is placed in a situation of dominance with regard to the other discourses of the text. The narrative discourse does not just dispose the other discourses, it compares them with the truth or falsity transparently available through its own operations. The political question of such a realism is then whether this dominant discourse is in conflict with the predominant ideological discourses of the time. I argued further, however, that this formal organisation of discourses is fundamentally comprised by the relationship between reader and text on which it depends. The simple access to truth which is guaranteed by the meta-discourse depends on a repression of its own operations and this repression confers an imaginary unity of position on the reader from which the other discourses in the film can be read. (pp. 98-9.)

MacCabe argues that Brecht's theory and practice are productive in challenging the erroneous epistemology and political entailments of the practice of classic realism. We do not dissent from his conclusion that Brecht has much to offer us but we see the productivity of the Brechtian heritage leading rather towards Ziewer and *Der aufrechte Gang* (which we suspect MacCabe would regard as 'classic realism'). Brecht in fact embraces much more of the lineage that MacCabe hints at in his use elsewhere in his article of the words 'totality', 'realism', 'Lukács' than MacCabe himself acknowledges and more than the title of the New Left Books translation of the Brechtian theses (that remained unpublished in Brecht's lifetime) 'Against Georg Lukács' allows.

Certainly there is a substantial critique of a pervasive aesthetic practice in MacCabe's article, but not of realism. It seems to us that his critique is actually of the practice of naturalism, a practice of which the Hegelianized Marxism to which he once refers offers various critiques, all adequate, whether the Frankfurt School's notion of 'one dimensionality' or, more substantially, Lukács's conception of naturalism as an aesthetic of the immanent and phenomenal. Lukács does distinguish between realism and naturalism and this central distinction is ignored in MacCabe's categories of 'classic realism' and often the even broader 'representation'. MacCabe's criterion is 'discourse which will fully adequate the real'. This seems to us a formulation that is close enough to pass muster to the classic Marxist aesthetic position on realism as articulated at successively greater length and sophistication by Marx Engels, Lenin and Lukács, but which seriously misreads, and misrepresents, that tradition. (But see MacCabe's interesting attempt to square this particular circle in MacCabe, 1979.)

The key problem lies in MacCabe's use of the word 'fully'. Broadly, the central tradition in Marxist aesthetics, Marx, Engels, Lenin, Lukács, argues for art as a mode of cognition and constitutes the central aesthetic/epistemological problem as one of devising or constructing a form or mode of representation that within the confines of artistic representation (mimesis) represents the totality of the *extensive* relations and determinations of the material world. This *intensive* representation of an *extensive* totality can never 'fully adequate the real'. Rather, the mimesis has to be constructed on sound epistemological principles (affirming the materiality of the world and the presence of structures governing its seeming heterogeneity) and comprehending the crucial determining forces and their relations to the extensive totality intensively, so that the artistic mimesis may function as a satisfactory heuristic device. The question hinges not on whether representation can ever 'fully adequate' that which it takes as a referent, but whether the structures and relations out of which the real is generated correspond to those present in the mimesis.

Der aufrechte Gang might, it seems, have been conceived as a refutation of MacCabe's central thesis that realism, because it subordinates all other discourses to the narrative discourse, which is the only one to guarantee 'truth', cannot accomodate contradictions within the text. Certainly we're happy to appropriate it as such. For not only does it treat a plurality of contradictions but those contradictions are articulated in such a way that 'the end is not guaranteed from the beginning nor does this certainty enable the reader to place him or herself in a position of unity from which the material is dominated'. (MacCabe, 1976, p.100.) Contradictions in *Der aufrechte Gang* are indeed unresolved. This indeed seems to us to be a classical aspect of a major mode of realism; one that Lukács categorises as critical realism and differentiates from a more fully adequate system of representation, socialist realism, precisely on the ground that the critical realist lacks the intellectual perspective, the consciousness, that is ultimately a class consciousness, to perceive how through social transformation and the achievement of the ascendancy of the working class contradictions perceived as irreconcilable might be resolved. But to demand simply that contradictions should be presented not only as unresolved but as *unresolvable* is to demand a presentation of them as immanent, without causation. The import of MacCabe's thesis is to deny any principles of relation, correction and integration in the fictional world other than that of pure contingency. It is the aesthetic of a conception of the social whole as one animated by 'no necessary correspondence' between its autonomous spheres of (at least) the political, the ideological, and the economic. Whilst a single narrative fiction film offers no conclusive rebuttal of that epistemology, at least it may demonstrate that there are devices of construction available to the realist film-maker in which the urgency and reality of social contradiction may be represented as both determined and unresolved, their resolution not 'closed' through the action of the narrative 'metalanguage' yet open to *future* resolution through the determination of human action and comprehensible in their source and effect.

In his presentation of the experience of alienation by the worker from the value created through his labour, Ziewer employs at an early point in the film a device which has some similarity to that which McArthur has argued does 'handle contradiction':

MacCabe's assertion [is] that the classic realist text is incapable of handling contradiction. In *Days of Hope* there is a scene in which Pritchard, the gentlemanly Northern coal owner, lectures Ben and the three arrested Durham miners on the excellence of the British tradition of peaceful gradual and constitutional reform while, in the background, the soldiers brought in to suppress dissent in the coalfield indulge in bayonet practice. I am not clear how such a scene fails to handle contradiction in MacCabe's terms. (McArthur, 1975, p.143.)

To this MacCabe rejoined:

What McArthur here confuses is the narrative's ability to state a contradiction which it has already resolved, and the narrative's ability to produce a contradiction which remains unresolved and is thus left for the reader to resolve and act out. In other words while McArthur looks simply for contradiction in the text, we must look at how contradiction is produced in the audience. In the example McArthur cites there is a contradiction between what the mine-owner says and what the picture shows. But this is exactly the classic realist form which privileges the image against the word to reveal that what the mine-owner says is false. In this manner our position of knowledge is guaranteed. (MacCabe, 1976, p.100.)

100

It is not clear to us from MacCabe's argument how an effect in the audience (the production of contradiction) is to be assessed from textual analysis if not by looking for contradiction in the text. But his argument about the specific textual feature in *Days of Hope* is clear: that one element of the discourse or one discourse in the text 'masters' the others and resolves them.

Now, whether or not *Days of Hope* does in fact present an unresolved contradiction, certainly there are such scenes in *Der aufrechte Gang*, as when Dieter first goes to the picket line. The camera presents the scene outside the steelworks gate from a variety of viewpoints, and no stable locus for identification is offered. The camera participates and it observes; the *mise en scène* itself enacts a dialectic of involvement and distanciation. The film proceeds with a series of shot/reverse shots between Vollmer of IG Metall and various strikers as they encourage him to press for the thirty pfennigs, the camera adopting the position of an 'invisible guest' among the strikers. A medium close-up of workers talking follows a shot of the management photographers (the camera taking the point of view of the photographers). It then successively adopts the point of view of the *Betriebsrat* inside the factory gates looking out at the mass of German and Turkish workers, then the point of view of the group, and finally rises above the group in which it has been immersed to observe and show workers outside, *Betriebsrat* inside the gate, and the furnaces themselves. The variety of points of view adopted by the camera in this simple sequence problematises the position from which events are narrated and related. Ziewer's method exemplifies a retention of openness in the narrative and avoidance of closure by the dominant metalanguage that MacCabe insists necessarily attends realism.

There is a similar moment in *Der aufrechte Gang* (in a sequence following that outside the steelworks), where Dieter is seen at home with manufacturers' catalogues for a VW Passat, calculating how he might afford one. Speech from the television insists on the irresponsibility of the workers' demands in the face of German industry's declining competitiveness. Image, as MacCabe argues, does seem to master sound. However, the conversation between Dieter and Hannah that ensues about how to afford the car opens a concern that animates much of the rest of the film and strongly problematises the reading of the contradiction between the ideology of the television news and that of the strikers. As Lukács observes (Lukács, 1963, p.17) no epistemology *necessarily* attaches to an aesthetic device; rather its purport is determined by the set of relations within which it is placed. And a consistent practice in *Der aufrechte Gang* is to replace, recontextualise and revise the judgements, values and readings offered elsewhere in the film; not finally in a 'truth' that sums up and resolves the contradictions but in a demonstration of the power and mode of operation of the forces that structure the way the

101

characters make their lives. It shows, in Ziewer's (1976) words, the process of 'people who want to make their dreams come true without escaping everyday life in the course of it'; the process of achieving an 'aufrechter Gang'.

Hannah and Dieter's relationship is one of considerable potentiality only some of which is realised because of the subordination of Hannah. Her emancipation offers her not only 'der aufrechte Gang' but a strength and clarity of mind that can be lent to Dieter. There is, though, characteristically in Ziewer's dramaturgy always a materiality to the postures that the characters strike and which may be readily interpreted by the viewer as ideological and inappropriate. It is easy, and correct, to perceive the relationship between Dieter and Hannah as patriarchal and to see as male chauvinism Dieter's attempted denial of Hannah's desire to take on an (again chimerical, ideological but nonetheless material) autonomy as shop manageress. Yet there is, the fiction states, a substance to Dieter's resistance just as there is to Hannah's choice. The change she initiates will mean (other things remaining the same and the film offers no concrete possibility of Dieter, for instance, giving up working on shifts as a maintenance engineer) that they see each other only once every three weeks.

The specific purport of MacCabe's articles has been to specify realism as a mode of representation that through its unquestioned prioritisation of the discourse of narration cannot 'deal with the real as contradictory' . . . 'in a reciprocal movement the classic realist text ensures the position of the subject in a relation of dominant specularity.' Both these statements seem to us to be open to objection as exemplifying a prescriptive formalism analogous to that which Brecht found in Lukács. Elsewhere in his article MacCabe rightly observes that artistic practices have different effectivities at different moments in history. To argue that there is a *necessary* relation between text and consumer, whether enforcing 'dominant specularity' or not, denies this conjunctural factor and is open to simple empirical objections such as the status of narration in Henry James' novels, the relation of subject to the text in Brecht's *The Mother,* or 'against the grain' feminist readings of patriarchal texts. It is, though, the question of contradiction that was specifically taken up in the attenuated debate between McArthur and MacCabe and it is in relation to this question and the implications for 'political cinema' of a kind very different from *The Nightcleaners,* backed in *Screen's* second issue on Brecht as 'the most important political film to have been made in this country', that it is instructive to examine the treatment of contradiction in *Der aufrechte Gang.* Ziewer's work is a film that external evidence leads us to suppose is no less a lesson learnt from Brecht than other more evidently fissured and alienated texts and which itself offers Brecht a brief homage in the programme schedule shown on a television set towards the end.

102

Der aufrechte Gang

Der aufrechte Gang

CHAPTER 7

The Demise of the *Arbeiterfilm*

The circumstances surrounding the demise of the *Arbeiterfilm* provide an object lesson in the contradictions between the liberal ethic of public service broadcasting and the ideological needs of a capitalist society which stretch beyond the documentary representation of contemporary life into the fields of art and culture; areas which although they are frequently seen as being above and beyond politics and economics are essential elements in the way a society understand itself and how it survives. The work of the WDR Cultural and Drama Departments under Klaus von Bismarck, Hans-Geert Falkenberg and Günter Rohrbach challenged the cosy cultural concepts of the German industrial establishment too directly for it to allow their work to continue. Accordingly a three-fold strategy was developed which drew on the classic elements of communication theory (see, for example Klapper, 1960, pp. 129-132). The three elements in the strategy were to discredit WDR as a broadcasting institution; to shackle the dramaturgy of the *Arbeiterfilme;* and to replace the senior personnel who were responsible for permitting the production of the *Arbeiterfilme* within WDR with new and more acceptable executives.

THE BID TO DISCREDIT WDR

To discredit a public broadcasting institution such as WDR was no easy task, given its explicit legitimation by the political establishment of North Rhine-Westphalia. Nevertheless, the very editorial independence asserted by Klaus von Bismarck in separating the WDR programming policy from continuing and detailed scrutiny by the political establishment represented by the *Verwaltungsrat* made that very area of WDR's activity extremely vulnerable to concerted political attack from *outside* WDR and from outside the political establishment. If it could be shown that public opinion was hostile to these programmes then indeed WDR's legitimation as a public service broadcasting station would be seriously questioned.

When the philosophy and ethos of public service broadcasting had been introduced into NWDR by the British authorities, it had had to take little, if indeed any, cognisance of public opinion in a Germany humiliated and disillusioned by its defeat in the Second World War. In the late 1960s and the early 1970s, however, the views and the opinions of the German industrial establishment, backed by their material successes in the social market economy, were ignored by WDR at their peril. Unemployment had peaked at 694,000 in 1968 and working days lost through strikes had peaked at 4.483m. in 1971. Although these figures seem ludicrously small when viewed from the perspective of Great Britain in 1980, they were the largest unemployment figures the Federal Republic had seen in nearly a decade and the largest number of working days lost through strikes for two decades. To many at that time, the future of the German economy looked distinctly problematic, and student disaffection both in the universities and elsewhere with the capitalist way of life simply reinforced that view.

'Public opinion' about television programmes is essentially articulated through four main channels: through audience surveys carried out by Infratest, through editorial and other opinions expressed in the columns of the German press, through directly partisan responses in magazines such as the Deutsche Industrieinstitut's regular newssheet *Fernseh- und Rundfunkspiegel,* and through 'spontaneous' external comment by politicians. Of these four channels, that of the audience survey is essentially passive, limiting its information to averaging individual comments into categories such as 'good' or 'satisfactory' (see Appendix 20). Although these replies do have a limited role in determining public opinion the real debate over 'public opinion' is fought out in the three other channels and it was in these that the German industrial establishment set out to change the course of WDR's programming policy.

The role of the German press in articulating 'public opinion' merits a more extensive study than is possible here, but for our purposes it is important to signal the role played in North Rhine-Westphalian politics by the *Frankfurter Allgemeine Zeitung.* The FAZ is the Federal Republic's most prestigious paper, drawing over 10 per cent of its circulation from abroad. Its network of foreign and domestic correspondents is unrivalled in Germany and it has a predominantly male readership coming from the worlds of business and finance. It can thus claim that 90 per cent of its readers are important decision-makers in the German economy (Sandford, 1976, p. 212). Of these many come from the Frankfurt area and from North Rhine-Westphalia. Although nominally a paper of the middle of the political spectrum, it is, as Sandford points out (ibid.), in fact a right-wing paper and a determined advocate of capitalism. It was from the columns of the FAZ that the first attack on the *Arbeiterfilme* came, and its target was *Rote Fahnen sieht man besser.*

The first transmission of *Rote Fahnen* on WDR's third channel had upset the Deutsche Industrieinstitut's *Fernseh- und Rundfunkspiegel* (see Appendix 4) but otherwise had occasioned very little overt comment.

However, when the film was rescreened on the first channel under the Radio Bremen flag some three months later on 14 December 1971, albeit in a shortened version, the FAZ swung into action. In an article in the economic section (see Appendix 6) it accused Schübel and Gallehr of rigging the film, of suppressing evidence favourable to the employers and of paying the sacked employees for their participation in the film. In the television section of the paper, a second article (see Appendix 6) dismissed the film as being neither a proper documentary nor a feature film but boring and repetitive publicity promoting co-determination and against capitalism. Some two months later, the FAZ returned to the attack, with another article in the economic section (see Appendix 7) which repeated the earlier accusations of tendentiousness by the film's makers in depicting the employers as wicked nineteenth-century capitalists. It also introduced new material into the argument by claiming that the makers of the film had deliberately omitted a number of 'facts' which did not support their case: namely that all the workers who had been made redundant had found new jobs; that they had received financial compensation; that a fund had been set up to compensate the sacked workers for losses in their income; that the workers were not evicted from their houses and almost all were given the option of buying them; and finally that all workers were given the option of remaining in the works pension fund. The article concluded by deploring the prizes awarded to the film, and in particular, the Gold prize of the German Workers' Education Association (Deutscher Volkshochschulverband).

Radio Bremen, which was responsible for the broadcast on the first channel, came under specific attack in a letter sent by Dr Albers and Dr Bischoff of the Phrix management in Hamburg to Hans Abich, the *Intendant* of Radio Bremen (see Appendix 12). The main burden of their complaint was the lack of 'objectivity' displayed in the film and its failure to present a 'balanced view'. Public service broadcasting should not, in their opinion, favour the interests of one social group and in their view the film contravened Article 7 of the law setting up Radio Bremen which demanded objectivity in its programmes.

The attack on Radio Bremen could equally well have been an attack on WDR except for one crucial difference. WDR's constitution did not have the stipulation of objectivity that Radio Bremen's did. Article 4 of the WDR constitution was much broader in its remit, since it was only news broadcasts which had to be impartial and objective. Defiantly, von Bismarck and Falkenberg returned to the battle and *Rote Fahnen sieht man besser* was screened for a third time on 11 March 1972, on the third channel. This time, however, the WDR Press Office released detailed documentation about the film, which included specific rebuttals by Schübel and Gallehr of the accusations made in the columns of FAZ and in the letter from Phrix in Hamburg to Radio Bremen, together with sworn affidavits by Fritz Thomas, Dieter Süllwold, Elly Scholz and Heinrich Göbel which stated that they did not appear in the film for money and that all their opinions were their own (see WDR *Pressestelle* 1972 and Appendix 13).

In reply to the attacks in the FAZ, Schübel and Gallehr hit back. They denied manipulating the truth. On the contrary, they accused the prestigious FAZ of precisely the crime of which it had accused them, insufficient scrupulousness in obtaining the true facts of the matter. No-one on the FAZ had actually spoken to any of the people, whether Phrix workers or film-makers, who were actually involved in the film. The unemployment figures quoted by the FAZ were unavailable at the time the film was made in January 1971 and moreover they were in fact wrong, as a DGB spokesman from Krefeld had pointed out in a letter to the FAZ two days later (see Appendix 8). Furthermore, at their request the film did not quote the compensation monies paid to the workers; the Heads of the Supervisory Board of Phrix Krefeld had had the opportunity to censor their own interview material and had indeed taken advantage of the opportunity so to do; none of the four workers featured in the film had in fact received any money from the special compensation fund; and none of the workers had mentioned the opportunity to leave their contributions in the pension fund.

Von Bismarck and Falkenberg had won the battle; *Rote Fahnen* while admittedly partial in its approach was nevertheless true and a valid film for a public service broadcasting institution both to have produced and to have broadcast; for had not the Constitutional Court recognised that every programme would have a certain tendency and that objectivity was an impossible goal to achieve? But although von Bismarck and Falkenberg had won a battle, the case of *Rote Fahnen* was only the opening skirmish in a long war of attrition between WDR (and later on NDR and HR) and the right-wing industrial establishment linked to the CSU and the CDU. Although the *Fernseh- und Rundfunkspiegel* continued to put out the views of the Deutsche Industrieinstitut the real threat to WDR from 'public opinion' came about a year later when an organisation called Tele-control was set up in Bonn.

Tele-control was the brainchild of Carl-Dieter Spranger, a CSU Deputy in the Bundestag whose plan was for it to monitor and record all broadcasts so that it could then feed to all politicians, but particularly those in the CSU and CDU, chapter and verse of every example of 'tendencies hostile to business in television and radio programmes' ('wirtschaftsfeindliche Tendenzen in Rundfunksendungen'). The economic structure of Tele-control remained obscure for several years, but it now appears that Tele-control is in fact owned by CDU Deputy Rainer von zur Mühlen. It publishes about 1000 copies of its newsletter and propaganda sheet. About 800 of these are bought on subscription at an annual contribution of 240DM (£60). The majority of these subscriptions are taken out by CDU and CSU politicians, and by CDU sympathisers in the broadcasting institutions and large industrial companies. The institution has a staff of 11 who monitor the output of WDR, NDR and HR but not that of Bayerischer Rundfunk. The names of the 11 staff are largely unknown, but one is Elmar Schubbe, who works for the conservative catholic *Rheinischer Merkur* (see Thomas, 1978). Not surprisingly, the right-wing politics of Tele-control now extend to monitoring and commenting upon anything which 'falsifies and defames our public and social economy; agitation against the social market economy and its bases; leftist church politics; pro-communist reports from abroad; feminism, sexuality and pornography as cultural centres of gravity in broadcasting and television' (quoted Skriver, 1978, p.19). Tele-control has cemented the links between the critics of broadcasting and the right wing of the political spectrum. 'Public opinion' as expressed through their opinions is briefed regularly and clearly on every move which is deemed hostile to their interests. As a result every word and every image in broadcasts is checked and double checked before it goes out. Caution rather than liberty is the watchword of the day.

If the early attempts to discredit WDR and *Rote Fahnen* in the columns of the FAZ came unstuck because they were inadequately briefed, the regular drip, drip, drip of hostile comment and outbursts from the CSU/CDU politicians do not, because today they are well-briefed by Tele-control. The battle to discredit the liberal tendencies in the public broadcasting institutions and in particular WDR is slowly but inexorably being won by the politicians of the right, as they continue to burrow away at the 'lack of objectivity' in public service broadcasting.

THE DRAMATURGY OF THE ARBEITERFILM

The transmissions of *Eight Hours Are Not a Day* between November 1972 and March 1973 proved comparatively popular, as the Infratest results in Appendix 20 show. Between 41 per cent and 45 per cent of the West German public had watched them and approximately 60 per cent of those watching had found them 'good' or 'very good'.

Of all the *Arbeiterfilme*, it was *Eight Hours* which conformed most closely to the popular stereotype of the bourgeois narrative and it is not surprising therefore that its message of populist self-management cemented into the cracks of a capitalist culture should have generated such widespread popularity. The television critics were not so impressed, however. In a detailed analysis of their responses, Wolfgang Gast and Gerhard R. Kaiser (Gast and Kaiser, 1977) analysed the reviews of 34 critics in daily and weekly German language newspapers published in the Federal Republic, in Austria and in Switzerland. They found that there was a generally negative response to Märtesheimer and Fassbinder's project of adapting an established television genre towards

108

progressive ends and that most critics objected to Fassbinder's 'stylistic mishmash', as Wolf Donner called it in *Die Zeit* ('Idyllen eines TV Jusos', *Die Zeit*, 23 December 1972). Most critics were also quite clear on what they understood by 'reality' but, as Gast and Kaiser point out, there was insufficient reflection on the differences between reality and fiction. As a result, liberal critics, although commenting favourably on the artistic merits of the series, judiciously distanced themselves from its political orientation. Furthermore, without exception, critics both from the right and the left criticised the instant appeal of the series, arguing that the realities of the industrial workplace were more complex than it allowed. Thus K. Korn writing in the FAZ ('Ein Spiel von der Betriebsgemeinschaft', FAZ, 24 December 1973) presents the argument that managerial structures must be orientated towards economic efficiency, while on the left most critics pronounced the series as anarchic. Thus Klaus Eder, writing in 1969, had described Fassbinder's *Warum läuft Herr R Amok?* as 'Revolution im ganz Privaten: dass das zur Flucht in die Krankheit führt, zu Anarchismus und Tod, belegt Fassbinder mit seinen eigenen Filmen' ('A completely private revolution that produces either a flight into sickness or anarchy and death, as Fassbinder is proving with his own films'). ('Revolution im Privaten. Gespräch mit Rainer Werner Fassbinder', *Filmkritik* no. 8, 1969.) In the same way *Eight Hours Are Not a Day* was criticised for being 'a private revolution' (Gast and Kaiser, 1977). Fassbinder was accused of having 'a notion of political activity which does not go beyond the realms of private experience into the traditional areas of political struggle and debate.'

This double criticism of *Eight Hours*, both from the right and from the left, was deemed to be of such importance that a specific debate on the series was held in the *Rundfunkrat*. The common ground between the left- and right-wing film critics was reflected in agreement on the *Rundfunkrat* between Günter Triesch, who represented employer interests in North Rhine-Westphalia, and Peter Michels, who represented the interests of the organised trade union movement. (This information comes from an interview by the authors with Günter Triesch in Cologne, 13 January 1978.) Their objection, endorsed by the majority of the *Rundfunkrat*, was that the dramaturgy of the series failed to follow in documentary detail the highly organised and articulated series of procedures that would have to be gone through in a realistic working situation before an industrial grievance could be articulated in industrial action. There was no detailed consideration in the dramaturgy of *Eight Hours* of the roles played in real life by the *Betriebsrat*, the *Vorstand* or the *Aufsichtsrat*. And this criticism in its turn entailed a clear dramaturgical exposition of the arguments of both the management and the workers, of both capital and labour. The makers of *Eight Hours* had not only been politically naïve in their portrayal of industrial relations, they had also been politically naïve in their understanding of the politics of the *Rundfunkrat*. In arousing the hostility of both the employers' organisations and the organised trade union movement, they had dealt a crippling blow to the future success of the series.

As far as can be ascertained, the *Rundfunkrat* did not actually forbid the production of the further three espisodes of the series which were contemplated by wDR, but it did stipulate that these three episodes should face up to the challenge of producing a dramaturgical structure which took account of their criticism of episodes 1-5, namely that any future episodes should deal coherently and realistically with the social institutions and structures at the workplace. In the event wDR did not proceed with the projected episodes 6, 7 and 8. Apparently Fassbinder found the problems of preparing new scripts which met these specifications too daunting and Rohrbach found them too debilitating dramatically. (Interview by the authors with Peter Märthesheimer, Cologne, 12 January 1978.) Since the series had been produced and marketed by wDR as essentially 'authored' by Fassbinder rather than by wDR it clearly presented a substantial credibility problem if the series were continued once Fassbinder had withdrawn, and so the three projected episodes lapsed. (This is an interesting sidelight on the problems and possibilities of the *Autor* aesthetic dominant in the West German film and TV industry.)

The decision of the *Rundfunkrat* concerning *Eight Hours* had, perhaps, a more profound significance than many realised at the time. Naturally its structures applied to all *Arbeiterfilme* produced by wDR after that time and in particular to the films of Lüdcke and Kratisch and of Ziewer. But the limits imposed on the dramaturgy of all future *Arbeiterfilme* stemmed from the critical premises and the ideological interests of the élites of West German society. In future the dramaturgy of the *Arbeiterfilm* had to handle the dialectic of the pros and cons of the arguments in the *Betriebsrat*, between the *Betriebsrat* and the *Vorstand*, and so on. If any romantics were hoping that the *Arbeiterfilm* was to be a genre that would form the basis of a workers' revolution in the Federal Republic, then *Eight Hours* was the last, indeed almost the only, film in the genre which was able to bypass the organisational intricacies of contemporary life in the workplace in the Federal Republic of the 1970s.

The implication of the decision of the *Rundfunkrat* was that in future all programmes would be required to adopt criteria of 'objective' and 'balanced' representation, even those based on traditional television genres where no such criteria normally applied. (Few police series would be made if the statistical profile of the crimes and clear-up rates represented had to correspond to those in real life.) Research into propaganda done after the Second World War showed that for the less educated the one-sided presentation of an argument was more effective than presenting both sides. For a highly-educated audience, however, the presentation of both sides was more effective, always supposing of

110

course that the 'right side' is seen to win (see Klapper, 1960, p.130). This general proposition was in fact borne out by the Infratest responses to the *Arbeiterfilme* (see Appendix 20). These indicated that *Eight Hours Are Not a Day* captured the largest audience share of any *Arbeiterfilm*. The shift away from the traditional dramaturgical practices of entertainment genres towards a structure built round analysis and contemplation meant a shift away from the possibility of affecting a more popular audience. The industrial establishment of North Rhine-Westphalia, both management and unions, had therefore headed off what seemed to them a threat by programmes as popular as *Eight Hours* to the very fabric of German industrial society.

Far from killing off the *Arbeiterfilm*, however, the genre acquired a new lease of life, drawing its dramaturgy from a more dialectical, marxist analysis of industry and society in the work of Christian Ziewer, and to a less overt extent in the work of Marianne Lüdcke and Ingo Kratisch. Far from being a limitation, the strictures of the *Rundfunkrat* were celebrated with positive glee by Christian Ziewer in *Schneeglöckchen blühn im September*. We have already discussed the dramatic and aesthetic felicities of this approach in Chapter 6, but it is necessary at the same time to point out that these virtues were not appreciated by the majority of German audiences whose expectations were tuned into the traditional dramaturgical patterns of bourgeois entertainment series.

How effective were the *Arbeiterfilme*? Evidence for this can be found in a study by Kohli, Dippelhofer-Steim and Pommerehne, who published a study of two *Arbeiterfilme*. They showed two WDR productions, *Die Wollands (The Wolland Family)* and *Schneeglöckchen blühn im September* to a sample of 54 respondents — male and female workers in two large engineering works in South Baden. The enquiry was designed to investigate the contradiction between the findings of effects studies — that media messages have little effect on their consumers — and the desire of film-makers (here Lüdcke/Kratisch and Ziewer) to influence the audiences of their films. Kohli *et al.* concluded that the conditions in which the films were seen and discussed affected the samples' response to them. Although the films produced little evident cognitive change in the respondents, the reality of the films' fictional world was acknowledged by the sample of interviewees. The films offered a 'vocabulary' and an interpretative paradigm through which the respondents' own experience could be ordered, and material for reflection and the furthering of the audiences' understanding of their place in the world.

The interviewees were approached through their trade union (IG Metall) and *Betriebsräte*. The authors of the study reported the respondents' view (shared by Kohli *et al.*) that their own 'militancy quotient' was lower than that of industrial workers elsewhere in West Germany — particularly, the sample thought, lower than the North German workers shown in the films.

111

In works A. two group discussions of *Die Wollands* took place, one between 5 repetitive piece workers, the other between 5 skilled maintenance fitters. In works B. there were 14 individual interviews — 10 production worker respondents, a cleaning woman, two women clerks and a storekeeper, of whom two were shop stewards and one a *Betriebsrat* — and two group discussions with a further 23 workers. The group discussions and viewings were held in the local offices of the trades union and the individual interviews and viewings were held in the respondents' homes.

Kohli *et al.* argue (i) that group discussions relieve the respondents of the tensions and anxiety of an individual interview; (ii) that it is known that in group situations a higher level of understanding of the material in question is achieved and that there is therefore a more satisfactory basis for enquiry; and (iii) that the group situation is intrinsically no less authentic and valid for research than the classical individual interview. They also conclude that a difference in the location of the interview affects the sample's response and that in the case of home viewing and interview the lower 'mediation' expressed in the respondents' attitudes to the films (e.g. little interrelation between the film and their own experience) stems from resentment of the intrusion of the world of work (the subject of the *Arbeiterfilme*) into the home; an area into which the respondents can retreat and exclude the tensions and antagonisms of work. The higher 'mediation' recorded in group discussions at the trade union offices is associated with the group situation *and* the site of the viewing and discussion; a place that is perceived by the sample as within the realm of work. And thus the greater evidence, at the group meetings, of the general assent to the realism of the films and the situations that they treat and the greater incidence of respondents interpreting their own experiences in the light of the films' paradigms and vice versa may be interpreted as a positive perception of the films at work (or at a place associated with work) as offering useful knowledge, pertinent to the world of work but not to the home.

The authors conclude:
(i) that research findings based on the technique of individual interview in the home require qualification in the light of different responses in group situations outside the home;
(ii) that the *Arbeiterfilme* put workers and their problems into the 'public sphere', that the profile of the 'world' offered by mass communications is skewed *vis-à-vis* the real world; that mass communications constitute a 'public sphere' in which the number of, for example, men, academics, members of upper income groups is over-represented *vis-à-vis* the real world. That this public sphere is perceived by audiences as real and only the problems recognised in that sphere count as 'real'. But that, conversely, *Arbeiterfilme* cannot be expected to be seen as pertinent by respondents when the overall tendency and flow of television program-

ming is to constitute a radically different 'public sphere'.

(iii) that, accordingly, the cognitive change in the sample was slight, although the 'reality' of the films' fictional world was generally acknowledged. The incidence of cognitive change ('mediation') was greater outside the home and in group discussions and the nature of the cognitive shift was predominantly to offer respondents a vocabulary and repertoire of interpretative paradigms through which the respondents' own experience could be ordered and which theirs could reflect.

Thus Märthesheimer's and Fassbinder's dramaturgical project of developing a series in which the protagonists could influence the reality of the workplace yielded to one in which the viewer was made to explore not one single character but the behaviour and the internal dynamics of all the protagonists at the workplace (see Appendices 14 and 18). That is to say, the viewer's experience was no longer in the subjective sphere but in the 'public sphere' and that consequently the cognitive change was slight. The dramaturgical limitations imposed from above which took an 'objective' or 'public' view of the reality of the workplace imposed an intolerable limitation on those film-makers who wanted to deal with the problem at an individual or subjective level.

THE REPLACEMENT OF WDR'S SENIOR PERSONNEL

The continuing political pressures of the CDU and the CSU, and in particular of former CDU Federal Minister Heinrich Windelen, who was by now a member of the WDR *Verwaltungsrat*, together with the continuing barrage of criticism fed by the selective monitoring of Tele-control, began to take their toll of morale in the senior management of WDR. Central to the structure was Klaus von Bismarck, who as *Intendant* had been responsible for the appointment of Falkenberg and Rohrbach, as he had indeed been for Werner Höfer, his director of television programming. As von Bismarck's third term of office as *Intendant* came up for renewal on 1st April 1976, the future of all these four key executives was in doubt. The split on the *Verwaltungsrat* was clear. The CDU faction — former *Land* Minister and chairman Konrad Grundmann, former Federal Minister Heinrich Windelen and *Land* Deputy Dr Theodor Schwefer — wanted a new *Intendant*. The SPD faction — deputy chairman and Minister-president of North Rhine-Westphalia Heinz Kühn, Johannes Rau, the North Rhine-Westphalian Minister for Education and Research, and Gunter Hammer, the chief editor of the *Westfalischer Rundschau* — saw no reason for change, while the FDP nominee, Dr Willi Weyer, the President of the Deutscher Sportbund, could not produce a candidate that would command majority support. Klaus von Bismarck gave the impression that he was undecided whether he even wanted to allow his name to go forward to run for a fourth term of office. Whether this was what he genuinely felt, or

113

whether this was part of a subtle campaigning strategy, is difficult to determine. In the event it became clear that the *Verwaltungsrat* could not propose von Bismarck to the *Rundfunkrat* without there being a split vote in the *Verwaltungsrat* and the consequent danger that the *Rundfunkrat* would reject the *Verwaltungsrat*'s nominee. Accordingly another candidate had to be found who would command the support of the SPD faction, but also of a wider section of the *Rundfunkrat*.

The candidate who emerged from this process of discreet consultations was Friedrich-Wilhelm Freiherr von Sell. At 50 years of age, von Sell had a solid and sober track record as a lawyer and broadcasting administrator first with Sender Freies Berlin and later in Cologne. He had taken key executive roles in the advertising subsidiaries of both Sender Freies Berlin (Berliner Werbefunk GmbH) and of WDR (Westdeutsches Werbefernsehen GmbH) and had been leader of the ARD delegation which negotiated a unified wages agreement with the broadcasting trade unions between 1970 and 1974. By all accounts, von Sell was much more closely involved with North Rhine-Westphalian party politics than von Bismarck, and his experience in the advertising subsidiaries of SFB and WDR and as a negotiator for the ARD as employers stood him in good stead with the CDU faction, who ultimately came to recognise that the best they could achieve was to replace von Bismarck with von Sell.

With von Sell's appointment, the old team of executives built on the liberal principles of public service broadcasting fell apart. Werner Höfer resigned from WDR at the end of July 1977 to become diplomatic correspondent for *Stern* in Bonn, and in a structural re-organisation von Sell deprived Hans-Geert Falkenberg of his responsibility for cultural programmes, giving him the nominal and derisory responsibility of liaison with cultural activities overseas. Although humiliated and insulted, Falkenberg refused to resign, believing that he had more to contribute to public service broadcasting by staying at WDR than by resigning to go elsewhere, and continuing to argue for public service broadcasting in a variety of fora. (Discussion with the authors, Cologne, January 1978. See also Falkenberg, 1979.)

Günter Rohrbach stayed on as Head of Drama, but during the next year his statements about the current needs of television drama began to change. By the end of the year both he and Peter Märthesheimer had left WDR and gone to Bavariafilm.

With the departure of von Bismarck, the CSU and the CDU and the industrial establishment had achieved its aims, the castration of a practice of public service broadcasting in WDR which could trace both its heritage and its lineage back to the Reithian ethic of public service broadcasting introduced into NWDR by the BBC at the end of the Second World War.

114

The *Arbeiterfilm* at WDR ended in 1976, not because the possibilities of the genre had been exhausted nor because of an impasse stemming from unresolved or unresolvable aesthetic problems, nor because of audience dissatisfaction. The genre ended because of the *Tendenzwende*, the change in the political balance in and around WDR.

To be sure a clear path cannot be traced between the comments of Tele-control, *Ferseh-und Rundfunkspiegel,* the efforts of Heinrich Windelen in the *Verwaltungsrat* and a shift in programme policy. We were surprised to receive in answer to our question to one of the *Redakteuren* in the WDR Drama Department, 'Why no more *Arbeiterfilme?*' the remark 'The film-makers didn't want to make any more'. It is true that the split up of Kratisch and Lüdcke, or Ziewer deciding that he could not afford to become stereotyped as an *Arbeiterfilme* director — hence *Aus der Ferne* and the Peasants' War project — had a real effect on the possibility of continuing the genre. But the necessary conditions for continuing with the genre had disappeared and it is a testimony to that change in conditions that Rohrbach's 1978 Mainz speech did not look back to the achievements of WDR's sustained engagement with the *Deutsche Alltag* but determinedly distanced the speaker from that moment.

It is notoriously difficult to account for the operation of power. We cannot conclusively show that the power relations in WDR were such as to permit in the first half of the 1970s the *Arbeiterfilm* genre and in the second half to preclude it. But we believe so. Certainly neither the aesthetic possibilities of the genre nor audience interest had been exhausted. To be sure *Arbeiterfilm* never commanded audiences to rival sport or men on the moon, but the Infratest ratings in Appendix 20 are hardly conclusive evidence of audience dissatisfaction. The only substantial study of audience response to the *Abeiterfilm* (Kohli *et al.*, 1976) did not suggest that, even though little effect on the audience could be measured, the audience rejected either the specific films shown or the programme form. Rather than degeneracy of the form or audience dissatisfaction, it was a change in the balance of political power in West Germany which killed the *Arbeiterfilm*.

It remains our view that although disappointing for those who perceive considerable aesthetic interest and artistic success in the *Arbeiterfilm* and greet it as a small step towards unskewing the representation of the public sphere offered by mass communications and therefore towards ushering the spectators into their own real world with attentive faculties, this ending is paradoxically a testimony to one of the most positive features of the post-war West German broadcasting order. Its representation of politics and of political control is much more explicit than in the UK. In Germany, by and large, you know who is talking to you, why and what they are saying. When the WDR station identification sign comes up then the viewer knows that the world to be presented is different from that which follows, say, the Bayerischer Rundfunk sign. To say that the viewer knows who is talking could never be said of the BBC.

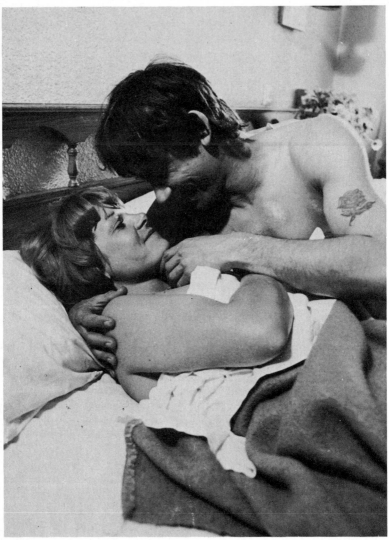

Familienglück

Der Angestellte

Appendices

I   WORKER REPRESENTATION IN WEST GERMANY

Unlike the situation in the United Kingdom, the worker in West Germany is not simply represented by his or her trade union. The methods and procedures by which the interests of workers are represented in German industry are closely specified in Federal legislation, and the activities of the trade unions, and indeed of the employers, are closely circumscribed by this legislation. In general, the trade unions make every attempt to ensure that they are law-abiding and are not in breach of the law, and thus normally actively dissociate themselves from activities such as pressures for a closed shop or from unofficial strikes, which are deemed illegal. The role of the trade unions in representing workers in West Germany is therefore more bureaucratic, more cumbersome and less sensitive to the direct concerns of the workers than that in the United Kingdom.

A further difference between the United Kingdom and Western Germany, is that while the Federal law makes legal provision for the interests of the workers to be represented in determining company policy, it makes no provision for this representation to be carried out by members of the relevant trade union, with the result that on occasion the workers' interests are represented by individuals who are not members of any trade union at all.

The senior board of a company is the *Hauptversammlung* (General Assembly of Shareholders). This board, on which the workers are not represented, is responsible for the company's bye-laws, for decisions on its capital structure and on the distribution or reinvestment of profits. The *Hauptversammlung* elects the shareholder representatives to the *Aufsichtsrat* (Supervisory Board) and ratifies the decisions of the *Aufsichtsrat* and the *Vorstand* (Management Board). It can also decide on matters relating to management of the company when requested by the *Vorstand*.

The *Aufsichtsrat* or Supervisory Board which meets quarterly is responsible for determining investment and financial policy within the parameters approved by the *Hauptversammlung*. The Board has no direct managerial powers but does have the power to insist that certain kinds of transactions should have its prior approval and it also has the power of appointment of membership of the management board itself — the *Vorstand*.

118

The Works Constitution Act of 1952 and the Co-determination Act of 1976 provide that there shall always be an odd number of members of the *Aufsichtsrat;* equal numbers of shareholder and worker representatives plus one neutral member. The *Montan* Industries (mining, iron and steel) Co-determination Acts of 1951 and 1956 and the Personnel Representation Act of 1955 made similar but slightly different arrangements for the mining, iron and steel industries and for government departments. The worker directors on the *Aufsichtsrat* are nominated and elected either by the *Betriebsrat* (Workers' Council) or by a secret ballot of all the workers, including most supervisory and middle management grades but excluding a limited number of top management who have a seat specially reserved for them from one of the places allocated to workers' representatives. Prior to the 1976 Act, the workers were only a minority of the *Aufsichtsrat,* but even today, parity of representation with the shareholders has only been achieved by reserving a separate seat for senior management represented as a separate and distinct group of workers.

Worker directors are forbidden to participate in industrial action and may only be concerned with the interests of the company or establishment. The main concerns of the *Aufsichtsrat* are with broad policy and with appointing and overseeing the *Vorstand.*

The *Vorstand* is responsible for the day to day management of the company and, like many boards of management in the UK, is chaired by the chief executive of the company. Members of the *Vorstand* are all full-time executives and may serve neither on the *Aufsichtsrat* nor on the *Betriebsrat.*

Worker representation is required by law in even the smallest companies (down to those with five employees). The *Betriebsrat* is elected every three years by secret ballot and consists only of worker representatives. The *Betriebsrat* is designed to operate at plant level. In multi-plant organisations there are provisions for *Gesamtbetriebsräte* (company works councils) and where the company is part of a larger industrial group there can be group works councils (or *Konzernbetriebsräte*).

The Works Constitution Act defines the duties of the *Betriebsrat* as 'seeing that effect is given to Acts, ordinances, safety regulations, collective agreements and plant agreements for the benefit of employees' and 'making recommendations to the employer for actions to benefit the establishment and the workers'. In addition, the *Betriebsrat* will have access to all plans for modifying or extending the works, its technical facilities, its work processes and its employment practices. In this last area, the *Betriebsrat* has the right of co-determination (*Mitbestimmung*) over all conditions of employment, and in all personnel matters including dismissals, except where specific provisions have been established by a separate collective agreement.

The *Betriebsrat* normally meets during working hours and has a statutory obligation to meet the employer at least once each month. In addition there is a meeting once every three months when the employer attends and at which he is entitled to speak. Employers may attend other meetings of the *Betriebsrat* only at its invitation, and so far as trade union officials are concerned they too must be invited to the meetings of the *Betriebsrat*. Naturally some members of the *Betriebsrat* will also be active trade unionists but this is not necessarily always the case.

Liaison between the *Betriebsräte* and the trade unions are carried out by the *Vertrauensleute* or *Vertrauensmänner* (shop stewards) who are trade unionists working at plant level. Their role is to provide a link between the workers and the *Betriebsrat* and to foster trade unionism on the shop floor. They recruit workers into the union, collect union dues and generally inform the workers about subjects under discussion at the *Betriebsrat*. They serve for three years. Some are elected by the workers, others are appointed by trade union officials.

It is only through the *Vertrauensleute* that the trade unions are officially involved with worker representation. Much power that normally accrues to trade unions at plant level in the UK is siphoned off to the *Betriebsrat* in West Germany, where the trade unions may or may not be involved. If they are, they soon tend to become part of the hierarchy of power within the company, continually balancing the interests of the

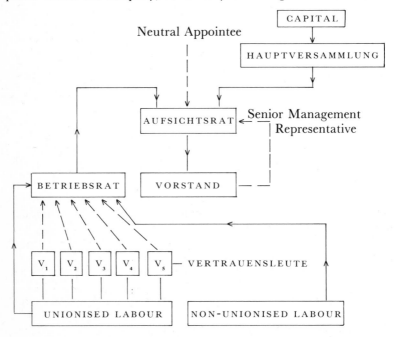

The structure of worker representation in German industry

workers against those of the company and thus channelling worker protest into bureaucratic compromise lost somewhere in the hierarchical structure of *Mitbestimmung*.

2 HOW DISRUPTIVE SHOULD A PROGRAMME BE?
COLLECTIVE INTERESTS AND INDIVIDUALISM — EXPERIENCES OF AN INTENDANT
BY KLAUS VON BISMARCK

Klaus von Bismarck has been Intendant *of Westdeutscher Rundfunk since 1961. We thought it only fair to give him the opportunity of expressing the opinions he has formed as a result of five years' experience in order to reply to a number of critical voices, in* Die Zeit *for example, following the decision to discontinue the programme* Hallo Nachbarn.

These days, a broadcasting *Intendant* has to beat his way through an undergrowth of very diverse expectations, all of which he is supposed to fulfil, and one of the main features of the landscape in which he moves is the strained relationship between intellectuals and politicians. The recent disputes surrounding *Hallo Nachbarn* have demonstrated this yet again.

Who is actually meant by the term 'intellectuals' when an *Intendant* is accused of allowing these people too much control over the programmes for which he is responsible? It means those who are constantly asking awkward questions, exposing abuses, uttering cries of doom and taking up an extremely critical stance towards the government and its decisions. All these people are lumped together under the heading 'intellectuals'.

Their criticism has — according to the powers that be — a 'disruptive' effect. By this is meant a pernicious, negative, devastating influence that undermines the authority of the State from within and without. One of them, Ulrich Sonnemann, has said in reply to this reproach: 'The mind should disrupt until it comes upon something which resists it, which it can respect and admire, and therefore we must say that anyone who does not disrupt even though he should in view of the facts and could in view of his personal talents, is quite simply a traitor to the mind and to humanity itself, a dishonest person and a moral coward.'

Seen in this light, disruption is a moral quality — the responsibility of the mind to expose evil, lies and hypocrisy. I know that intellectuals like Ulrich Sonnemann are impelled by such a spirit of truth when they repeatedly question the *status quo*. But should and must the mass media give extensive space to this kind of critical questioning? The answer is 'no' if we stress the word 'considerable', but 'yes' if we replace the word

121

'considerable' by 'definite, but appropriate'.

The very nature of mass communications puts programmers under an obligation constantly to think about the extent to which the ideas, statements and questions which are broadcast are liable to be misunderstood. Statements like Sonnemann's can only be understood by a mass public to a certain extent. Moreover, intellectuals are of course themselves very much a motley crew. It is said that even highbrows are not exempt from narrow-mindedness where politics are concerned. Some are specialists in the art of coming to completely the wrong conclusions with kamikaze bravura and brilliance. And there are doubtless other intellectuals who tell themselves: 'Be a realist, don't speak the truth!' Then of course there is also the temptation to use a satirical revue, for example, to convey a downright political message, not just as a general critical forum but with a very specific political aim in view.

But it would be wrong for programmers to take universal comprehensibility as the absolute criterion for their overall programming schedule in accordance with the maxim 'Keep out of trouble' or to aim for a cosy compromise on the very lowest level. Acceptability varies widely in accordance with the time and the type of the programme. Critical intellectual comment which is most appropriate in a broadcast on the third radio programme will be inadvisable in a popular programme at another time. So, for radio and television, the acceptable limits to this kind of questioning which is keenly critical, i.e. 'disruptive' in a positive sense, vary depending on the time and 'place' of the programme. Given that public corporations are responsible for broadcasting in the Federal Republic, these limits must be narrower than those, for example, of an exclusive magazine. A public corporation is not allowed to make a principle of constantly questioning the *status quo*. The duties of a public servant call for a balance between critical detachment and the encouragement of continuity. The answer to the problem of whether the broadcasting companies should be permitted to give space to critical intellectual questioning is 'yes' if by this is meant the freedom of independent critics to describe things as they really are, even if politicians of all parties sometimes do not find it expedient for tactical reasons. A wit once described politics as a 'Derby for Trojan Horses'. All over the world there exists within politics the temptation to paint things in a rosy light, to play 'let's pretend' in order to take in the masses. It is essential to a living democracy that responsible critics are on the alert in order to provoke thought in as many citizens as possible by making unbiased observations on radio and television that may frequently annoy those they concern. But it is inevitable within mass communications that groups with a mania for bitter criticism can also form when the space for such criticism is allocated to individual critics on a long-term lease, like a piece of land (e.g. in *Hallo Nachbarn*).

122

But of course there are many examples of cases where courageous individuals have expressed an opinion which was widely attacked to begin with but which cleared the way for an insight that subsequently found more and more tacit acceptance. (I am thinking of Karl Jaspers, for example, and his thesis that anything which could further the liberalisation and humanisation of conditions in the Zone [i.e. the Soviet-Occupied Zone, pre-*Ostpolitik* term for the German Democratic Republic — translator] must take precedence over political considerations.) And so the independence of broadcasting must constantly reaffirm itself through the provocative, critical questioning of the widest possible variety of individual independent minds. This thesis may be at odds with the 'leasing out of land' to critics of a particular persuasion (although this is obviously effective with the public!), but it does provide a reference point for an *Intendant's* decisions about programmes and personnel.

Part of the touchiness with which many politicians react to the influence of intellectuals within broadcasting can be accounted for in historical terms. When broadcasting was re-established after 1945, an especially large number of key positions were initially entrusted to intellectuals who had proved themselves during the Nazi period by their critical democratic convictions. But these often very worthy men did not always possess the ability to make innovations or improvements in the practical politics of post-war Germany, and in any case were not given the task of doing so.

And so there arose a discrepancy between aims and actual achievements in the democratic reconstruction of our country. The belief in Kuby's theory of the 'watchers' and the 'doers' (which, in my opinion, is wrong) still haunts some editorial departments even though the heyday of our faith in the democratic education of the people primarily through broadcasting is long past.

It is clear that politicians both in parliament and within the parties are increasingly inclined to react with irritation to critical comment from independent journalists. Often, my colleagues in the broadcasting companies are seen as 'intellectuals' or even 'disruptive intellectuals' whereas in reality they are merely 'open' and capable of talking things over, and therefore condemned by all those with inflexible opinions. The broadcasting institutions appear as unknown quantities to anyone who thinks purely in party terms. They are regarded with suspicion because they cannot be pinned down by the usual criteria of party politics. Particularly for the CDU, the NDR programmes *Panorama* and *Hallo Nachbarn* caused so much hurtful bitterness throughout the party, even among the ranks of its local dignitaries, that a sizeable proportion of its members see red whenever they hear the words 'television' or 'autonomous broadcasting corporations' even when these refer to other television companies within which there is no 'crusading' bias as happened with the early *Panorama* programmes. And even today politicians involved with the cause of refugees [i.e. Germans from east of the Oder-Neisse line and from Czechoslovakia expelled to the West in 1945 — translator] react with equal touchiness to NDR's *Neven-du-Mont* programme and Hessischer Rundfunk's *Stehle* programme although a remarkable number of other programmes have represented the refugees' cause very much in a positive light.

In this way each side goads the other on to further excesses. So it is not surprising that journalists who find themselves inordinately under attack (the usual reproaches are 'fouling their own nest', 'indulging in disruptive criticism' or even 'betraying their country') are all the more tempted to declare their opinions with, so to speak, one foot on the barricade.

The nature of politics on the parliamentary 'front' and the conflicts between the parties are such that we must make some degree of allowance for the element of emotion. Moreover it is obvious that German politicians are particularly tempted sometimes to shroud themselves completely in such emotions as if in a fog of their own making. Many are clearly so fond of their tried and proven pathos that the actual meaning of their words becomes of less and less interest to themselves and to their supporters. A head-on clash is then inevitable when a sober intellect penetrates through the fog to the heart of the matter.

The basic attitude of a journalist is a crucial factor in forming an opinion about him. We must support him, even when his views are extremely critical, if his cutting remarks and radical questioning of current beliefs are prompted by a concern for the matter itself. But the situation looks rather different when a journalist hits out around him irrationally out of sheer malice. Every day an *Intendant* has to make new decisions between these two basic attitudes and their countless permutations and on the degree of criticism for which in the last analysis he will have to answer. It would be a complete misunderstanding of the principles of freedom of speech and of the press to see these as threatened by censorship whenever an *Intendant* happens to cancel a programme, something which, in the case of current affairs programmes, is frequently only possible at the last minute.

New decisions are always being required, not only on explicitly political programmes, but also, in different ways but to the same extent, on cultural and entertainment programmes. In the large category of entertainment, we have to take into account not just the dictates of journalistic honesty but also the very elusive concepts of 'taste' and 'tact'.

Whose taste should be the criterion? We all know that 'one man's meat is another man's poison'. Something which appears harmless enough to a couple of bright sparks producing entertainment programmes for a

124

broadcasting company can be quite offensive to people living in rural areas; something which is acceptable in a private cabaret is not necessarily suitable for transmitting to millions of viewers. Irony is frequently misunderstood, and besides, in the sphere of light entertainment the gift of tact is often not accompanied by those of imagination and know-how. And so it is inevitable that programmes not infrequently meet with strong objections because a group of people feel themselves to be shocked, offended or under attack, and this can lead to trouble of varying degrees of seriousness which calls for self-critical reflection and conclusions.

Let me quote two examples which clearly illustrate how difficult it is to steer the ship of light entertainment through the rocks represented by these divergent concepts of tact and taste. Of course it would be easy to enumerate the many programmes which brought the broadcasting houses fame and honour, but the problems we face are more apparent from the bad examples. The first case is a report on an explosion in which several workshops in a factory were destroyed and 18 workers lost their lives. Shortly after the accident a reporter interviewed the local manager of the works where it happened and also the district manager. Both men assured him that everything humanly possible had been done to minimise the damage and to resume production without delay. Another colleague then took it upon himself to 'gloss' these tape-recordings by combining them with his own commentary in such a way that the result was a gross slander on the two persons interviewed: the local manager accompanied a description of the accident with blatant propaganda for his production which was to be continued without loss of time or fall in quality, and the district manager mainly congratulated himself on the precautions he had taken while supervising the emergency operation. This 'imputation' of attitudes that had only been conjectured was an inexcusable manipulation of the evidence. Such crude violation of fairness and tact should not happen again.

The second case was the programme *In diesem Sinn Ihr Knigge II*, a cultural history of courtesans with a text by Herman Mostar accompanied by music and incorporating famous historical examples from antiquity to the present day. This time it was a Christian church that strenuously protested against the 'frivolous' nature of the programme. Of course this criticism was exaggerated, but certain passages were in fact not acceptable for some listeners. This means that a public corporation must carefully consider the extent to which the shock effect on certain groups of viewers or listeners can be justified, especially where entertainment programmes are concerned.

When these two cases were investigated in a spirit of self-criticism, we came to the conclusion that somewhere along the line we had not been sufficiently aware of our own responsibility, even though our negligence was very much more serious in one instance than in the other. However,

125

the *Intendant* himself was prompted by these cases to reassess the extent to which light entertainment programmes can be justified as well as the chain of responsibility for keeping a check on them, in order to forestall if possible any future blunders. But there is no foolproof control system and we should beware of wanting to invent one. If we are going to attract authors of wit and *esprit* to work with us, we shall have to accept a certain degree of risk.

The tension between collective interests and individualism is even greater within television, whose influence is still constantly increasing, than within radio. More and more people get their information from television and it is having a stronger and stronger effect on viewers' living and consuming patterns and on their political opinions and decisions. So it is understandable that in almost every country pressure groups are attempting to reduce television to a vehicle of group or of state interests; the Federal Republic also has its share of such attempts to break down the monopoly of the public corporations.

Two conflicting tendencies may be discerned in television programming throughout the world. There are programmers who apply the democratic principle of 'majority rule' to programme planning and essentially want to comply with the wishes of the viewing majority. Advocates of a differentiated programme structure oppose this with the democratic principle of equality: minorities and numerically inferior groups also have a right to be given the programmes they require. The opposition of popularity and quality also exists on an international level where as a rule it is only the independent broadcasting companies which are prepared to defend the principle of quality.

Experience has shown that programmes tend to ossify when the demands of society have reached a state of perfect balance; programme patterns become inflexible, planning is carried out on a sweeping, long-term basis and productions are safely mediocre, without risks, gambles or experiments. In this situation it is again and again the initiative of a few individuals which is needed in order to break through the blockage caused by routine, by opening up new paths with boldness and imagination. Their wings should not be clipped by the fuss about an occasional programme (*Hallo Nachbarn,* for example).

So, groups and individualists are complementary forces which both have their rôle to play in forming our view of the world as reflected in the mass media. The *Intendant* of a broadcasting company which is free of both governmental and commercial influences must take on the difficult task of protecting many different interests both from within and without. But when in doubt he should opt for taking the risk of providing a platform for the widest possible variety of well thought-out opinions. In the last analysis society will benefit more from this willingness to take risks than from an excessive timidity.

(from *Die Zeit,* 4 February 1966; translation by Sheila Johnston)

3 THE RED WEEK

(WDR 3RD PROGRAMME, 17 SEPTEMBER, 9.05 P.M.)

On five days during the week of the 3rd of September the red flag was unfurled by the WDR. Commentaries, reports, documentaries, films and discussions were broadcast with the aim of making the 'wage slave' of 'capitalist society' conscious of his 'situation'. Dr Hans-Geert Falkenberg, Head of the Department of Culture and Entertainment, claimed responsibility for this crash-course in Marxist politics and for this 'red week' in the WDR. Artists and workers, troupes of actors and cabarets, trade-union officials and film-makers were mobilised, not merely to demonstrate the shortcomings of our social order but, in the last analysis, to condemn the entire system of the social market economy.

In *Ende Offen*, the discussion led by Friedrich Wilhelm Räuker on Friday evening, in which Dr Falkenberg participated together with the chairmen of works councils, trade-unionists and a scientist, the spotlight was turned on this week's agit-prop experiments by the spokesmen for the employers. Then it became clear that all the manoeuvring that had been going on during this week of programmes had not succeeded in writing off a system which, though capable of improvement, has been tried and proven. The dynamic economic process within an industrial society has to be affirmed independently of the system. Even so, the legislation of the Federal Republic provides for more aid and greater security during factory closures, for example, than do socialist states. The humanisation of factories is a social process which should be developed and sustained irrespective of demands for co-determination and attempts at socialisation. The critics of the so-called capitalist systems had above all to admit that socialist economic systems could not compare with that of the Federal Republic, either in economic output or in social status. They refused to voice any utopian concepts of their own. In the end, all they could do was repeat the well-worn slogan about manipulation by means of compulsive consumerism. Whereupon they were informed that the WDR's red parables (*Lehrstücke*) were themselves a prime example of manipulation. Finally the WDR was told that it had been exploited as a vehicle for ideological and utopian dogmas. Falkenberg's reply that all of that week's programmes had served primarily as information was quite inadequate since the left-wing slant of both words and images had the function of developing not consciousness but one-sided opinions. Ideologues who have cut no ice either with the populace in general or with workers in particular here tried to voice their opinions in public with the help of the WDR. The failure of their scheme is perhaps the only positive result of this red week.

(from *Fernseh- und Rundfunkspiegel*, no. 181, 23 September 1971; translation by Sheila Johnston)

The Adolf Grimme Prize, which has been awarded to *Rote Fahnen sieht man besser* and which the WDR covered at some length in broadcasts on the 9th, 10th and 11th of March, has yet again fuelled the debate on the propagandistic content of this film (cf. *Fernseh- und Rundfunkspiegel* of the 17 December 1971). The unpleasant aftertaste left by its first screening has since become even stronger. Two complexes of questions require immediate clarification both within and outside the broadcasting houses. What forces, tactics and deliberations were the real criteria behind the decision to award the prize to a programme that grossly violated those principles of television journalism which had always, at least up till now, been respected? For example, could the jury only come to a decision after the programme had been extracted from the category of 'documentary' and rebaptised a 'documentary television play'? To alter the function of a programme in this way would — and this is indisputably the more important complex of questions as far as the future is concerned — confront those working in television with a serious problem. Either a programme is a documentary, in which case it should include all the facts important for the viewer and essential to the subject of the documentary, or else it is a television play which must be designated as such. The intention of *Rote Fahnen* was, as the sub-title expressly states, to represent the closure 'from the point of view of those who lost their jobs'. This, precisely, is the problem. For there is, simply, not just one point of view, and one might ask when, where and to what extent the other points of view can be heard. A 'counter-presentation' or a supplementary programme are precluded by the shortage of air-time and experience has shown that when films are followed by a discussion this is watched by only a fraction of the audience. Moreover, the 'counter-presentation', which would in any case be extremely difficult to obtain on television, could not begin to inform the viewer of all the relevant facts and arguments.

Rote Fahnen sieht man besser was certainly no documentary. There was no elucidation of the overall economic background to the closure of the Phrix works. There was no comprehensive account of the 20 million DM social welfare plan which brought everyone entitled to it an average of 6,400 DM. And there was, more particularly, no reference to the handsome compensation, totalling almost 30,000 DM, received by the four protagonists of the film. The authors' statement in defence of this omission that the indemnification was not mentioned by request of those concerned is (always assuming that there was no intention to manipulate the evidence) either the expression of a most uncommon delicacy or else an avowal of plain journalistic incompetence. Should it really be impossible for an experienced television man to impart a fact so crucial to the viewer as the handsome compensation received by the workers who lost their jobs in a form which would not encroach upon their privacy? It looks as though *Rote Fahnen sieht man besser* might become a text-book example of German television journalism. Seldom was a film so skilfully and deliberately edited, cut and pieced together. If the Grimme Prize in this case helps those responsible within television to re-sharpen their sense of the limits set the individual categories of what appears on the screen by the law, the statutes, the programme guide-lines, a sense of fairness and the journalistic ethos, then at least it will have achieved something.

(from *Fernseh- und Rundfunkspiegel*, no. 48, 10 March 1972; translation by Sheila Johnston)

5   EDITORIAL NOTES ON THE FORM AND CONTENT OF THE FILM BY THEO GALLEHR AND ROLF SCHÜBEL: ROTE FAHNEN SIEHT MAN BESSER

The closure of a factory from the point of view of the victims
In the first weeks of August 1970 press reports suddenly appeared about the intention to close the Krefeld Phrix works, which in the main produced chemical fibres. Following this, Theo Gallehr and Rolf Schübel, the documentary film makers, famous for their social reports about living conditions in the provinces ('The Small German Towns') and workers' conditions ('Between Prosperity and Class-Struggle'), made their first television drama-documentary for WDR/Westdeutsches Fernsehen.

The television film *Rote Fahnen sieht man besser* is an attempt to further extend the boundaries of the traditional television play. The significance of this attempt is dependent on the authenticity given the film by the ethnographers Gallehr/Schübel and on the distance, both in form and content, from the artificial, not artistic form of stylisation of previous television-drama which attempts to imitate life. However, in everyday politics and in society there is proof that political life contains its own inner drama which makes it tangible and useful if you want to make reality transparent when for many people it is opaque.

The television film *Rote Fahnen sieht man besser* was not produced but constructed. Not actors but the employees who had been hit did the talking.

With the example of the closure of the Krefeld Phrix works, where 2100 employees lost their jobs at short notice after August 1970, Theo Gallehr and Rolf Schübel present the recorded developments connected with the closure, and also describe how the consciousness of those hit changed. For a period of five months the authors visited and accompanied four typical Phrix families. Each of these people sees himself in a different relationship to the liquidation of the Phrix works.

Rote Fahnen sieht man besser constitutes teaching and learning material in so far as it exposes large economic and small private situations of conflict. The major contradiction between wage labour and capital in our society is stated and its effect on consciousness is made clear.

Concepts like exploitation, alienation and social injustice seem to have become slogans which are often dismissed sardonically by the strong minority, to extract the wealth for themselves, or seem passé through the apparent logic of reactionary ideology which in its turn tells lies with concepts like social partner, works family or works atmosphere.

It was necessary to make abstract concepts concrete by means of an example from real-life experience in order to ensure that other potential victims would have no difficulty in understanding.

So the film *Rote Fahnen sieht man besser* attempts to take the dramatisation of social reality seriously. From September 1970 to January 1971 the authors shot 31,000 metres of film in the Phrix factory in Krefeld and of the families of the employees who were laid off. This material was put together on the cutting table in the five months which followed, with the aim of combining and interpreting social concreteness and political reality.

The film was transmitted for the first time on Westdeutsches Fernsehen on 13th September 1971 at 8.15. p.m., at the beginning of a week when several productions dealing with conditions, contradictions and difficulties in the world of work were transmitted. Walter Jens followed the transmission with a critique of the film. Then followed a live discussion among the employees with the title 'The World of Work On Television — Workers See A Film'. On 17th September 1971 a second discussion took place at 9.00 p.m. on Westdeutsches Fernsehen, this time between employees and employers, with the title 'Contradictions in the World of Work'.

On 14th December 1971 the co-producer Radio Bremen, 1st Channel transmitted the film at 9.00 p.m. but cut the ending, which was significant both in terms of form and content.

Martin Wiebel

(from WDR Presstelle, 1972; translation by Scilla Alvarado)

6   SEEN FROM A RED POINT OF VIEW

Television writers do not take on an easy task when they tackle economic matters. Economics is particularly difficult to translate into the visual medium. For this reason one should be tolerant toward less successful attempts. However, there is a particular form of economic and socio-political film production which is not made by experts, does not actually clarify relations and does not criticise the bases of expertise. Its aim is purely defamation. The film *Rote Fahnen sieht man besser* shown on Tuesday on the First Channel of German television was an obvious example of this. A camera team filmed 31,000 metres about the closure of the Phrix works — from which a very biased selection was made showing how those involved viewed the events. The aim was clearly to attack the whole free economic system with the comments of four of those affected, who were encouraged without much effort, due to their difficult personal situation, to make bitter comments. Yet neither a sufficient presentation of all the aid in this particular case was given (10 million DM for 2100 employees) nor was the viewer informed about the really tightly-woven safety net that is spread out generally for the employee on the closure of a works.

Certain explanatory passages, for example where a spokesman for the employers explained the necessity for the closure, especially in a market economy in the interest of the consumers, were cut. From answers to about forty questions practically only a single sentence remained, one which compromised the interviewee, and this was completely taken out of context. Finally the interviewee was asked to relinquish in writing all claim to compensation, a charming practice meant obviously to somehow legally guard against lack of seriousness.

The film had a small epilogue. One of the four 'protagonists' who had cursed the most about the market economy and employers stated when applying to another firm (this was confirmed as genuine) that he had received a sum of about 20,000 DM from the enterprise. In repayment for his participation he received an incredible amount of marks (he was filmed over several days) and this was the reason he had cooperated. That says a lot; for this was not reported but staged.

TELEVISION COLUMN: THE HYBRID GENRE

Theo Gallehr and Rolf Schübel advertised their film *Rote Fahnen sieht man besser* as a 'sort of television film made in a documentary style'. In this way it was made known from the beginning that it was going to be a hybrid genre and so one could not complain that a true documentary was not transmitted about the Krefeld factory closure (at Phrix AG) but rather one of those films which belong to every weekly programme pushing for participation and a stand to be taken against capitalism. What was lamentable was the transparency of the methods used and how unclear the whole event remained, as well as the visual boredom and the vague content of the eternal conversations in the local pub between the four employees (obviously selected as typical) and their

131

friends. No more enlightening were the usual faded-in interviews with union representatives, members of the board of directors and of the executive committee. There was also a song about struggle performed in front of the factory gate — that is, as much as was left after Radio Bremen had cut it. In this way the film was able to end with the authors' direct protest against this intervention (from the First Channel).

CM

(from *Frankfurter Allgemeine Zeitung*, 16 December 1971; translation by Scilla Alvarado)

7 AGITATION WITH THE CAMERA
PHRIX THROUGH RED-COLOURED TELEVISION SPECTACLES

These gentlemen know of course how to use the camera effectively for their desired political aims. So they made a film to teach us about the horrors of capitalism. If you saw the film *Rote Fahnen sieht man besser* a few weeks ago on the First Channel you will remember these scenes. A black flag fluttered over the works. 'Now you stand there shattered. Your work place has gone up in smoke. Neither tears nor tricks will help. There is nothing more for you at Phrix', sang the red protest singer Süverkrüp in front of the factory gate. It was November 1970. The final closure of Phrix, the artificial silk works in Krefeld, was imminent. 2100 employees lost their jobs.

'When the representatives of capital no longer acquire the expected profits then they make decisions without taking the interests of the employees into account . . . Bang, without a suggestion of partnership . . . laws and justified claims are ruthlessly ignored and are often arrogantly derided, as was the case with Phrix.' This was how television viewers learnt about the closure from the mouth of an IG Chemicals spokesman. Both the authors, Theo Galleter [*sic*] and Rolf Schiebel [*sic*] had intended that the protest singer should appear again at the end of the film, to draw the conclusion: 'There only remains one thing for you, don't remain quiet anymore / Chuck sand into the damned mill / of capital which churns you into money. / Just stop cowering in private. / Start to take a stand together.' This call to class struggle in the style of the last century was sacrificed because it was censored by the director of Radio Bremen as politically inflammatory.

But even without this concluding point it was clear where the journey was to lead according to the ideas of the authors. They wanted to encourage the viewers to believe that nothing has changed since a hundred years ago when another protest singer (Georg Hergh) composed the poem for the German Labour Movement: 'Man of work

132

awake! / And recognise your power!!' Has nothing really changed? Has this economic system in the case of Phrix really been exposed as so ruthless and inhuman, as an ingenuous viewer would have to believe according to the film?

Let us discuss a few facts, facts which were not mentioned in the film because they did not fit in with the authors' intentions:

1. Of just about 2000 employees who were employed at the time of the decision to close down the Krefeld works of Phrix AG, only 112 were unemployed three months after the dismissal of the last batch at the end of June 1971. Over half of them were older than sixty. In the interim most of them also found new work. In mid-January of this year only between 20 and 25 were without work, all of them over 60 years old and thus after 12 months of unemployment entitled to draw their old age pension.

2. Because of the social plan worked out between the works council and the management of the company, 1571 employees received altogether the amount of 10-12 million DM. On average each employee in Krefeld who was entitled to compensation received 6443 DM. The highest sum for a wage-earner in Krefeld amounted to 20,858 DM for a 60 year old worker who had been employed since 1939. The highest sum of compensation for a salaried person amounted to 34,885 DM for a 62 year old skilled engineer, who had worked there for 32 years. At the other extreme the lowest sum paid out, of 325 DM, was for an apprentice, who was able to continue his training without interruption in another works. The three Phrix workers who cooperated on the film have received sums of 3306 DM, 5665 DM and 16,573 DM.

3. Furthermore a 'hardship fund' was set up which was administered on a footing of equality, with the aid of which temporary losses in income were fully compensated for. With the help of the fund the amounts for those entitled to receive it were increased so much for the period of 12 months, that they amounted to at least 75 to 95 per cent of their former Phrix net-income. These allocations presupposed however, a minimum age and were worked out according to the period of time the person had been working at the company and varied according to age. From 50 years up the time was no longer of importance.

4. The loss of a job is frequently connected with the loss of a flat. At Phrix in Krefeld practically all the houses were sold to former members of the company as long as they were not situated directly on the works site. All the contracts of sale for the houses included a clause for security of tenure, some for a life-time and some for five years.

5. All 2200 members in the superannuation scheme had the possibility of remaining in the scheme under the protection of the owners. For those retiring, amounts were raised to around 30 per cent because of the

closure. 225 pensioners, who had no claims to pensions from the company, yet had received voluntary benefits before the closure, were compensated with the accumulated amount of their pensions according to actuarial principles.

Either all this information was known to the authors of the television film or they could have known about it. They made no use of it because it did not fit into the image of the brutal rule of 'capital' which they had undertaken to paint. The quoted commentary of the IG Chemicals spokesman ('laws and justified claims were ruthlessly ignored and . . . arrogantly derided') and furthermore all the lamentations about the supposed unbridled rule of profit in this land would have forfeited much of their strength of conviction had this background been presented.

  For this 'courageous' falsification of reality the authors received subsequently yet another golden prize from the 'German Workers' Education Association'. What actually is journalistic courage in this country? When one cuts out of a few thousand metres of film everything that does not fit into a preconceived theory of life and suppresses everything which could possibly make one's own position appear questionable? When one sets up scenes for which the cast are paid and present them as documentation? Our liberal economic and social order is certainly not aided by uncritical reverence and the ship-wreck of an enterprise would be the most unsuitable advertisement for it. However, criticism is somewhat different from agitation.

Hans Jürgensen
(from *Frankfurter Allgemeine Zeitung* 9 February 1972;
translation by Scilla Alvarado)

8 COMMENT FROM THE GERMAN TUC (DGB) SPOKESMAN IN KREFELD, HEINZ STEINKE, ON THE *Frankfurter Allgemeine Zeitung* ARTICLE, 'AGITATION WITH THE CAMERA'

To the editors of the *FAZ*
Attention of Mr Hans Jürgensen

Stk/Ka.   1st March, 1972

Re: Article in the FAZ, 'Agitation with the camera'

Dear Mr Jürgensen,

We learned about the planned closure of the Phrix works from an article in your newspaper about the statement made by the managing director

Timm and so were able to take measures to help the workers concerned earlier than the management of the company had wanted.

You are correct when you state in your article that both sides should be heard. The authors Gallehr and Schübel certainly did this, and even let both sides have their say.

But it could well be argued that had you listened to both sides equally you would not have made some of the statements you did in your article.

It must be stated that a ridiculously small sum was made available by the board of directors for the 'social plan'. It was only when the union lodged massive complaints to the Krefeld industrial tribunal that negotiations started and changes were made in the 'little plan' set up by the company's management.

You specify sums of compensation in your article. These sums are roughly 30 per cent under the limits which the industrial tribunal worked out in constant legal consultation, and that even includes the highest sum for the 62 year old skilled foreman engineer.

It had not been possible for the DGB to arrive, with the aid of the industrial tribunal, at the usual settlement, as the complaints would have lasted for several years right up to the last stage of the proceedings. The very purpose of compensation, to help over a transitional period, could not have been accomplished. As far as the hardship funds go, it must be mentioned that only those who claim unemployment benefit are entitled to hardship funds. A married woman for example, mother of 2 children, who alternated working for six hours in the morning shift and seven hours in the afternoon shifts for eight years at Phrix in order to take it in turns with her husband to look after the children, was not entitled to unemployment benefit because according to the labour exchange, industry does not have jobs with these working hours. Hence she did not receive anything from the hardship fund. The complaint against the labour exchange is now at the social benefits tribunal.

None of the Phrix flats have been given over to former employees of the firm. The flats belong to a housing society; some of the rents were immediately doubled as soon as the works closed and they merely agreed upon security of tenure for five years.

The fates of different individuals, of the older people, of those injured in the war and in accidents, of the invalids and of the blind and of those with criminal records cannot be presented here.

The film was a product of the general impression that the biggest problem was to confront the indifference of the public: e.g. with 10,000 vacant jobs at the labour exchange it cannot be difficult to accommodate 2000 workers from Phrix. It was a long time before this official opinion, which was shared by the local government, could be corrected.

It also must be emphasised that the employees from the works manager to the youngest apprentice had been completely unprepared for the closure because of the recent investment of seven figure sums.

135

The Krefeld closure was completed a few weeks ago when the works site was sold. Having previously refused an offer of 15 million DM made to the town council, the town was later given first refusal for 100,000 sq. m. (at 18 DM per sq. m.) of undeveloped industrial land and a further 300,000 sq. m. (12 DM per sq. m.) was sold to a private firm.

According to the 1971 BASF industrial report the trades union and shop committee concern about not being able to go to the legal limit for compensation was unfounded since the existence of the other Phrix works would also be endangered by such greed. But everything that you describe in your article as the special benefits given out by the capitalists (who are persecuted by us) is retrieved again in tax rebates.

With best wishes,
(Steinke)
(translation by Scilla Alvarado)

9   GOLDEN SCREEN 1971
THE TELEVISION CRITICS' AWARD

For Theo Gallehr and Rolf Schübel

Rote Fahnen sieht man besser
('The Closure of a Factory from the Point of View of the Victims')
(WDR/WDF)

The basis for the jury's decision:
For over five months during the closure of the Krefeld Phrix Works Theo Gallehr and Rolf Schübel stayed with four of the people affected, chief witnesses so to speak. They portrayed themselves, and the authors let them report on their situation of having lost their place of work, let them talk about their existence, their relationship to their employers and the possibilities for solidarity among the workers.

Thus we have a rather tough play which is constructed out of reality, from a society of human beings, acted and conceived in a dramatically intelligent and extraordinary manner, employing filmic techniques which project it back into the reality of everyday television and so make it intelligible to a society which can now be involved. Or as Martin Wiebel of the WDR, the editor of this programme, put it, the authors 'have tried to take the dramatic presentation of social reality seriously'. They have succeeded.

(translation by Scilla Alvarado)

136

(German Television, 14th December, 8.15 p.m.)
A chemical works which employs about 2100 members of staff can no longer cope with the fall in profits caused by the revaluation of the DM in 1969, the devaluation of the French franc and increases in the cost of labour and raw materials. It has to close down. It is true that the decision comes as a surprise, but dismissals are staggered over a period of nine months, and many workers are kept in their jobs even though there is no more work for them. A total of 20 million DM, that is, an average of approximately 10,000 DM per member of staff, is spent on a social welfare plan and individual workers receive up to 30,000 DM. By far the majority of employees quickly find new jobs, even if they do not always or immediately enjoy their previous high earnings. One year after the closure has begun, about 110 former employees (about 5 per cent of the staff), mainly older men and women, are still without new jobs.

That is the story, as shown on television, of the closure of the Phrix works in Krefeld, or rather, that is how it could have been shown. Theo Gallehr and Rolf Schübel cannot feel themselves to be misinterpreted when we describe their film *Rote Fahnen sieht man besser*, now broadcast again on the First Programme as a contribution from Radio Bremen, as an unequivocal attempt at writing off 'capitalism' lock, stock and barrel. In the course of the 100-minute film, the four protagonists selected by them reiterated almost tediously similar variants of accusations from the arsenal of late Marxism and the stock arguments of the German Federation of Trade Unions: 'Those in charge' do just as they like; the reconstruction of the BRD has only been achieved thanks to the ordinary worker; the capitalists are not interested in people, only in profits; all this could only happen because there was no co-determination. Conclusion: Abolish this system of private capitalism.

When over 2000 people lose their jobs, this fact should not be glossed over. Each fate is of grave concern. But a works which no longer manages to make sufficient profit can no longer offer good wages and welfare benefits. And the expectation that greater co-determination will solve this problem is — if expressed in good faith — touchingly naïve. The four protagonists of the film received a total of 30,000 DM under the social welfare plan. But not a word of this was breathed to the viewer. It is true that Radio Bremen had the courage to cut, under strong protest from the authors, the Süverkrüp Song, which was intended to conclude the film on a militant climax; the details, which followed the film, about the fate of the four speakers and the number of workers still without jobs were also of some use. However this information belonged in the film; it would have been an apposite way of filling the 'minutes of silence' which occurred at the end of the film as a result of the deletion of the Süverkrüp Song. (from *Fernseh- und Rundfunkspiegel*, No 240, 17 December 1971; translation by Sheila Johnston)

For Theo Gallehr and Rolf Schübel
Rote Fahnen sieht man besser
('The Closure of a Factory from the Point of View of the Victims')
(WDR/WDF)

The bases for the jury's decision:
The team observed the closure of a works for over five months. The result
is a convincing presentation of social processes and their effects on those
concerned. These self-portrayals enable the viewer to identify with them
to a great degree, to emulate and to learn and this helps him to
understand comparable situations and to use this knowledge appropriately.   (translation by Scilla Alvarado)

12   LETTER FROM THE MANAGEMENT OF PHRIX TO HANS ABICH,
INTENDANT OF RADIO BREMEN

Dear Herr Abich,   12 January 1972
The film *Rote Fahnen sieht man besser* which described the effects of the
closure of our Krefeld works was broadcast on the WDR Third
Programme on 13 September 1971; your organisation was subsequently
responsible for its being screened on the First Programme on 14
December 1971. Given the extent to which this screening may influence
public opinion, we should like to make one or two comments in the light
of numerous criticisms voiced by the press and of a number of individual
letters from impartial television viewers.

The film was shot in the period between 4 September 1970 and 5
January 1971 during which the authors Theo Gallehr and Rolf Schübel
were allowed complete freedom of movement within the works on the
strength of their stated intention to represent events in an objective light.
Unfortunately our trust in the professional ethics of journalism was to be
sadly disappointed.

As far as we know it is one of the principles of the ARD to guarantee a
minimum of balance, objectivity and mutual respect in the content of its
programmes and not to deliver itself into the hands of one social group.

In the case in question, the bias in the presentation and the
manipulation of the evidence in text and image is patently obvious. In
view of the openness which we always showed towards the team during
the shooting of the film, we feel that we ought to have been able to expect
a similar propriety from them in the way they represented the closure. In
the *Glashaus* programme broadcast by the WDR on the 13 September
1971 Professor Jens expressed the criticism that the film *Rote Fahnen sieht*

138

man besser concealed its intention deliberately to manipulate the viewer. And indeed, according to the *Redakteur* Martin Wiebel in the subsequent discussion, material had been selected on the basis of 'enlightenment, interpretation of reality and political tendency'. We particularly noticed this lack of objectivity in the following matters:

1. To begin with, an objective presentation would have required greater consideration of the economic context. The film gives the impression that the closure of the Krefeld works was the result of capitalist intrigues; the truth is that the Krefeld works had to be closed down because losses had steadily increased as a result of economic developments, in particular the revaluation of the DM in 1969, and because there was no longer the remotest possibility of marketing the products of the works at prices that would even cover our costs. The film gives the impression that a closure of this kind would only be possible within a capitalist economic system; the truth is that there is no economic system within which it is not necessary from time to time to close down a production plant because it no longer makes economic sense to keep it open. The film gives the impression that it is a characteristic of our present economic order that job security is ruthlessly subordinated to the interests of capital; the truth is that there is no economic system which can guarantee every single person a specific job to all eternity; the closure of individual works and thus the regrettable necessity for some workers to change their jobs are inevitable within any economic system; it is economic policy alone which can ensure that new jobs are created elsewhere to replace jobs that are no longer economically required, by means of implementing a policy of full employment.

We should like to illustrate our train of thought with a (fictitious) example which, we believe, will make our meaning quite clear. Let us suppose that things should develop to a point when all transatlantic passengers travel by aeroplane and nobody by ship. Would it then make sense to keep the ships in operation without passengers in order to maintain jobs for the members of crew? If in such a case a passenger ship is withdrawn from service, is it then justified to reproach the management of the shipping line with acting purely out of avarice? A reproach of this kind would be particularly grotesque if the shipping line in question belonged to a public joint-stock company whose hundreds of thousands of shareholders — almost all of them medium or small savers — would suffer losses for absolutely no reason if such a passenger ship were to be allowed to continue operating without any passengers.

We would recall in this connection that the two companies which held shares in Phrix-Werke AG at the time of the closure of the Krefeld works — BASF AG and the Dow Chemical Company — are both public joint-stock companies whose shares are owned in each case by several hundred thousand small savers.

2. An objective presentation would have furthermore required a more detailed account of the payments made under the social welfare plan. At least one fact essential for the viewer to form an opinion has been suppressed here. We regard this as another infringement of the ARD Programme Principles. We would also point out in passing that payments under this social welfare plan were the largest ever made in the Federal Republic. The total amount came to 21 million DM, of which over 10 million DM was allocated to the Krefeld works.

Three out of the four Phrix workers who collaborated in the film found new and on the whole suitable jobs after leaving the company. Even so they received compensation of between 3206 DM and 5665 DM net under the social welfare plan. In the particularly serious case of our former colleague Fritz Thomas, we paid compensation of 16,573 DM net which fully supplemented his Social Security benefits. We would point out in this connection that here too the film did not give an objective presentation of the facts since it did not take into consideration the system of welfare benefits in the Federal Republic, paid for by our market economy and acclaimed all over the world, which came into effect in precisely this case.

For a journalist to disregard all these facts is a violation of his code of professional ethics. Dieter Süverkrüp's song was particularly derogatory about our social welfare plan. His appearance in the film was intended purely to rouse the emotions since he contributed nothing to the documentation of events. We are pleased that at least you did not broadcast Dieter Süverkrüp's performance which had been planned to end the film.

It cannot in principle be the function of a public corporation to influence public opinion with a programme which is without even the remotest objectivity; that is, which only represents the interests of a specific social group. Its content, style and interpretation are in flagrant contradiction of Article 7 of the Law regarding the Establishment and Function of Radio Bremen, which expressly stipulates that 'all news items and reports' must be 'true and objective in respect of content, style and interpretation'. We can understand that the regrettable fact that a works had to be closed down is of such great public interest that this theme was taken up by television over and above its coverage of current affairs. But this problem is too serious to be dealt with one-sidedly, from only one particular socio-political viewpoint and without regard to the economic context or to the welfare benefits provided both by the company concerned and by the market economy.

Yours sincerely,
The Management (Dr Albers & Dr Bischoff),
Phrix-Werke AG.

(translation by Sheila Johnston)

13 STATEMENT BY THE FILM-MAKERS THEO GALLEHR AND ROLF SCHÜBEL IN REPLY TO NEWSPAPER ARTICLES IN THE *Frankfurter Allgemeine Zeitung* ABOUT THEIR FILM *Rote Fahnen sieht man besser*

The *FAZ* has devoted three articles to the film *Rote Fahnen sieht man besser* since the screening of 14 December 1971. Two of these articles appeared in the business section, the first on 16 December 1971 two days after the screening and the last on 19 February 1972 about two months after the film had been broadcast on the ARD First Programme.

The *FAZ* articles reproached us with, among other things, 'falsification of reality', 'manipulation', the tendentious selection of material and violation of our code of professional ethics. For example, it was alleged that we had set up certain scenes and then passed them off as documentation. The source of this information was not acknowledged. We made inquiries and found out that no-one had asked the people who collaborated in the film how it had been made. There were other facts too that these attacks neglected to verify. So the *FAZ* reporter does not waste much time on something very basic to the ethics of journalism, i.e. conscientious research. He passes off as facts things which he has invented himself or learned through hearsay, but accuses us of neglecting our duty in this respect after we have spent ten months of the most conscientious work on our film.

The very point of departure of these articles is wrong. The film is treated by the *FAZ* as though the things said in the film had been invented by us. The sub-title, 'The closure of a factory from the point of view of those who lost their jobs' has been ignored by the reporter. It is correct that almost a hundred per cent of the film was shot with direct sound. In editing the film we selected extracts from conversations between the four protagonists and members of their families, friends, colleagues and the film-makers. In addition to this, the film contains excerpts from interviews with a member of the Works Council, a trade union spokesman and gentlemen representing the management.

The shooting work on our film was completed in the middle of January 1971. Events which took place after this date were not dealt with in our film. So, for example, the number of workers still without jobs in June 1971 could no longer be relevant to the film. The figures quoted in the *FAZ* regarding this are false, according to information from Heinz Steinke, spokesman for the German Federation of Trade Unions in Krefeld. Further details may be found in Steinke's letter, which is included in the documentation.

The amount of compensation received from Phrix by our four protagonists was withheld not by us, as the *FAZ* states, but by the protagonists themselves, who did not consent to the disclosure of the sums involved. We respected their wish, just as we respected the wishes of Herr Selbach of the Supervisory Board and of Herr Dr Morawski of the Board of Directors. Both these gentlemen were shown their interviews in their entirety on the editing table. They had the opportunity of cutting out entire passages from their statements, and indeed made use of it.

None of our protagonists received an allowance from the hardship fund even though only one of them was under thirty. In fact the worker Fritz Thomas was 57 years old.

None of the four protagonists bought a house (or could have afforded to buy one). In fact a trade unionist from Krefeld — a former employee of Phrix — told us that a hundred per cent rent increase was imposed on employees living in the former Phrix houses. According to him, only two houses belonging to the works have been sold, and these to employees in managerial positions.

None of the four protagonists made any statement regarding the pension fund. We must repudiate the accusation, both that we had falsified reality and that we had pieced together out of our couple of thousand metres of film only those bits which fitted into our preconceived view of the world. The following criteria were used in selecting our material from the total footage:

a) restriction to a prescribed length, which was in fact exceeded by about ten per cent;
b) restriction to the themes and arguments important to our protagonists (a works closure from the point of view of those who lost their jobs !!); and finally
c) the need to document the learning process of the four protagonists. We are moreover convinced that even an impartial viewer of our total footage would find nothing in the statements of the four protagonists which fitted into the preconceived view of the world held by the editors of the *FAZ*. Indeed we were extremely wary about using statements which bitterly abused 'those in charge'.

The allegation that we 'set up scenes, paid those collaborating in them and then passed them off as documentation' is a vile calumny. All four protagonists have made affidavits that during the entire period of shooting they were neither given a set-up scene to act out nor asked to make a statement dictated by us.

The fees received by some of those collaborating in the film bore no relation to their expenses. For example, the four protagonists received 1100 DM each. In return, they had to be available during the entire shooting period (five months!). We were frequently in their homes, both with and without the film crew, used electricity and were now and then even offered something to eat or drink. None of the four protagonists even knew during the first few weeks of shooting that they were going to be paid a fee. In fact we deliberately avoided using people who offered to do anything we asked in return for a large fee. We did not want actors, either professional or amateur, but people who were interested in our work. They helped us not least because they had confidence in us and were certain that their interests, i.e. the workers' interests, would be represented in this film, something that happens all too rarely in the mass media.

The accusations made against us in the *FAZ* are false. This is proved by the material contained in the documentation.

Munich, 29 February 1972
(from WDR Presstelle, 1972; translation by Sheila Johnston)

14 WHAT CAN THE HERO DO? HE CAN CHANGE THE WORLD!
A FEW PROBLEMS CONCERNING DRAMA PRODUCTION

Many television plays, good and bad, have come about because a drama producer or script-writer has said at some time or other, 'Something ought to be made about . . . ' Then a so-called 'theme' usually follows, a 'problem' which the person who thought it so serious that he wanted to 'make something about it' considers relevant. This approach, which surely has something to do with the proximity of the television editorial staff in the drama department to those of current affairs, features and the political journal ('I've got a programme on Monday — do you know of any more grievances?') has in recent years made a definite impact on the 'television play' genre and has set it apart from the cinema film, probably not always to its advantage. Now there would be nothing against this approach, which cautiously and discerningly commits itself to the subject matter of the film, if this fixation with bringing the facts to light were always extended to consider the question of how the facts should be presented, how the bare theme becomes a living story, how the content finds a form and the one mediates the other.

One can well imagine that Heinrich Böll was at some time annoyed about the particular practices of a certain newspaper ('Something really should be made about that'). Had the character of Katharina Blum not occurred to him, it would have remained at that. One can well imagine that Bernard Sinkel had at some time or other become annoyed about how abominably society treats its old people. Had the character of Lina Braake not occurred to him, just one more of those 'Isn't-it-bad-for-old-people' films which have flooded the channel for some time would have emerged from the theme. In both cases, and that is why I have mentioned them here, a social problem was attached to a person who related to her social environment in a particular way, who was suffering as an object of that situation, and yet who, as a subject at the same time also stood firmly against it, resisted it, attempted to influence it in her

143

own way. Both are also interesting because they are supposed to deal with a quite definite social reality known to all viewers, while at the same time abandoning this reality through a narrative device, thus clearly making it problematic. The character assassination practices which Böll or Volker Schlöndorff and Margarete von Trotta describe are well known; everyone knows the situation of old people with which Sinkel is concerned. What is not so clear is that the victim of such a character assassination would ever have shot a journalist; neither is it obvious that an old woman would have taken revenge on a bank in the way Lina Braake did. Thus the films do not merely imitate reality; on the contrary, they add to it, they include within the subject the resistance to it. This has become, so to speak, the meat which goes beyond the mere duplication of reality and is striking for its utopian, unreal and even irrational element. Here we are talking about the hero. (The fact that they are both heroines is, by the way, no accident but possibly deliberate, even though there are definite inherent romantic features.)

This use of drama, which attempts to deal with reality by means of utopia, is not unproblematic, as is evident when one thinks maybe of Fassbinder's *Eight Hours Are Not a Day,* a working-class series whose hero certainly does not act as workers generally do. Nevertheless, reality was intended, but this reality was not to appear as natural and unchangeable but as part of a process which might be influenced by human beings. In order to make this clear and accessible, the 'hero' Jochen was conceived of as a fictional figure possessing the principal characteristics of being able to move everything which at first sight appears to be fixed, to resist all the opposition which had appeared so sacrosanct; in short he acts absolutely in his own interests and always tries to see the possibilities for changing bad situations. The 'upright stature' ('aufrechte Gang'), as we then called Jochen's mode of behaviour, quoting from Ernst Bloch, did not last long of course and soon had to end on account of its own contradiction: Jochen's scope for development as subject of the story was limited from the beginning; it was actually to be anticipated that he would have to come up against limits which despite everything tended socially to make an object out of him — a victim of social processes which possibly allow compromises but not victories. The utopian character of Jochen was too strongly programmed for victory for him to have accepted the compromise which probably would have been more true to reality.

I think the decision made at that time, to provide a 'working-class' series with such a strictly utopian element, is correct even today, although, at the same time, it did make the continuation of the series impossible; the majority of viewers enjoyed it and many critics were upset by it. If Jochen once more wanted to go about bashing his head against the wall, both groups could at least learn where the walls stand in this world and how massive they are. Finally, it must not be forgotten

144

that *Eight Hours* was also a reaction (if not an 'over-reaction') to a whole tradition of mouse-grey films before it which had merely portrayed the life of the worker as that of a powerless victim. Then after *Eight Hours* a whole line of films about the working class emerged handling the subject/object problem in drama more carefully and cleverly and these in so doing perhaps were able to learn particularly from the bizarre elements of *Eight Hours*.

In *Smog*, Wolfgang Menge has incorporated quite the opposite approach to the dramatic technique of *Eight Hours;* that is, not only is there a total absence of a 'hero' but also of active subjects. This film is just as didactic as it is extremely critical. *Smog* was, in its genesis, the classic case of a 'theme' film ('Something ought to be made about pollution'); it needed well over half a year of researching, reflecting, reading (pursued, by the way, in an unsystematic and haphazard fashion), until suddenly and quite compellingly, there was the dramatic concept: the North Rhine-Westphalian plan of emergency in case of smog, an insignificant, dry official directive which one could read like a scenario if one wanted to make a film on this theme: it begins here and ends there, and something happens in between. All this was in the 'Administrative Directive to the Authority responsible for Public Order: Measures to be taken when weather conditions do not change'. No human beings other than officials and functionaries appeared in it. There were no 'human beings' as such in *Smog*, but rather suffering, passive creatures, powerless victims of an event which this time literally took place above their heads.

The fundamental position of *Smog* was described sometimes in discussions with film students at adult extra-mural classes and at universities as 'fatalistic' or 'cynical'. This may be a correct observation as far as the symptom is concerned; incorrect, however, when one looks for the cause. The reason for *Smog* giving some people a 'fatalistic' impression is to be found in the subject itself, because it simply dictated the corresponding form. A smog catastrophe is essentially a sort of natural event, certainly produced by human beings indirectly, but not literally induced by them nor are they directly responsible — the emergency situation 'sets in' or it 'occurs' as is written so precisely in the official documents. All that human beings can do about it is just prevent the worst, or endure it. The dramatic organisation of this theme copies this event exactly: the meteorological office sees the so-called situation of inversion approaching, the bell-shaped haze (warm air above, cold beneath — no circulation of air) turns upside down over the Ruhrgebiet and beneath it the oxygen is reduced and harmful agents increase. Thus the first day passes, and the second day. On the third day the authorities follow the alleviation measures prescribed in the plan, on the fourth day the weather situation changes, wind comes up and 'blows the whole nightmare away', as it says in the film; life goes on, as is expressed 'cynically' by the cheerful closing music. In my opinion it would have been 'cynical' had the people who experienced all this as passively suffering objects been transformed at this point by some heroic trick into active subjects; a totalitarian event of this kind just has no space for this, the content itself could only be depicted as terrifyingly as possible so that it would perhaps be changed outside the film. Within the film this would have been idealistic eyewash.

Eight Hours on the one hand and *Smog* on the other are certainly extreme cases of dramatic forms, but because of this one can describe particularly clearly how a conceptual decision about form, which is inevitable in a dramatic work, also effects the content. This problem has again become evident for me in the two productions I am preparing at present at Bavaria Studios for WDR. Both of these 'disparate' films basically have a social theme: one deals with the rise of the German bourgeoisie in the 19th Century; the other takes place in the present and deals with the Federal Defence Forces. One is a film of the novel *Soll und Haben (Debit and Credit)* by Gustav Freytag and is narrated by a 'hero' in a straightforwardly classical way despite its theme which is that of the history of a large business firm of the period. In the other film, Wolfgang Menge describes the execution of a so-called Federal Defence Forces map manoeuvre. Naturally a great number of people act in it, but not one of them stands out in a way which would make him interesting as an active subject so that he could be described as a 'hero'. Instead, this film reproduces in a nutshell its subject matter as it is and records it instead of dramatising it through external intervention, as would have been absolutely possible technically, most probably through the introduction of a dominant character with whom one would identify. What is the reason for these concepts of narrative being so extremely different from each other? Let us ignore the fact that the one film naturally follows the concept of the novel already in existence — even a film conceived independently certainly would have similarly linked its theme to one character. On the contrary in both cases the actual structuring is clearly defined by the theme of the film. One deals with a period in German history which was characterised by individuals who behaved confidently, were active and mass produced: the early German bourgeoisie. What could be more obvious than to express what is essentially a social phenomenon in drama? The other film, the simulation of a military conflict on the soil of the Federal Republic, played out by the 'orange' and 'blue' parties, executes an operation which in reality simply does not take into account the concept of the 'individual', for all the participants follow rules which are not theirs and which they, moreover, could not influence or even change. In one film the hero changes the world — the feudal society is severed by the bourgeoisie; in the other even the supposed 'heroes' are in fact only executors of military and political logic. They, and even more so the rest, are possibly only the unheroic

146

victims of this logic. The dramatic category of the 'hero' can, if a rule is to be made, only be genuine when it is legitimised by social reality; where this is so well established in the content that the subject can do nothing about it, it is more correct to take this up in the form of the film as well.

Peter Märthesheimer
(from *Fernsehspiele,* WDR, Jan./June 1976, translation by Scilla Alvarado)

15 THE OCCUPATION OF A BOURGEOIS GENRE

Standardisation and Serialisation in Television

For some time there has been a marked tendency in television for the culture industry to standardise and serialise all its productions; even those which are clearly autonomous works of art tend to be labelled with the series rubric of 'The Autonomous Work of Art'. This development began with the importation from the advanced television countries — the USA and England — of popular series for the early evening and then for peak-viewing programming too. But soon we too learnt how to produce our own series or rather to somewhat violently clamp together programmes which were quite disparate in form and content with common labels ('The location film', 'The studio film', 'The Monday play', or even for example 'The Scene of the Crime'). The reasons for this are only partly to be found on the production side, the production of a series being relatively more economical than the production of plays. In the first place the series (whether it is the Western which only varies in minor details, the high-quality paperback, or the television series in several parts) has an advantage on the distribution side; even the cheapest and best product and the most relevant and most interesting television programme must first of all make a name for itself if it is to attract attention at all. This is achieved most easily if it is introduced as something blatantly familiar to the public — like a western, a high-quality paperback or a television series. If they watch the first five episodes then they will continue to watch the next eight.

It is in the Third Channel, which has shunned the world of commerce, that television most often displays its non-domestic potential for imaginative and creative uniqueness. Television lost its purity some time ago in the majority of its programmes and adjusted to the commerical mechanisms which came into play from the day the two channels began to compete with each other for viewers. Consequently this readjustment constituted an attempt to reach as many viewers as possible, for television was established from the start as a mass medium, its total technical range being closely linked to demand. In its efforts to create an audience for itself, television is of course dealing with an intrinsic characteristic which distinguishes it qualitatively from other media. A

147

film can still be seen in the cinema three days after the première, a novel can still be bought three years after its appearance. Television, on the other hand, lives only through the transient minutes of its programmes, which only exist for the short duration of their transmission and generally cannot be repeated, and if they are, already seem dated. Television is forced, more than other media, to make its precise and ever new productions appear to have continuity and above all familiarity for the public, in order to have them on its side. It is easier to win people over to one's side if they think *their* interests are represented: 'their' master of ceremonies or 'their' star is appearing; a quiz programme is shown in which, without fail, the same questions are always put, always eliciting the same responses; a thriller is put on where the hero hunts down different criminals using different ruses and yet one is led to suspect that it is basically no different from the last one; finally there is the family series, the characters being so familiar to the viewers after the first episode that they not only know their problems but also the very way in which they will solve them.

The objectives of programmes which are to be accessible to the viewers inevitably work against themselves. When a programme succeeds in winning over the viewers, it is promptly appropriated by them and furthermore they actually control it — it has to surrender itself to them. As a mass medium television is constantly exposed to the temptation of subjecting its programmes to the law of the majority and creating a level of consensus. If one defines a 'borderline viewer' as the person whom television can still just about reach without sacrificing a certain level of quality in the programmes, the question arises whether the quality level should not be lowered in order to reach the last possible viewer whose level of reception then determines the programme. Serialising a programme is only part of this attempt to reach the largest possible audience. It is particularly in the series that television has always up until now lowered its standards so strikingly. This cannot be explained purely by the quantity of viewers. Reasons for this drop in quality must be found in the genre itself; a genre which has to be as familiar to its public as a series (and the so called 'family series' even more so), can for a short time avoid the demands of its fans, but it seems that sooner or later, it must succumb to their embrace.

'Eight Hours Are Not a Day'

The series *Eight Hours Are Not a Day*, conceived of from the beginning by Rainer Werner Fassbinder together with WDR, gave itself coyly (bearing in mind the dialectic intrinsic in a series) just like some young girl. Of course it did not want to remain quite unloved, it wanted to flirt with the favour of the people; it did not want to surrender, but then again it wanted to be desired. This conflict expressed itself clearly not only in

148

some of the peripheral characters, for example, in Aunt Clara, the stereotype of the comic old spinster or in Mr Meier, the stereotype of the subordinate official, but also in the central figures like Grandma and Gregor, who in their splendid rarity leave no doubt that they have escaped straight from a farce and would not be dissuaded from introducing its devices and techniques even into the serious world of a working-class family. The dramatic strategy of the series is most clearly recognisable in the behaviour of Grandma and Gregor, which appears eccentric and extravagent. In the genre of the bourgeois farce or comedy, the technique of which they so dramatically exploit, Oma and Gregor would have remained comparatively inconspicuous. They only become so striking because the forms of expression which formerly belonged to the bourgeois and petit bourgeois milieu are in *Eight Hours* introduced for the first time into the proletarian milieu, and with these forms stories are told in a completely different way. This transplantation has two advantages — one of aesthetic effect: how the characters behaved was very striking, 'distanciated' against the given background; the other of ideology: the apparently unlimited scope for action and behaviour which bourgeois culture allows its heroes in the novel, the theatre and even in the family series, addicted to eclecticism and the cult of the private, offers an effective lever to make problematic the established, regimented and constrained working-class milieu.

The Bird's Eye View of Films About the Working Class

Films about the working class which had previously appeared on television, despite all differences in content and actual forms of presentation, can be distinguished by a common ideological view of milieu and characters. The milieu was portrayed as grey, sad and cheerless, especially the work situation, which was depicted as totally unbearable and inhuman yet essentially unchangeable. The characters were conclusively part of this bird's eye view, which was compassionate and sympathetic but in reality must have appeared arrogant at times from the victim's point of view; deprived and resigned human beings, objects and victims of a social situation which presented itself through the alleged stasis as a natural condition against which it seemed from the beginning pointless to rebel. And for those who dared to rebel in these films, perhaps out of sheer foolhardiness, failure was so absolutely certain that change for a worker was inconceivable.

The New Position: The Reality Which Can Be Changed

Thus from the beginning *Eight Hours Are Not a Day* was intended to create an alternative to the simple assumption that the worker is not only the 'underdog' of this society, but must inevitably remain so. Certainly the workers are the negroes, on whose bones this society reproduces itself;

certainly the official nomenclature is correct in labelling the workers as 'dependents', and certainly this dependence has an effect on the consciousness of the victims, which at times is as pitiful as the conditions from which it emerges. Yet the tendency to be limited to reproducing and repeating what has been found to be the case suppresses the contradictions inherent in relations which are not just conditions but processes, to which human beings are not simply subjected but which they keep in motion, whether through resistance or through initiative. *Eight Hours Are Not a Day* has thus provided its characters with qualities which general opinion formerly had not wanted to acknowledge in proletarian characters and which are rather carefully sketched: self-confidence, activity, tenacity, courage, smartness, cunning — qualities which one needs and must develop all the more if one's social situation is difficult. Furthermore this series made available to its workers actions and experiences which up to now had seemed to belong to the catalogue of behaviour and experience of another social group. So the workers in *Eight Hours* are actually interested in their work instead of just confronting it with disgust and suffering; they have happy experiences; they actually reflect on their living conditions and how they could improve them; they actually try to settle a conflict for themselves and sometimes they are even successful, or slightly successful. *Eight Hours Are Not a Day* is made as if workers are not mere objects of history, but could also be its subjects, as if they are not subjected to blind fate, but could take fate into their own hands.

Bourgeois Freedom in the Proletarian Milieu: the Proletarian Hero

Formerly the bourgeoisie had always seen itself as the sole subject of the history of bourgeois society, and consequently this was also reflected in bourgeois culture, which was concerned incessantly with its own kind in its novels, plays, films and also in its television series. The open and excessive rage which occasionally met *Eight Hours* can only be explained in this context. Clearly our characters have here stepped into alien territory; a playground of bourgeois freedoms, which until now seemed to be reserved for the bourgeois individual, as though the demand of this society had not taken into account the development of *every* individual. The reaction must have appeared all the more vehement because the bourgeoisie had already related its final family histories with *Buddenbrooks* or *Debit and Credit*, of which it could still be proud, and ever since has reflected more and more its decline and uncertainty. This social disorientation has found its most concrete expression in the family series, and there the former proud claim to be master of history has totally declined into the helpless and pointless struggle to remain master of a pitiful private destiny in the middle of an impenetrable and overwhelming world. Jochen and Marion and the other working-class characters who suddenly occupy this playground with such naïvety as if the world belonged to them are, through this behaviour, imitating nothing more than the proud conduct of the former bourgeoisie. And as this playground has been vacated for some time by their predecessors, it offers an excellent opportunity to slide into the old behavioural patterns and to test them out in a new world. This world, introduced into the genre by *Eight Hours*, was certainly one which encouraged an analysis of reality and was not the world of the private pseudo-conflicts which had previously dominated the genre and which were basically only an expression of the socially diffuse position of the petit bourgeoisie and its shaky, ill-defined and uncommitted consciousness.

The only interesting family series to have come out of the petit bourgeois milieu are those where the characters have emerged as socially critical liberals, who do not so much gaze at their own private navels as at socially relevant problems. The characters of *Eight Hours* were from the start at an advantage, taking into account incidentally the difficulties of attempting to be socially useful in the interests of others (because one's own interests are so difficult to define due to the heterogeneous nature of social grouping). The interests they fought for always represented the majority position as well as their own; they could thus act in solidarity, because 'solidarity' is not a foreign word to their class, but derives from the situation which is fundamentally common to them all, and to a great extent is perceived as such from the start and so may easily be made problematic. This had frequently been depicted in other films, namely the traditional films about the working class. What was new about *Eight Hours* was that the two concepts were brought together: the proletarian milieu on the one hand and the bourgeois hero on the other, a sociologically clearly definable social class and a fictional character whose very mode of behaviour had up until now always been attributed to another class.

The Didactic Effect of the Series

The contradiction intrinsic in this perspective, which the critics quite succinctly labelled as 'painted proletarians', in the first instance proved to be extremely productive (its limitations will be discussed later) as far as the possible didactic effect of the series goes. Learning through television is certainly a very complex process which is difficult to measure in any case, especially when the teaching material is an entertaining family series. It is probable that the mode of behaviour attributed to a popular and familiar character in a series requires from the start a relatively high degree of attentiveness. This attentiveness will probably be greater the more clearly the behaviour is perceived as something irregular, abnormal and unconventional, which nevertheless stimulates identifications or, further still, discussion. It may provoke

151

discussion about those aspects of identification (how one once wanted to be and yet was not; how one should have liked to have acted and yet did not) and so this is made problematic and thereby requires examination. It was this critical relation to reality in *Eight Hours* which constituted the interest for the viewers (who watched faithfully for the five episodes of the series despite the attractive alternative offerings on the other channel, zdf), because here reality was depicted — through the deviant and non-conformist behaviour of the characters — as something which could be changed, provoking thought instead of reproducing yet again what exists in its apparently overwhelming entirety; because identical human behaviour was presented in a world intent on obstructing such behaviour, if not bent on its destruction; because here was being affirmed the refusal to endlessly adapt — for a limited time at any rate — when it would have been better to apply the principles of realism; because a direction which had been considered correct was not denounced as incorrect merely because it proved to be difficult to achieve.

The Limitations of this Perspective

Eight Hours Are Not a Day represented the first stages in establishing a working-class series on television reaching a public who would like to avoid confronting its own problems, meeting the representation of itself with disinterest and apathy — the numbers of those who switch on pertinent films being only too clear evidence of this. *Eight Hours* could only take this first step because it takes up the offensive at the same time as it retreats, in as far as the position of the proletariat is presented by a basically bourgeois character. This device, although necessary in view of the inarticulateness and powerlessness of the workers themselves, whose social position does not tolerate the self-confident hero made possible by the range in the arsenal of characters of the genre, at the same time points to the limitations of such a perspective. It has been criticised, not without justification, for the 'upright stature' of its characters, now and then exhibiting modes of behaviour which were 'individualistic and competitive' or 'hostile to organisation' — just those characteristics which they had of necessity acquired through borrowing from the bourgeois hero and which are now a hindrance. If the first five episodes of *Eight Hours* have succeeded nevertheless in making the figure of the 'proletarian hero' plausible in the consciousness of the public, if the resistance to a working-class series has been reduced a little with this first attempt, then one can more easily think afresh about how the proletariat could be more realistically portrayed from its own position.

Peter Märthesheimer
(from *Fernseh und Bildung*, no. 13, 1974; translation by Scilla Alvarado)

Gong, 'the television magazine for the beautiful hours at home', rated the last but one episode of *Eight Hours Are Not a Day* as 'very good'. And then followed word for word: 'A shame that we have to wait until November for the continuation'. We must wait, but three more episodes are definitely coming. The director Rainer Werner Fassbinder declared with frankness that the series had been planned for a long time. First of all you have to make contact with the viewers, create a 'potential audience', and then you can 'try to include political content. *This is done in such a way that the viewers might possibly be prepared to join the German Communist Party (DKP) with the characters.*' So Fassbinder sees himself as the fifth column within television.

Günter Rohrbach, Head of television drama and entertainment in WDR, sees the programme as a model for independent action. Consciousness-raising cannot be achieved with a wooden hammer, but in small doses. In fact: allusions to worker interests have been consciously very sparing in the programmes so far but they are going to become 'more obvious' in the autumn. In the eighth and penultimate episode the central issue will be a wages settlement struggle. Hanna Schygulla refers to the kind of ideological unity which exists between the head of the channel, the director and the main actress: *'One of the many criticisms was that a worker does not bring about a revolution on the screen. Who is going to throw stones next to bring about the avalanche?'* Schygulla has, however, recognised the alienating aspect of her work. 'The director, who is far from being a worker, makes films about workers with actors who are also far from being workers, films which show the world of the workers not as it is, but how it could and should be.' She is frustrated. But, she says, 'The really new things come from the East.' Fassbinder spells out how one can agitate for class struggle on television: 'WDR is a fairly spongy institution. For example the intendant von Bismarck was against the series. And then there are other people who have the same objectives as I do. In other words, to make things that are dangerous for the so-called ruling class. *The reason for my series getting through probably lies in the fact that it went on in the entertainment slot.* The same content packed into a single film and without the entertainment value would probably not have been transmitted'.

So this was how it was made. One can agitate easily in the entertainment slot. Because the control body, especially the party representatives, are concerned with political programmes, their personal-political thoughts do not reach the entertainment sector. It is particularly in this area that the overcoming of the system is sold in small doses. *Gong* finds this 'very good'.

Stama-Studio, Munich carried out a lightening survey on behalf of Tele-Control in 20 towns in the federal area to find out the reaction of the audience to the last episode of the A R D-series *Eight Hours Are Not a Day* (18 March, 20.15 hours). Here are the results of the survey: 51 per cent of those who had seen the programme were of the opinion that class struggle between employees and employers had been emphasized a great deal. 23 per cent, just under a quarter of the viewers questioned, were of the opinion that *the attempt* in the tapes shown *to propogate control over the means of production by the workers, i.e. the usage of surplus value in the communist sense, was subliminal.* According to their answers the viewers saw the employer image portrayed in the programme as follows: 74 per cent saw the employers complying with the suggestion of the worker group in this film *as it was in their own interests.* 9 per cent thought that the employer only wanted *to avoid unpleasantness with the staff, i.e. the works council;* a further 9 per cent were of the view that the employer only complied with the suggestion of the group of workers in the hope that the venture would fail so that further attempts of the labour force in the direction of 'more independence' could be quashed; 14 per cent represented the view that the employer was acting out of *social responsibility.* A few of the interviewees stated several motives and the rest had no opinions. *Almost half* (47 per cent) finally described the group of workers portrayed in the film and their behaviour as *distorted or completely unreal* and were thus not convinced by the accuracy in the presentation of the milieu.

(from *Tele-Control* no. 6, 29 March 1973; translation by Scilla Alvarado)

17 CHRISTIAN ZIEWER: THE ORIGINS OF LIEBE MUTTER, MIR GEHT ES GUT

Two ideas were the starting point for this film:

1. It had become very clear to my colleague Klaus Wiese and myself, when investigating the situation in factories during the recession 1966/67, how great the difficulties were for most of those workers hit by lay-offs, short-time work or cuts in wages if they wanted to get beyond the experience of their individual fates in order to acquire more extensive knowledge of the politics of the running of their factories, of the economic aspect of the total social framework and of the possibilities for the employees of changing their situation.

2. In the English and Italian films which we valued and even the few German television productions which analyse similar problems, there has not been sufficient concern either with individual fate or with social problems over and above the personal.

In addition to this came the experiences which I had had in my work with target groups in the Brandenberg area. There it had become clear how receptive, almost zealous, the people we were addressing were when films confronted their concrete situation, their direct needs. For needs did not just arise out of passive consumer attitudes but also from self-awareness and knowledge — that is, if the viewers had their situation presented as being open to change, as a situation to which they do not have to succumb. Then the workers gained access to sophisticated points of view, to principles of analysis, to abstractions. The saying that 'they cannot think beyond their four walls' was no longer valid.

Guide lines for the script were as follows:
— Extreme accuracy in the description of everyday life.
— Analytical deductions about the different interests which are clearly defined and thus determine social conflict.

I tried to take both these aspects into account in the first drafts of the script by taking up the dialogue with those who had initially assisted me with reports of their work situation after I had made lengthy investigations: organised and unorganised workers, shop stewards, shop committees. The final form of the shooting script gradually emerged through a process of proposals and counterproposals and revisions being made after much criticism and deliberation. In this way a range of scenes changed and developed.

The longer we looked for ideas for scenes where the dialectic of production and worker existence (which is generally viewed as 'something personal and individual') could be posed, the more we were compelled to give up the dramatic technique of story as continuous action. We had to introduce the 'epic I', which took up a position outside the events (commentaries, titles, self-portrayals). Where connections were not made openly transparent in the human relationships, montage and editing produced new forms of narrative. In this phase of work places in the filming became significant where, during the *mise en scène*, the action was protracted and had to be brought to a standstill. Breaks should encourage the viewer to take up a position and by referring to his own experience, he should reach a greater understanding at these moments.

It was surprising to see how ready the workers were to forego a well-formed 'dramatic plot' once they were motivated to use creatively their own fantasy. This concern with taking control of one's own destiny led to the form of an 'epic film'.

At the same time as trying to provide the viewer with the appropriate stimulus I was also trying to achieve a similar image of change in the filming of material which embraces elements some of which are spontaneously authentic and some of which are constructed and static. Each of the four sections in the film contains some of the naturalism and obsession with detail of other television plays. Yet the realism does not

155

arise as a result of pure imitation. The inclusion of information which was beyond the immediate experience of the viewers provides a context for each of the everyday events so that these may be sifted, appraised and revised. A multi-layered complex of signs mediates each piece of information. Its clearly constructed nature makes the author very evident. He is not supposed to persuade but rather to encourage greater perception.

(translation by Scilla Alvarado)

18 CHRISTIAN ZIEWER: MORE ABOUT THE USES OF FILM

Preliminary note

'Useful films are those which show us *how* our conditions of life can be changed, by . . . developing out of the movement of reality a consciousness of this reality and . . . by starting new initiatives.'

That was what we wrote about our first film, *Liebe Mutter, mir geht es gut.* We should now like to add a reply to the question: How can an attitude be produced in the viewer that will encourage him to develop a 'consciousness of this reality'? For we do not believe that just looking at films will automatically awaken a need to relate them to our own lives and to take 'new initiatives'. Different principles of constructing films have different effects on the viewer. With the help of a few examples from *Schneeglöckchen blühn im September,* we should like to expound the methods with which, in our view, 'consciousness can be developed' and a connection established between film and our existence within society.

When we start work on our subject matter the formal structures we shall employ are only predetermined (from previous experience) to a limited extent. In most cases they do not emerge until we actually begin shooting and are often spontaneous and therefore intuitive. And so we should like to filter out and explain these methods in retrospect so that they can be 'appropriated' and utilised in future film-making. It is possible to find features in common with other films of the so-called 'Berlin School'. *Die Wollands, Lohn und Liebe, Wer braucht wen?, Der lange Jammer* and *Liebe Mutter* . . . have been important stimuli. If the people who make films like these are unable to clarify their inner logic, they will be in danger of instinctively longing for 'entertainment', 'suspense' and 'three-dimensional characters' and of succumbing to the fascination of thread-bare aesthetic models and all they imply.

I. The film does not present a 'character' drama

Originally we had planned to begin *Schneeglöckchen* . . . with an introductory scene showing Ed Malchow acting in a particular way towards his colleagues. Ed was the focal point of the scene and the function of the other figures was to explain him. But now the film starts off with a *collective* action. In this way the viewer is made to explore, not one single character, but the behaviour and internal dynamics of a whole group.

The entire film is structured on the same principle as this single scene. Protagonists are lost from view and 'incidental' characters take over the main action. The film is a network of collective relationships and projects: Diemal (the member of the works council) joins in activities started up by Hannes the *Vertrauensmann;* Grandpa Emil hands out leaflets; and Bertram collects signatures (the camera shows mainly him and not Hannes who initiated the campaign!). This juxtaposition of events reflects the basic experience of the workers' movement, which is that history is not made by great individuals but by collective action. The author should therefore avoid looking for the truth about society in the portrait of a single hero or in the interpretation of his characters.

In the middle section of the film it becomes particularly clear that the course of history has little to do with individual persons. As a result of certain movements of capital (the threatened close-down) the piece-workers accept a cut in wages. This puts a stop to Hannes' activities. He tries to stir up his colleagues against this pressure to economise, but without success. In the end he falls silent — not because he has run out of arguments but because he has to recognise the power of material repression, and because the conditions under which the workers have been fighting have taken such an extraordinary turn for the worse. His colleagues are numb with resignation, taking refuge in a flood of empty words. Now, unlike the earlier situations, Ed is on Hannes' side and recognises the futility of moral indignation.

Plots composed of collective activities are not likely to produce figures with whom the viewer can identify throughout the whole film. He can no longer put himself in the place of individual 'heroes' when his attention is being claimed by the relationships between a number of characters. The efforts of many people are needed in order to resolve conflicts, so how could identification with a single protagonist be adequate to answer the questions that have been raised? The traditional methods of identification are not called into question wilfully by the authors; rather is the old 'character' dramaturgy that tried to draw generalised conclusions from 'typical people' in 'typical situations' made obsolete by the laws of reality itself.

Another example from quite a different source may help to demonstrate that we are compelled by history to tell stories in other ways than with omnipresent characters and masterful heroes. The authors of *Andrei Rublev* felt that it was impossible to represent a whole epoch in the portrait of one central figure, and so other characters stepped into the foreground for long periods and became indices of social change.

157

There is another reason why confidence in the 'positive hero' has been shattered: people cannot be depicted realistically through images which are unequivocal and totally without contradiction. They are made up of all kinds of opposing aims and attitudes and have to create the future out of the ambiguous potential within themselves. Ed Malchow's self-assurance and capability make him do something (the repair work) that runs counter to an improvement in the collective situation. He gets a bonus from the foreman (in the dismissal scene) which has the effect of cutting him off from his colleagues. But under other conditions he puts just as much energy into the common cause. He calls for collective action against the wage cuts (in his own interest) and refuses to carry out repairs because he does not want to stab his striking colleagues in the back. (However, the camera does not dwell on him in admiration, but shows Hannes, who sees the result of his 'agitating'.) Ed Malchow has not undergone a personality change or received inspiration from above; instead he has drawn on existing potential that had hitherto been suppressed.

At the end of the film, Ed demands that his colleague, Udo, account for his actions; the workers' call for solidarity is absolute and its other face is an aggressive reaction against those who do not join in, an aggression which, by dividing the workers, prevents what it is trying to achieve: collective action.

These examples should show how important it is to represent people as full of contradictions. The viewer must be able to recognise that he does not necessarily have to reject everything as it is at present in order to change his conditions of life. Instead he must examine what is already there and develop qualities which have never been called upon before. In this way he will be able to look to the future with optimism.

II. The film does not present a 'drama'

The conclusions we have drawn about the characters in the plot also apply to the structure of the plot itself: fragmented, divided into chapters, broken up by inter-titles that suddenly announce what is about to follow, divorcing work from private life. With a structure like this, the proverbial 'unity of action' is no longer feasible. In order to represent a complex reality, it is necessary for the film to be more like a chronicle than a drama in which the scenes develop out of and lock into each other. The viewer has to make deductive leaps, connecting a number of different and only distantly related levels. The closed, linear form of classical dramaturgy precludes him from doing this. 'The main problem with my play is the fact that it will not lend itself to being organised in a few large units, as I would like, and that I have to split it up into too many parts discrete in time and space, a structure which . . . is always resistant to tragedy.' In these words Schiller complained that it was impossible to meet Aristotle's requirement for a centralised plot-structure if he wanted to represent a complex historical subject. The autonomy of the individual parts and the range they covered in time and space were incompatible with classical drama and were characteristic of the epic.

If even the classical writers could no longer meet the requirements of classical form in certain circumstances, it is clear that the modern author has far less justification for depicting his reality in accordance with that system. The meaning of our world is not revealed in a few great moments; it demands a wide perspective that draws together apparently unconnected events.

When authors believe that to show catastrophes will be enough to convince the viewer (as in Costa-Gavras' *Z*) or that brilliant dramatic effects can be used to put over a point, it is because they place their hopes in 'learning through catharsis'. But the labour movement has always learned its lessons by examining and organising its struggles. This called for a critical attitude towards its conditions of existence.

So the 'alienating' distance that results from the structure of our film is not due to a decision on our part to impose arbitrary aesthetic principles but to the method by which our viewers appropriate their reality. When the negotiations between management and works council are directly juxtaposed with events at the works, the viewer is invited to make connections between the two complexes of actions. (Eisenstein knew a lot about the way in which cross-cutting can be used to activate the viewer, as can be seen from his discussion of Griffith's montage technique.)

The confrontation between Diemal, representing the works council, and Schröder, representing the management, is an account of divergent interests rather than the dramatisation of a dynamic piece of action. In this way the viewer is not made to jump on a train on which he is trapped once it has started off. Instead the film tries to prompt him to see the conflicts from a distance and to assess the relationships between the various people.

However, the flow of the narrative is not interrupted only by the breaks between individual episodes, by commentary with music and songs and by the impact of contrasting scenes. Sometimes the course of events stops for a moment (less obviously but still perceptibly) within scenes and even within shots. We have already drawn attention to the wage-cutting scene. No more action seems possible and the scene turns into a tableau, exposed to the viewer's enquiring gaze. It does not place him 'under its spell' but challenges him to comment on it. One of the things that leads us to conclude that the viewer of our film does not cease thinking for himself (because of getting involved in the fictional drama for example) is the fact that an audience of workers could criticise through laughter the words with which Heinz tries to placate himself and the others: 'If they cut our wages now I'm sure the works won't be closed down'. The viewers laughed, although they had just been shown the defeat of the piece-workers. They did not pity themselves because they did not imagine themselves in this situation. They took up a critical stance. Nor is the effect of the final tableau of the film, showing the motionless workers and the gap left by Udo whom they were unable to accept, one of resignation because it embodies contradiction, making the viewer feel that 'things will get better'.

What is it that motivates the public to take on the considerable problems posed by a complex and self-reflexive epic narrative form? We believe it is his pleasure in the *operative* nature of the film that encourages the viewer to come to grips with it. The film shows him situations that have to be interpreted, commented on and completed from his own experience. Only through a critical engagement with the film, through working hard at it, can the viewer achieve an overall perspective. But this is not alienated labour: it is fundamentally different from the other problems in his life. By looking at and thinking out solutions to complex situations the viewer experiences the pleasure of being able to make history — *his* history. [Play on the double meaning of *Geschichte*: history/story — translator.]

III. The film does not build up 'suspense'

The viewer has learned from Hannes that the repair-workers have gone on strike. Then he hears in the course of negotiations between management and works-council that 400 workers have marched through the works on a demonstration. Not until he has been given this information does the viewer actually see the struggle of the workers.

It is apparent from the dramatic structure of these events that the audience's interest is not focused on the moment at which the workers' hesitation suddenly tips over into a wide-spread strike. Instead, we first show the piece-workers and their inability to take action (Ed's refusal to carry out the repairs is the only declaration of solidarity with the workers who are already on strike, but it is an individual act and so has no real effect) and then the attitudes of the negotiating parties. So precisely those facts which could elicit an emotional response in the viewer and which could have been built up into a 'suspenseful' *peripeteia* [sudden change of fortune] and climax are instead conveyed only in the form of reports. Since the negotiations are not systematically pushed towards a climax either, the news of the demonstration does not make the viewer feel that excitement described by Eisenstein as the aim of a 'pathetic composition'. The method used to develop the subject obviously breaks Aristotle's law that 'those elements with which tragedy should prefer-ably touch the heart are . . . the *peripeteia*'. We have already explained why it is not our aim to 'touch hearts'. 'Pity and fear' and 'catharsis by these same emotions' may be able to give the empathic viewer a deeply-moving experience but they are hardly a suitable basis for changing the world, and our audience's daily confrontations with its surroundings suggest that precisely this is its main concern.

So why does the public keep on going to the cinema of 'suspense' and exciting adventures? Because this cinema promises clear-cut situations that are so refreshingly different from the complexities of everyday life. Because it offers relaxation and resolution of the conflict it sets up, whereas all reality has to offer is one conflict after another in endless succession. The viewer even enjoys the catastrophe in a masochistic way because it vindicates his own feeling of impotence.

This cinema provides plenty of excitement and sorrow, but not much in the way of insights — may that be drummed into all the cinéastes who hope to put over political messages with old methods. No doubt they would have invented a purpose for the rallies, a race against the clock or other drivers; or they would have used the urgent music in the last third of the film not only to interpret the workers' actions as a prospect for the future but primarily to lend the demonstration the necessary impetus. But our viewers have no use for authoritarian film forms that prevent them from giving rein to their ideas and from mobilising their own experience, film forms which hold them fettered to the story.

But our refusal to submit the viewer to the usual 'suspense' does not necessarily mean that we have to lose his suspenseful interest. People are constantly asking themselves, 'How can we gain control over reality?', addressing themselves to this question with ever-renewed zeal. The *methods* of our films aim to pose this question correctly and to provoke some answers.

For example: when Diemal sets out to mobilise the men who work on the excavators the viewer does not know *how* he is going to do it. He can identify neither with Diemal because he is not yet familiar with his way of tackling things, nor with the young worker whom he hardly knows. He remains an observer at a distance from events, wondering 'How will he (Diemal) do it?' If we had told him about Diemal's 'trick' beforehand, he would no longer be interested in his method and would have waited maliciously for the worker to fall for it. But the way we decided to show it, he tries to guess what will happen, thinks out solutions and evaluates the result that is finally provided. In this case we find the method of 'suspenseful expectation' appropriate to encouraging a creative attitude in the audience.

Conclusion

We should have made it clear by now that we want to demolish the traditional principles of composition not only because of our conception of social relations but also because we are concerned to produce a certain

161

attitude in the viewer. Films should be judged by the extent to which they are able to change the consciousness of the viewer and to reduce 'false' consciousness. So realist films can only be described as 'imitations of reality' if this term also includes the independent activity of the viewing subject. Aesthetic methods must be seen in relation to the thought processes they start off; they derive their power from the contradictions they express.

Ed Malchow is exposed to the pressures of consumerism if he wants to fulfil himself in his spare time: he has to make sacrifices for his rallies. And conversely: if he wants to satisfy this need, he must fight for it and, at certain moments, not *against* his fiancée and colleagues but *with* them. This is a characteristic of the dual nature of reality and of its explosive nucleus, thrusting towards liberating action. This nucleus is not kept hidden from the viewer. It gives him the confidence expressed in *Schneeglöckchen* by Grandpa Emil: 'The workers have a long way to go before they wage the class war properly — but there are some short-cuts'.

(translation by Sheila Johnston)

19 EXPOSED

Christian Ziewer, one of the two authors of the 'Workers'. Drama' *Schneeglöckchen blühn im September*, which was shown on German television (WDR) on the 12th November, exposed in a single sentence the aim of all films of this type: 'Films should be judged by the extent to which they are able to change the consciousness of the viewer and to reduce false consciousness.' So according to this, the aim of the television dramas which have been broadcast, mainly by the WDR, over the past two years is not the representation of the working world as it really is but the political manipulation of the viewer.

It is apparent that fewer and fewer critics are inclined to go along with the left-wing caprices of militant authors and producers. When, according to a recent report in the weekly *Das Parlament*, the WDR producer responsible for these films claimed that so far no critics had accused them of being unrealistic and one-sided, he must have read only a few reviews that suited him; surely he had overlooked what *Das Parlament* had to say about *Schneeglöckchen*. Although Herbert Lilge of the Hessen Centre for Political Education concedes that this 'typical testimony to the proletarian film' has a 'certain merit', he also calls it a 'fashionable caricature of employers and managers'. Hans-Jörg von Jena, teacher and lecturer, makes no bones about it: 'The film is partisan, and deliberately so. It is an incitement to class warfare'. And he continues: 'Anyone who tries to copy reality from ideological stereotypes

162

ends up with a cliché'. Dr Erich Röper, scientific assistant to the CDU group in the Bremen City Parliament, doesn't mince his words but describes *Schneeglöckchen* as 'cheap and nasty agit-prop'. Even Wolfgang Ruf, an advocate of this 'new and independent genre' — as he calls it — had to admit in *epd-Kirche und Rundfunk* that 'each character is there to illustrate a thesis'.

Dr Günter Rohrbach, Director of Programming for Drama and Entertainment in the WDR and Head of the Television Drama Department, said in a lecture at the beginning of 1973 that in future there would be fewer plays about managers on German television 'and in their place series with a new protagonist, the worker'. These series have now started up — but the 'protagonists' are not workers but synthetic proletarians whose function is to declaim left-wing catch-phrases and slogans. The 'worker as protagonist' has not yet appeared on our screens.

(from *Fernseh-und Rundfunkspiegel*, No. 235, 11 December 1979; translation by Sheila Johnston)

20 WDR ARBEITERFILME — AUDIENCE REACTIONS

Film	Transmission Time	Transmission Date	Percentage viewing share	Viewers' Reactions (%)						
				very good	good	satis-factory	unsatis-factory	bad	very bad	average rating
Warum ist Frau B glücklich?	23.15	16 Dec 1968†	5*	..	..	..	..	..	..	..
Ich heisse Erwin und bin 17 Jahre	21.00	19 May 1970	19*	..	..	..	..	..	..	3.0
Rote Fahnen sieht man besser	20.15 / 21.00	13 Sept 1971† / 14 Dec 1971 / 11 Mar 1972†	13*	..	..	..	..	..	..	..
Der Angestellte	21.05	13 June 1972	14	10	59	24	4	2	1	3.7
Eight Hours Are Not a Day Ep. 1 'Jochen und Marion'	20.25	29 Oct 1972	56	10	46	29	9	5	2	3.4
Eight Hours Are Not a Day Ep. 2 'Oma und Gregor'	20.20	17 Dec 1972	41	17	50	25	5	2	1	3.7
Eight Hours Are Not a Day Ep. 3 'Franz und Ernst'	20.15	21 Jan 1973	42	14	47	31	6	1	1	3.7
Eight Hours Are Not a Day Ep. 4 'Harald und Monika'	20.15	18 Feb 1973	65	13	47	29	7	3	1	3.6
Eight Hours Are Not a Day Ep. 5 'Irmgard und Rolf'	2015	18 Mar 1973	43*	..	..	..	..	..	..	..
Liebe Mutter mir geht es gut	20.25	1 May 1973	32	12	45	31	10	1	2	3.5
Lohn und Liebe	21.20	12 Feb 1974	45	15	55	24	4	1	1	3.8
Schneeglöckchen blühn im September		12 Nov 1974	32*	..	..	..	..	..	..	..
Familienglück	21.00	30 Sept 1975	39*	..	..	..	..	..	..	..
Shirins Hochzeit	21.00	20 Jan 1976	37*	..	..	..	..	..	..	..
Der aufrechte Gang	21.00	19 July 1977	25*	..	..	..	..	..	..	..

*No Infratest figures available
†WDF only
Source: Infratest/WDR

Glossary

Alltag
Everyday life

ARD
(Arbeitsgemeinschaft der öffentlich-rechtlichen Rundfunkanstalten der Bundesrepublik Deutschland)
The Joint Association of Public Broadcasting Corporations in the Federal Republic of Germany. An association of nine *Land* broadcasting institutions — BR, HR, NDR, RB, SDR, SFB, SR, SWF and WDR (qq.v.) responsible for the first national television network

Bavariafilm
Munich-based film production company in which WDR is a majority shareholder

Bereich Kultur
Culture department

Berliner Luft
Berlin Air

Bundesanstalt für Arbeit
Federal Labour Ministry

Bundesregierung
Federal Government

Bürgerinitiative
Citizens' initiative

BDI
(Bund deutscher Industrie)
Confederation of Germany Industry

BR
(Bayerischer Rundfunk)
The Bavarian broadcasting institution

Bundesministerium des Innern
Federal Ministry of the Interior

Bundesrat
The upper chamber of the Federal Parliament

Bundestag
The lower chamber of the Federal Parliament

CDU
(Christlich-Demokratische Union)
Christian Democratic Union, right-wing political party outside Bavaria

CSU
(Christlich-Soziale Union)
Christian Social Union, right-wing political party inside Bavaria

DFFB
(Deutsche Film- und Fernsehakademie Berlin
The West Berlin Film School

DGB
(Deutsche Gewerkschaftsbund)
The West German TUC

DKP
(Deutsche Kommunistische Partei)
German Communist Party

165

Fernseh- und Rundfunkspiegel des deutschen Industrieinstitut	Television and broadcasting review of the German industries institute
FDP (Freie Demokratische Partei)	Free Democratic Party, German liberal party
Filmbewertungsstelle	Agency which establishes cultural value and hence eligibility for tax relief of films
Filmförderungsanstalt	Film Development Agency, disposing aid to film-makers
Gastarbeiter	Immigrant worker, often of Turkish origin
Gremienpolitik	Committee politics
Geschichte	History
HR (Hessischer Rundfunk)	The Hesse broadcasting institution
IG Chemie	Chemical Workers' Union
IG Metall	Metal Workers' Union
Intendant	Director-General (of a Broadcasting institution)
KPD	Communist Party of Germany (now a maoist group, previously the main communist party in Germany, which became the DKP in West Germany)
Kölner Stadt-Anzeiger	A Cologne newspaper
Kuratorium junger deutscher Film	Trustees of the young German film (a film development agency)
Land (plural Länder)	One of the eleven states — Baden-Württemberg, Bavaria, Berlin (West), Bremen, Hamburg, Hesse, Lower Saxony, North Rhine-Westphalia, Rhineland-Pfalz, Saar and Schleswig-Holstein — which comprise the Federal Republic of Germany
Landesregierung	*Land* Government
Landtag	a *Land* parliament
NDR (Norddeutscher Rundfunk)	A broadcasting institution established by inter-*Land* treaty between Hamburg, Lower Saxony and Schleswig-Holstein
NWDR (Nordwestdeutscher Rundfunk)	The broadcasting institution set up by the British occupation authorities to broadcast throughout the British Zone
Programmbeirat	The Programme Advisory Council (of WDR)

166

Programmbereich Spiel und Unterhaltung	Drama and entertainment programme department
Proporz	The system whereby senior broadcasting posts in an institution are split between supporters of the main political parties in proportion to the party-political mix of the *Land* government.
Rathaus	Town Hall
RB (Radio Bremen)	The Bremen broadcasting institution
RFFU (Rundfunk-Fernseh-Film-Union)	The German film and broadcasting union
Rotes Lehrstück	Red didactic play
Rundfunkrat	Broadcasting Council, the body which represents the community in the supervisory structures of broadcasting institutions, and which speaks for the overall interests of broadcasting and the public
SDR (Süddeutscher Rundfunk)	The broadcasting institution for part of Baden-Württemberg
SFB (Sender Freies Berlin)	The (West) Berlin broadcasting institution
SPD (Sozialdemokratische Partei Deutschlands)	Social Democratic Party of Germany
SR (Saarländischer Rundfunk)	The Saar broadcasting institution
Verfremdungseffekt	Alienation effect (a central term in Brecht's dramatic theory)
Verwaltungsrat	Administrative Council, the body which supervises the business and administrative functions of the *Intendant* of a broadcasting institution
Volksbühne	People's Theatre. A subscription theatre established in 1890 to bring 'art to the people'
WDF (Westdeutsches Fernsehen)	The 'third' channel of WDR broadcasting only to North Rhine-Westphalia
WDR (Westdeutscher Rundfunk)	The broadcasting institution of North Rhine-Westphalia
ZDF (Zweites Deutsches Fernsehen)	Second German television network which broadcasts nationally

Bibliography

Bartsch, A. and Bispinck, R. (1977), 'Communication Media Under Pressure' in *Democratic Journalist*, no. 7/8, originally published in *Blätter für deutsche und international Politik*, Cologne: December 1976.

Bazin, A. (1967), *What is Cinema?* (trans. H. Gray), Berkeley: University of California Press.

Benjamin, W. (1973), 'The Work of Art in the Age of Mechanical Reproduction' in *Illuminations* (trans. Harry Zohn), London: Collins and Fontana.

Berg, E. (1977), 'Fernsehen-ökonomisches Standbein der Filmwirtschaft: Fernsehumsätze der Filmwirtschaft weiter hinsteigend' in *Media Perspektiven*, June 1977.

Bloch, E. (1977), 'Non-Synchronism and its obligation to Dialectics' in *New German Critique*, no. 11 (trans. M. Ritter), originally published as part of *Erbschaft dieser Zeit*, Zurich: 1935.

Bloch, E. *et al* (1977), *Aesthetics and Politics*, London: New Left Books.

Bronnen, B. and Brocher, C. (1973), *Die Filmemacher*, Munich: Bertelsmann.

Brecht, B. (1961), 'The Experimental Theatre' in *Tulane Drama Review*, vol. 6, no. 1 (trans. Carl Richard Müller), originally published as part of *Theater der Zeit*, no. 4, 1959.

Brecht, B. (1977), 'Against Georg Lukács' in *Aesthetics and Politics* (trans. Stuart Hood), London: New Left Books, originally published in *Schriften zur Kunst und Literatur*, Frankfurt: 1967.

Canaris, V. (1975), 'Style and The Director', in R. Hayman (ed.) *The German Theatre*, London: Oswald Wolff.

Collins, R. and Porter, V. (1980), 'West German Television' in *Sight and Sound*, vol. 49, no. 3, Summer 1980.

Comolli, J. L. and Narboni, J. (1971), 'Cinema, Ideology, Criticism' in *Screen*, vol. 12, nos 1 and 2.

Corsepius, D. *et al* (1977), *Filme der Arbeiterbewegung*, Berlin W.: Medienzentrum Kreuzberg.

Druck, H. (1980), 'The end of an era for German Broadcasting' in *Intermedia*, May 1980.

Elsaesser, T. (1979), 'The Post-War German Cinema', in T. Rayns (ed.) *Fassbinder*, London: British Film Institute.

Falkenberg, H-G. (1979), *Is there still some hope for Television?*, Liège: Co-opérative Internationale de Recherche et d'Action en Matière de Communication, mimeo.

Gallehr, T. and Schübel, R. (1971), '*Rote Fahnen sieht man besser:* Protokoll einer Sendung' in *Fernsehkritik*.

Gast, W. and Kaiser Gerhard, R. (1977), 'Kritik der Fernsehspielkritik. Das Beispiel von Fassbinders *Acht Stunden sind kein Tag*' in Jörg Drews (ed.) *Literatur Medien Kritik*, Heidelberg: Quelle und Meyer.

Grosser, A. (1979), 'Federal Republic of Germany: From Democratic Showcase to Party Domination' in A. Smith (ed.) *Television and Political Life,* London: Macmillan.

Guback, T. H., (1960), *The International Film Industry,* Bloomington and London: Indiana University Press.

Habermas, J. (1969), 'Ernst Bloch: A Marxist Romantic' in *Salmagundi,* vol. 10, no. 11.

Hess, W. (1970), 'Massenmedien wandeln sich, Die Filmwirtschaft und das deutsche Fernsehen' in *ARD Jahrbuch 1970,* Munich: ARD.

Himmelweit, H. (1979), 'Social Influence and Television' in S. Withey and R. Abeles (ed.) *Television and Social Behaviour,* New York: 1979.

Itzfeld, J. (1977), 'Meinungsfreiheit oder Schwarzfunk?' in *Konkret,* no. 9.

Jansen, P. W. and Schütte, W. (1974), *Rainer Werner Fassbinder,* Munich: Carl Hanser Verlag.

Jaspers, K. (1967), *The Future of Germany* (trans. and ed. E. B. Ashton), Chicago and London: The University of Chicago Press.

Johnston, S. (1979), 'The Author as Public Institution' in *Screen Education,* no. 32/33.

Klapper, J. T. (1960), *The Effects of Mass Communication,* New York: New York Free Press.

Kohli, M., Dippelhofer-Steim, B. and Pommerehne, B. (1976), 'Arbeiter sehen Arbeiterfilme' in *Leviathan,* vol. 4, no. 3. (translated by Sheila Johnston, Polytechnic of Central London mimeo.)

Lukács, G. (1963), 'The Ideology of Modernism' in *The Meaning of Contemporary Realism,* London: Merlin.

Lukács, G. (1970), *Writer and Critic* (trans. A. Kahn), London: Merlin.

MacCabe, C. (1974), 'Realism and the Cinema. Notes on some Brechtian Theses' in *Screen,* vol. 15, no. 2.

MacCabe, C. (1976), *'Days of Hope:* A Response to Colin McArthur' in *Screen,* vol. 17, no. 1.

MacCabe, C. (1979), 'Karl Marx and Friedrich Engels on Literature and Art' in *Red Letters,* no. 9.

Märthesheimer, P. (1973), 'Die Okkupation eines bürgerlichen Genres' in *Fernsehen und Bildung,* no. 13. (See Appendix 15.)

Märthesheimer, P. (1976), 'Was kann der Held? Er verändert die Welt!' in *Fernsehspiele WDR,* Jan/June. (See Appendix 14.)

Märthesheimer, P. (1979), 'Wirklichkeit und Fiktion im Fernsehspiel am Beispiel Arbeitswelt' in *Rundfunk un Fernsehen,* no. 4.

McArthur, C. (1975), *'Days of Hope'* in *Screen,* vol. 16, no. 4.

Preece, R. J. C. (1968), *Land Elections in the German Federal Republic,* London: Longmans.

*Public Opinion (*1971), (ed.) Press and Information office, Bonn.

Ratajcszak, H. (1976), 'Das Bild des Arbeitnehmers im Fernsehen' in *Deutsche Post,* no. 10/11, June 1976.

Rohrbach, G. (1976) 'Arbeitsplatzbeschreibung' in Brüssau, Stolte and Wisser (eds.) *Fernsehen: ein Medium sieht sich selbst,* Mainz: Hase und Köller Verlag.

Rohrbach, G. (1979), 'Plädoyer für mehr Fantasie im Fernsehspiel' in *Kulturbrief,* no. 1/2, Bonn: Inter Nationes.

Röhl, W. (1973), 'Kommt die Proletwelle?' in *Konkret,* no. 13.

169

Sandford, J. (1976), *Mass Media of the German Speaking Countries*, London: Oswald Wolff.

Skriver, A. (1978), 'Fragwürdige Medienkritik' in *Luthersche Monatschafte*, April 1978.

Smith, A. (1977), 'The Relationship of Management with Creative Staff' in *Report of the Committee on the Future of Broadcasting* Appendices (Annan Committee), London: HMSO Cmnd. 6753-1.

Thomas, M. W. (1978). ' "Linke" Sendungen werden aufgespiesst' in *Frankfurter Rundschau*, 22 February 1978.

Truffaut, F. (1967), *Hitchcock*, London: Secker and Warburg.

Ungureit, H. (1976), 'Zur Entwicklung des Verhältnisses Film/Fernsehen' in *ZDF Jahrbuch*, Mainz: Zweites Deutsches Fernsehen.

von Bismarck, K. (1966), 'Wie zersetzend darf eine Sendung sein?' in *Die Zeit*, 4 February 1966. (See Appendix 2.)

WDR Pressestelle (1972), *Dokumentation auf den Film von Theo Gallehr und Rolf Schübel*, 'Rote Fahnen sieht man besser', Cologne WDR mimeo, 8 March 1972. (See Appendix 5.)

Williams, A. (1976), *Broadcasting and Democracy in West Germany*, St. Albans and London: Bradford University Press and Crosby, Lockwood Staples.

Ziewer, C. (1972), 'The origins of the film *Liebe Mutter*' in *Materialien über 'Liebe Mutter'*, Berlin W.: Basis Film. (See Appendix 17.)

Ziewer, C. (1974), 'More about the uses of film, in *Materialien über Schneeglöckchen blühn im September*', Berlin W.: Basis Film. (See Appendix 18.)

Ziewer, C. (1975), Lecture at Polytechnic of Central London, 2 November 1975.

Ziewer, C. (1976), Interview in *Film in der Bundesrepublik Deutschlands*, March 1976.

Filmography

1968   **Warum ist Frau B. glücklich?**
(*Why is Mrs B. Happy?*)

Production	WDR
Director	Erika Runge
Photography	Horst Bever
Running Time	42 min.

1970   **Ich heisse Erwin und bin 17 Jahre**
(*My Name is Erwin and I'm 17*)

Production	WDR
Director	Erika Runge
Photography	Rudolf Körösi

Erwin Walther (*Erwin*), Heinz Günther Penckmann (*Father*), Irmgard Penckmann (*Mother*), Dirk Penckmann (*Brother*), Iris Hertisch (*Gisela*), Hermann Stemann (*Master*), Theo Dahlke (*Theo*), Siegfried Zeitler (*Siegfried*).

Running Time	74 min.

1971   **Der Angestellte**
(*The White-Collar Worker*)

Production	WDR
Director/Screenplay	Helma Sanders
Photography	André Dubreuil
Designer	Herbert Labusga

Ernst Jacobi (*Klaus Thieme*), Giselheid Hönsch (*Frau Thieme*), Peter Arens (*Kirsch*), Wolfgang Kieling (*Quentin*), Alf Marholm (*Bruchmüller*).

Running Time	99 min.

1971   **Liebe Mutter, mir geht es gut**
(*Dear Mother, I'm OK*)

Production	WDR/Basis-Film
Director	Christian Ziewer
Screenplay	Klaus Wiese, Christian Ziewer
Photography	Jörg Michael Baldenius
Editor	Stefanie Wilke

Clause Eberth (*Albert Schefczyk*), Niklaus Dutsch, Heinz Herrmann, Ernst Lenart, Kurt Michler, Horst Pinnow, Hans Rickmann and many others.

171

Prizes: Film Critics Prize, 1972; Film of the Month of the Evangelical Film Guild, October 1972; Adolf Grimme Prize (Silver), 1972; Berlin Artprize, 1973.
Running Time   87 min.

1971   Rote Fahnen sieht man besser
(Red Flags Can Be Seen Better)

Production	Radio Bremen/ WDR/Cinecollectif Hamburg
WDR Producer	Martin Wiebel
Directors/Screenplay	Theo Gallehr, Rolf Schübel
Photography	Karsten H. Müller
Camera Assistant	Harald Reetz
Editor	Christel Suckow
Sound	Klaus Amann, Udo Bick
Music	Dieter Süverkrüp

Prizes: Goldener Bildschirm 1971, Adolf Grimme Prize (Gold) 1971.
Running Time   99 min.

1972   Die Wollands
(The Wolland Family)

Production	DFFB (German Film and Television Academy, Berlin)
Directors	Ingo Kratisch, Marianne Lüdcke
Screenplay	Ingo Kratisch, Marianne Lüdcke, Johannes Mayer
Photography	Ingo Kratisch, Martin Streit
Running Time	92 min.

1972   Acht Stunden sind kein Tag
(Eight Hours Are Not a Day)

Episode 1	Jochen und Marion
Episode 2	Oma und Gregor
Episode 3	Franz und Ernst
Episode 4	Harald und Monika
Episode 5	Irmgard und Rolf
Production	WDR
WDR producer	Peter Märthesheimer
Director/Screenplay	Rainer Werner Fassbinder
Photography	Dietrich Lohmann
Design	Kurt Raab

Gottfried John (*Jochen*), Hanna Schygulla (*Marion*), Luise Ullrich (*Grandma*), Werner Finck (*Gregor*), Anita Bucher (*Käthe*), Wolfried Lier (*Wolf*), Christine Oesterlein (*Klara*), Renate Roland (*Monika*), Kurt Raab (*Harald*), Andrea Schober (*Sylvia*), Torsten Massinger (*Manni*), Irm Herrmann (*Irmgard*), Wolfgang Zerlett (*Manfred*), Wolfgang Schenck (*Franz*), Peter Gauhe (*Ernst*), Herb Andress (*Rüdiger*), Rudolf W. Brem (*Rolf*), Hans Hirschmüller (*Jürgen*), Grigorius Karipitis (*Giuseppe*), Karl Scheydt (*Peter*), Rainer Hauer (*Gross*).

| Running Time | Episode 1: 101 min., Episode 2: 100 min., Episode 3: 92 min., Episode 4: 88 min., Episode 5: 89 min. |

1973 Lohn und Liebe
(Wages and Love)

Production	WDR/Filmverlag der Autoren
Producer	Regina Ziegler
WDR Producer	Wolf-Dieter Brücke
Directors/Screenplay/ Photography	Ingo Kratisch, Marianne Lüdcke
Editor	Susanne Lahaye
Sound	Christian Moldt
Music	Peter Fischer
Costume	Ulrike Thursch

Erika Skrotzki (*Roswita*), Evelyn Meyka (*Barbel*), Nicholas Brieger (*Gerhard Markgraf*), Hans Peter Hallwachs (*Bernd*), Gisela Matishent (*Roswita's mother*), Elfriede Irrall (*Brigitte*), Dagmar Biener (*Marlies*), Horst Pinnow (*Betriebsrat Chairman Danner*), Lilli Schonborn-Anspach (*Berta, Betriebsrat member*), Inge Herbrecht (*Anna*), Edeltraut Elsner (*Sonja*), Ute Gerhardt (*Tina*), Susanne Tremper (Gisela).

| Running Time | 98 min. |

1974 Schneeglöckchen blühn im September
(Snowdrops Bloom in September)

Production	WDR/Basis-Film
WDR Producer	Joachim von Mengershausen
Director	Christian Ziewer
Screenplay	Christian Ziewer, Klaus Wiese
Photography	Kurt Weber
Editor	Stefanie Wilke
Music	Lokomotive Kreuzberg

C. Eberth, H. Rickmann, W. Liere, C. Jurichs, P. Fischer, M. Meurer, G. Konzack, K. Siefart, W. Kratzmann, N. Dutsch, K. Michler, W. Wagner, M. Pagels, H. Lange, H. Pinnow, U. Langen, H. Schinke, B. Morawiecz, H. Giese, H. Kammrad, K. Stieringer, E. Koyro, D. Riedel, F. Bauschulte.

| Running Time | 108 min. |

1975 Familienglück
(Wedded Bliss)

Production	WDR/Regina Ziegler Film
Producers	Regina Ziegler, Dieter Melzer
WDR Producer	Wolf-Dieter Brücke
Directors/Screenplay/ Photography	Marianne Lüdcke, Ingo Kratisch
Director of Photography	Hartmut Kohler
Camera Operators	Ingo Kratisch, Wolfgang Knigge
Editors	Siegrun Jager, Ursula Hof

173

Production Assistant	Brigitte Rochow
Sound	Christian Moldt, Helmuth Rottgen
Music	Peter Fischer, Ebehard Mathies
Costume	Hildtraut Warndorf, Ilse Stripp
Makeup	Martina Schwedas

Tilo Prückner (*Manfred*), Dagmar Biener (*Manuela*), Ursula Diestel (*Manfred's Mother*), Otto Machtlinger (*Manfred's Father*), Hilda Wensch (*Manuela's Mother*), Werner Eichhorn (*Manuela's Father*), Werner Rehm (*Wolfgang*), Hildegard Schmahl (*Monika*), Henrike Furst (*Sabine*), Ingeborg Wellman (*Inge*), Claus Theo Gartner (*Rainer*), Eberhard Feik (*Wulle*), Gunter Meisner (*Hektiker*), Irmgard Paulis, Beate Kopp, Ilse Marggraf (*Manuela's colleagues*), Gerhard Wollner, Monika Bleibtreu, Peter Herzog, Edith Robbers and many others.

Running Time	107 min.

1975 Shirins Hochzeit
(*Shirin's Wedding*)

Production	WDR
Executive Producer	Fred Ilgner
WDR Producer	Volker Canaris
Director/Screenplay	Helma Sanders
Photography	Thomas Mauch
Editor	Margot Lohlein
Designer	Manfred Lutz

Ayten Erten (*Shirin*), Jürgen Prochnow (*Aida*), Aras Oren (*Mahmud*), Aliki Georgoulis (*Maria*), Jannis Kyriakidis (*Janis*), Peter Franke (*Foreman*), Hilde Wensch (*Barmaid*), Renata Becker (*Hostel Warden*), Grete Wurm (*Official*).

Location	Cologne and Munskermaifeld (Mosel)
Running Time	120 min.

1976 Der aufrechte Gang
(*Walking Tall*)

Production	WDR/Basis-Filmverleih
Producers	Clara Burckner, Klaus Wiese
WDR Producer	Joachim von Mengershausen
Director/Screenplay	Christian Ziewer
Photography	Ulli Heiser
Editor	Stefanie Wilke
Music	Erhard Grosskopf
Designer	Will Kley
Costume	Anette Ganders

Claus Eberth (*Dieter Wittkoski*), Antje Hagen (*Hanna*), Wolfgang Liehre (*Georg*), Mathias Eberth (*Andi*), Walter Prussing (*Grandfather*), Martina Hennig (*Gabi*), Rainer Pigulla (*Werner*), Heinz Hermann (*Betriebsrat Chairman*), Kurt Michler (*Manager*).

Locations	Berlin, Gross-Ilsede
Running Time	115 min.

174